WOMEN, MONEY & POWER

WOMEN, MONEY & POWER

by Phyllis Chesler
and Emily Jane Goodman

WILLIAM MORROW AND COMPANY, INC.
NEW YORK

Copyright © 1976 by Phyllis Chesler and Emily Jane Goodman

All rights reserved. No part of this book may be reproduced or utilized in any form or by any means, electronic or mechanical, including photocopying, recording or by any information storage and retrieval system, without permission in writing from the Publisher. Inquiries should be addressed to William Morrow and Company, Inc., 105 Madison Ave., New York, N.Y. 10016.

Printed in the United States of America.

Dedication

Economic and spiritual poverty condemns and destroys human life. We dedicate this book to a Woman's Battle for Bread and Roses.

Acknowledgments

Phyllis Chesler would like to express her special appreciation to Nachmy Bronshtien, Margaret Taylor Boyle, Joyce Conigliaro, Helene Gross, Marian Howard, Janet McLeod, and George Sideris.

Emily Jane Goodman deeply appreciates all who, in different but special and loving ways, helped. Especially: Doreen Abraham, Rose Buschi, Connie Cuttle, Susan Demers, Suzanne DePlautt, Joseph Little, Pat Maddalone, Patricia A. Maloney, Lynn Outwater, and Micki Scherer.

The authors would like to thank all the people interviewed, and Neal Gantcher and David Lubell for their assistance.

Authors' Note

This book is a collaboration. However, the responsibility for and attribution of chapters is as follows: Phyllis Chesler: Chapters 2, 3, 5, 6, 8, 12, 13, 14, 16; Emily Jane Goodman: Chapters 1, 4, 7, 9, 10, 11, 15, Epilogue.

Although laws do not change quickly enough to meet the needs of women, there is constant activity which may result in some changes in the laws between the time this book was completed and its publication. The reader may note, for example, Proposals and New Developments may now have in fact become law.

Contents

1. Options — 11
2. Women and Money: The Psychology of Ambivalence — 17
3. I'd Rather Be Dead Than Ugly: The Psychoeconomics of Beauty — 39
4. Who Really Controls the Purse Strings? — 51
5. Wealth: A Tale of Two Sexes — 61
6. Women at the Financial Top — 66
7. Women and the Internal Revenue Conspiracy — 75
8. Marriage and Motherhood: The Psychology of Total Commitment — 92
9. Survival Tactics: Marriage and Divorce — 104
10. The Myth of Alimony: Why Is It the Husband Gets the Stocks and Bonds, and the Wife Gets the Children? — 128
11. Women and Credit: Neither a Borrower Nor a Lender Be — 152
12. The Compassion Urge: The Psychology of Volunteerism — 167
13. Sexual Economics: Who Profits? — 176
14. Women and Work: The Crisis of Psychic Survival — 185
15. Out of the Supermarket and into the Job Market — 203
16. Women, Money and Power — 238
    Epilogue — 245

1. Options

> "Revolution may also arise when persons of great ability, and second to none in their merits, are treated dishonorably by those who themselves enjoy the highest honors."
>
> —Aristotle

Why a book on money and power? Because women have neither. Because books are written about women and sex. Women and children. Women and men. Women and women. Women and cooking. Women and love. Women and orgasm. Women and the pill. But, by conspiracy, design, omission, or accident, little is written about women and economics and power.

This book is about the psychoeconomic condition of women and is an exploration into impotence and power, myth and reality. It is a look at how our institutions developed and continue to function in the service of the status quo. This book is *not* a guide to balancing budgets or even to getting a better job.

It is widely believed that through consumption, investment, inheritance, alimony or marital support, women control this country's wealth. The book looks at the facts, at why women do *not* control American wealth, or anything else, how they feel about money, power, what they do with money, what it is they do to survive.

Many men have been determined to make lots of money; historically, quite a few have done so, though room "at the top" is extremely limited. Very few women have even stated the desire to acquire wealth, much less fulfilled it.

When men or women are asked directly, "If you think women

have money and power in this country, who are they?" the fact that it can take a half hour for a couple of women to be named answers the question. Usually women are mentioned who are close to men with money and power, or sometimes have married or *inherited* money but are not in control of it. Very occasionally, very rarely can anyone name more than perhaps half a dozen women in America who have acquired power through *any* means.

Approximately equal energy has gone into creating the illusion, fabricating the myth that women have money and power, and, on the other hand, making sure they don't. In addition to the assumption that women *control* the money is the opposite one: women don't know anything about money and power and couldn't care less, anyway. In other words, it is a common assumption that women are not only "different," but incapable. This seeming contradiction contains its own logic: as long as the myth is kept alive that women are already in charge, women can be kept in the bedroom, in the kitchen, in the laundry—anywhere *but* in power.

Even to disagree with the concepts underlying our system and its institutions, to function within it, to change it or to function outside, if that is possible, requires information about its nature. At the same time it must be recognized that information is not enough. But that is how options are ascertained and possibly power to change achieved.

Most of the world's human energy is devoted to the struggle for survival. In the United States this is especially true for women. While male strategy is directed toward survival and success, women function on a tactic-by-tactic, technique-by-technique basis, which does not necessarily form a larger strategy or plan beyond "How do I survive?" Female "options" are so few and so narrow as not to be real options or choices. A woman's "choices" are among the available ways to survive.

All female survival tactics function to reinforce the status quo—not to challenge or redefine it. Beauty, sex, youth—and the various "appearances" that can be purchased with money, education, and time—do *not* result in any woman's becoming Pope, President, or Commander of the Armed Forces. What they *can* result in, given class and race origin, ambition, and "luck," is the opportunity to help or serve men who are Presidents or military chiefs. And this "power" to serve, or this "power" to be bought, is often confused, by women and men alike, with power itself.

Women do not act out of choice, despite what we are asked to believe. Women "choose," we are told, to be housewives, secretaries, teachers, librarians, nurses, social workers. But even where women ostensibly have made choices, the options are horizontal, not vertical or lateral.

A woman doesn't decide that she would rather make $5,000 a year as a nurse than a quarter of a million as a physician. Women don't *decide* they would rather be housewives with no income, or recipients of welfare, than be economically independent. No one is *born* believing that her destiny is to await being overtaken by the "maternal instinct." Yet it isn't necessarily because of economic philosophy that women have remained outside the American capitalist mainstream. As a matter of fact, women have been very much a part of "the system," but as its victims, and not as its beneficiaries.

When we hear, "But-I'm-doing-exactly-what-I-want-all-I've-ever-wanted-is-to-be-somebody's-wife-mother-and-I-don't-care-about-having-my-own-money," and, "I-just-love-asking-my-husband-for-money-so-I-can-buy-him-a-birthday-present," the question is what that woman viewed as her options, if she even had the option to think about it at all. If she says, "Well, even after I graduated from school, what kind of job could *I* get?" or, "My parents wanted me to be a teacher, but that just didn't appeal to me," or "I never got my degree because I was putting my husband through school," or, "There are no job opportunities for women," or "How could I ever have any financial security on my own?" or, "I love animals, but who ever heard of a woman veterinarian?" or, "I was always good at math and even thought of becoming a CPA like my brother did but, as a woman, maybe I'd have gotten a job as a bookkeeper for ninety dollars a week," or, "My father's a dentist and he was always telling me to marry a boy he could take into the practice," or, "I always felt my job would be my children," she correctly perceived that she had no real options. She'd be lucky to survive.

The survival techniques available to women have not carried access to power bases, ways of changing or influencing the world, much less their own lives.

When boys say, "What shall I be when I grow up?" their horizons (if they are white and middle class) are unending. But even if they are not white and middle class, men, in addition to their survival techniques, also have "escape routes." Men, even poor men whose social and economic mobility is limited, have more escape routes than women of their class. Thus, even poor and third world men who cannot ultimately improve their position through inheritance or employment, for example, still have greater mobility than poor women who are left at home with the children. Men can escape their class, their background, their family, their neighborhood. It is through existing institutions that men acquire their temporary and permanent escape routes. Travel. School. Sports. Military.[1] Bars. Clubs. Career. Money. Sex. Some men have more escape routes than other men.

For example, some men create escape routes which are foreign to women such as corporate alter egos. Men can divert liability for their actions through use of the corporate veil[2] which, unlike female veils or apron strings, is both seductive and protective. It is men who have corporate know-how—lawyers, accountants, consultants.

Few poor white and almost no nonwhite men are ever among the rulers, except as humanity is divided along sex lines. For men who are not part of the propertied class within the male aristocracy, divisions along sex lines may be their last chance to be among the oppressors rather than the oppressed.

What options do women have, and what are the inherent compromises of each? *Are* they options? Can women really be wives and mothers and students and workers? Can women really have careers *and* families?

For most women, the opportunities to survive through the acquisition of money are derivative rather than direct; that is, women do not inherit businesses, or acquire high-paying jobs. They marry or in some other way use their looks and their bodies. For most women, some variation on this theme has been the only option—and therefore not an option at all. And, interestingly, when women in marriages or marriagelike situations perform the work required in keeping themselves and their houses looking beautiful, and sexual and other services, it is assumed that they are doing what they *want* to do; when, done for money, the same tasks become very déclassé.

Generally women can improve their position by marriage only. Relatively few men have been able to achieve class change; for women the number is infinitely smaller. A mistress may get jewels, but little else. Being born female eliminates, except via marriage, class change, which is, after all, the great American dream. The appearance of female mobility and options is more illusory than real.

[1] *Even* military.
[2] See Morton Mintz and Jerry S. Cohen, *America, Inc.* (New York, Dial Press, 1971), and C. Wright Mills, *The Power Elite* (New York, Oxford University Press, Inc., 1957).

Women who marry believing they will always be taken care of find that "it ain't necessarily so." Husbands lose jobs and income, die, abscond, refuse to or even become unable to support dependents. Even without such events, the wife may not get wages, health insurance, pension, her own Social Security or tax benefits. If she gets divorced, she may lose even the pitiful economic security she thinks she has while married.

It is essential to recognize that in all probability a woman didn't really "choose," since there was so little to choose from. However, neither freedom nor equality for women begins with women sacrificing what little they have.

When women work *outside* (employment versus involuntary servitude) the home, they get lower paying jobs, fewer pensions, lesser disability benefits. A woman's body is used against her. She can become pregnant: she is a liability to the employer. She is already a mother: her children will keep her off the job. She is not a mother: something must be wrong with her. Circle. If she is married, she can't get bank loans because she *might* become pregnant. If she is *not* married, she still can't get bank loans because she doesn't have job security, high enough salary, or collateral. (Besides, what can a woman alone even do with the money she would borrow if she *could* borrow money? What woman goes out and buys a Porsche? Where can she take vacations alone? If she buys a house in the suburbs and lives there alone, she is a community outcast. What *is* wrong with her!)

There are many women "celebrities," some of whom even make money. Show business success, for example (name a successful woman-who-has-made-money-on-her-own and chances are she is in show business or the beauty business), can supply a woman with outlandish sums of money. But "stars" often don't even make the decisions that directly affect them, much less others. They have men who do that for them.

Women, by definition, have been shut out of the male aristocracy, in which a few have greater power than the many, but in which all members, as men, have more power than almost all women. This holds true even of "upper-class" women who, though they may have the illusion of power, access to the ear of power or some derivative power in noneconomic ways, have little direct or real power.

Women need to understand money and power and institutions and options; they have not been exposed to how the major systems and institutions of our society, other than those surrounding the home, operate. Men say it is enough to understand bingo, or buying and selling at the local fruit stand, without extending this information to the "abstraction" of the economy. As a result there are women—even now—who have never written a check, never handled money except an "allowance," never paid a bill or read a tax return. However, they have been working both in and outside the home for their families, for strangers.

Women are beginning to realize that they may have to—may be allowed to—look after themselves, to manage their own lives, plan their own futures. And, as women, conceive of lives in which they are responsible for, and dependent on, themselves. Having their own futures to take care of, they must deal with questions which previously would have been left to men.

Women have got to understand the system under which we live in the United States. That happens to be money and profit for a few. And in every system, it is power.

Many people in America and the rest of the world are literally starving to death. People who cannot find jobs or shelter live by searching out leftover or damaged food; old people, especially our women, have spent their lives working, only to find themselves living on the inadequate income of Social Security (if even that) and surviving by absorbing dog or cat food into their diets.

It is a peculiar time in the history of the world to be writing about money. We are living in a period which is extreme: it offers opulence and affluence for some, and poverty for most others.

Almost no women have participated in the decision making that brought us to the edge of disaster which we are now treading. Would it have been different with women in charge, or even involved? No one knows that yet.

2. Women and Money: The Psychology of Ambivalence

> "The King was in his countinghouse,
> Counting out his money.
> The Queen was in the parlor,
> Eating bread and honey."
> —Sixteenth century; *Oxford Dictionary of Nursery Rhymes*

Dolores Smith:
"To a woman, family life and children are more important than making money. Money is for food for the children, for rent, and for clothing for the family. . . . Pretty good money is anything over eighty dollars a week cash. A lot of money is two hundred and fifty dollars a week before taxes. Financial security is having enough money to bury the kids" (personal interview, 1974).

Katharine Graham:
"If one is rich and one's a woman, one can be quite misunderstood. . . . I get a lot of flak at the *Post*, too, when I talk about profitability. They get pretty up tight at the mention of M-O-N-E-Y; they think I'm some heartless bitch."—Quoted in *Ms.* magazine, October, 1974

Lynn Caine:
"Martin was dead. That was all that mattered. But I felt the loss of money almost as much as the loss of Martin. . . . I have come to recognize that money is important. Women should know more about it.

"Just a little security would have made my bereavement less frightening. The prospect of bringing up two children all by myself on my salary was terrifying. No figment of a nightmare or an anxiety attack. Fact.

"I know I am better off than most widows. But why should any woman face deprivation, anxiety, and financial terror because her husband dies?"—*Widow*

Why are women of all classes so ignorant about money? "I don't know anything about income tax, life insurance, or the stock market —my husband (or my father) handles that for me." Or: "You're asking *me* about money? I'm glad I can pay the rent and feed my children. Why should I snoop into the boss's books? I wouldn't understand all those numbers anyway."

Why are so many women almost *against* money? Or afraid of knowing too much about it? When pressed, why do women say that money is "not really important" and paradoxically, that "money is evil"?[1] How can women yearn so romantically and so desperately for precisely what money buys in a money culture—beauty, health, a home, security, comfort—and yet be so ignorant about how money works?[2] Why do so many women seem almost proud of their ignorance, as if economic ignorance, like sexual innocence or timidity, is somehow a moral and economic asset?

Women are supposed to feel the same way about sex as they do about money. Traditionally, women are not supposed to say they want to *make* money or *make* sex. It is something that women are not supposed to do, or are not supposed to say they do. Sex or money is something that is supposed to "happen" to women. Psychologically, women's attitudes toward money fall into two categories. "Real" money is what women have to earn and/or spend on themselves. This is never very much money—nor is it obtained in an exciting way. "Magic" money is what men spend on women. This ranges

[1] A 1972 study found that women, especially nuns and female college students, "poohpoohed" money and also thought it was "evil." Paul F. Wernimont and Susan Fitzpatrick, "The Meaning of Money," *Journal of Applied Psychology*, Vol. 56, No. 3 (1972).
[2] A 1974 study found that only money or affluence in America had a significant and positive effect on reports of "happiness." The author notes that "we know money talks and our research suggests it also makes us happy. Apparently, affluence is one of the few things that generally improves life satisfaction." Paul Cameron, *Psychology Today* (August, 1974).

from the cost of a drink, a meal, and a hotel room, to frivolous or expensive gifts such as liquor, candy, jewelry, vacations, or real estate.[3]

It is an ancient drama, a miracle of currency—this buying of women. Women themselves experience being paid for or bought as sexual, as practical, as shameful, or as wonderful. Being bought, especially for a high price, or for a lifetime, is exactly how most women learn what they are worth. In a money culture, their self-knowledge can be very exact.

To men, women are as universal a commodity as money. It is said that women have power because men work for them. But this is like saying that men work for money. Men are not so much enslaved by women as they are enslaved to the uses to which they put women. Men work to "have" women—for sexual, domestic, emotional, and reproductive reasons. They also work to "have" women for reasons of status.

To women, a man (i.e. money) is not a universal, interchangeable commodity. Psychologically, women are taught to want one *irreplaceable* man; one *irreplaceable* set of biological children; one *irreplaceable* family unit. Women also recognize certain other "irreplaceables"; their youth, their youthful beauty, their virginity, their childbearing years. But none of these "irreplaceables" can be transformed into major assets. Female attempts to do so are limited, and usually confined to indirect approaches. The female pursuit of either sex or men (i.e. money) must be "romantic," rather than rational. For example, women are *supposed* to marry for money and/or financial and social security—but they are not supposed to say so. They must say—and believe—that they marry for love, for children, and for God.

Psychologically, female financial ambition or the female need for economic self-sufficiency is completely at odds with the female need to either *be* or be *seen* as a Lady: protected, respectable, bought at a high price by one man.[4]

Ladies are not supposed to work. Ladies do not have to labor in public for vulgar cash. *Real* Ladies, the daughters of wealthy men, come already paid for. And a Real Lady is the best kind of woman

---

[3] Women who pay for their own meals or buy their own homes may do so shrewdly or greedily or realistically. But it is not often experienced as "magic": as an exhilarating and transforming moment in which time stops.

[4] Women also want to be seen as girls: shy, cute, young, seductive—and innocent. But the image of the Lady—the perfect "little lady"—still hovers, like a halo, around the youngest of female heads.

there is. Or so women have been made to feel.[5] Female inherited wealth is somehow "invisible" and, as such, is not threatening. Women *working* for cash, or having to, is as vulgar and embarrassing to our traditional minds as is the sight of a woman exposing a bank roll at a dinner table.

Thus, most women deny that they work. "I'm only a housewife and mother—I don't work." Or after cooking a dinner for ten people a woman will say: "This was no work at all." Or after spending hours—or years—trying to look beautiful or sexy or classy, a woman will respond to the hoped-for compliment by insisting that "this hairdo took only a minute." And most mothers reject the idea that bringing up their children is "work" or that they should receive money for their "labor of love."

Working in public for small wages—*having* to do so—fills most women with shame—not pride. Such public disgrace, such an obvious fall from grace in Protestant capitalist America, must be due to some sin committed, some God not properly honored. The sinner is definitely to blame. She is probably ugly—or no longer young. Probably, she wasn't "clever" enough to get a man to support her. Perhaps she was too clever—too outspoken, too pushy for her own financial good —but not "smart" enough to get ahead on her own financially without a man. Perhaps she has committed the sin of being born black or to a poor father. Maybe her sin is that of having too little luck.

Women bow their heads over their inadequate paychecks, welfare checks, and household allowances: how can they complain when the fault is their own? Why call further attention to their failure, to their poverty? The least they can do is accept their fate like Ladies: without protest, without vulgarity. Queens have accepted exile, prison towers—even execution—like Ladies. Grandmothers didn't "complain"—and they at least survived. Why scream economic or sexual rape when that only makes matters worse?

Such philosophical resignation is an attempt to avoid something "worse" from happening, not an attempt to bring about something "better." Such fatalism or masochism is neither surprising nor biologically based. Women are not usually rewarded for doing what they are told to do. Their reward is avoiding the punishment they would receive if they didn't obey orders. Housewives do not get congratulated each night for "keeping up the good work." Rather, they get criticized if the expected "appearance" or "service" is lacking or ab-

---

[5] See Chapter 5, "Wealth: A Tale of Two Sexes."

sent. Women who receive degrees in physics are usually punished for not being "feminine," rather than rewarded in keeping with their accomplishment.

Most women do not receive medals of honor for keeping their sexual virginity, or their spotless reputations. This is expected behavior. Women are only punished when they fail to perform it.

Most women are not economically rewarded by a money culture because they reproduce people. Women are simply called "unnatural" and are ostracized or impoverished if they don't become mothers.

Female labor and female economic poverty are so prevalent, and yet so culturally tabooed, that many ways have been found to deny or minimize this reality. Both women and men say that women do not work, that women do not *have* to work, that women do not *mind* working. That is why men can, in good conscience, pay no money or very little money for female labor.[6] If women actually *needed* the money they earned or were "granted"—to support themselves and their families—they couldn't survive economically. Men can't. Ergo: if women work for less without rioting or dying, it means they don't really need any more.[7]

Women deny the *productive* labor involved in creating and maintaining homes and children. They also deny their denial by first saying they don't think of mothering as work and then that they think it is *more* valuable than money. Women are genuinely confused by a money culture that depends on their labor completely, but does not reward them for it economically. Not to earn money directly in a money culture is equivalent to nonexistence, or at least to worthless existence. To have to sell your time or labor for money may be "bad enough": to have to sell it cheaply is worse.

The phrase *a workingman* denotes an inferior class member in a class society. Middle-class professionals do not like to be called workers—although they are workers. A workingman has to work in order to survive. He definitely has been banished from paradise. But a man, even in class society, may take pride in the *fact* of his work.

---

[6] Of course, in capitalist countries, private greed is the economic motivation for cheap labor as is public greed in Communist countries. But here we are talking about how the human mind rationalizes or translates economic forces.
[7] Women do die for economic reasons and some even attempt riots. Their deaths go unnoticed as such, their riots are squashed. Also, apathy and listlessness set in after enough economic deprivation—and eerie, compliant silences are maintained forever after.

Through wage labor, he gains the only or greatest importance he has —that of a provider for a family.[8]

The phrase *a working woman* or especially *a working mother* is a negative judgment. Psychologically, women sense that their *real* work is to expiate Eve's sin—by helping men relive the fantasy of paradise. Women must stifle their childbed screams, cosmetize their labor sweat, try to *look* as if they still inhabit paradise. Women who don't or can't hide the sweat of their brow, women who can't quite look like Real Ladies, know there are economic penalties for looking the "wrong way."

Women's Body Language

> "Fie, fie upon her!
> There's language in her eye, her cheek, her lip,
> Nay, her foot speaks; her wanton spirits look out
> At every joint and motive of her body."
> —Shakespeare, *Troilus and Cressida,* IV. v. 55

"Nonverbal communication represents a micropolitical system of control that mildly rather than violently reinforces as well as expresses existing power relationships. . . . However, looks and postures are considered illegitimate in analyzing communication. Legal transcripts and newspaper accounts don't record them, and [few nonverbal signals are] allowed in personal arguments ('*What* look? *What* tone of voice? Look, did I say okay or didn't I?')."— Nancy Henley, unpublished manuscript, "The Politics of Touch"

Women of all classes, within the home and in public, and at all levels of financial skill, employ a basic body language in order to survive economically. Women communicate deference, inconsequentiality, helplessness, and maternality—visually, verbally, and nonverbally. For example, many different "poses," the exaggeration of sexuality or its denial, via clothes, voice tone, and eyes, may help a woman communicate her basic deference—a stance which is supposed to put others at their ease, and men "on top."

---

[8] This is one of the reasons that working-class families are suspicious of Marxist or Feminist tracts against the family. The family unit is probably the only place in class or Communist society where powerless people feel some degree of safety or pride. Also, women feel lucky if they can avoid poorly paid and dangerous work outside the home, especially when male workers or employers can also abuse them sexually. Most women have always had to work in factories, in mines, or on other people's farms. They were treated like animals—and *also* had to bring up children at home. Women now consider themselves lucky if they can avoid a life of difficult manual labor, a life that has always been woman's as well as man's fate.

Women over thirty who work as clerks, secretaries, waitresses, teachers, or entertainers often wear short skirts (or tight pants), high boots (or high heels), and essentially "girlish" makeup. Here, no matter what else such a woman actually does (or feels), she is trying to say, "I am not a threat—I am a desirable girl." And she gets to keep her job. As wife and as a salaried employee.

Women who work for more money or at high prestige levels often dress in another way—but to accomplish a similar goal. Their style of female deference is a more suggestively expensive one: a touch of "casual" gold somewhere on the hand or throat, a decorous, immaculate look. A woman so dressed is trying to say: "I am not a threat either. I don't really *have* to work. My family has money. I am working out of choice and because my husband permits it. Of course, he—and my children—come first." And she gets to keep her job.

When women at various salary levels adopt sternly dowdy and/or "asexual" clothing, it is not the deference of "femininity" or marital status that is being communicated. Another type of deference is. At a "high" salary level, the woman is saying: "I have chosen a career instead of sex, instead of a family, or instead of emotional abandon. Trust me to be morally conservative and serious. I've paid my dues, I've sacrificed in order to work. You can count on me to work hard. After all, I have nothing else." And she is somewhat forgiven her rather unsettling financial success.

At a "low" salary level, dowdy, plain, or asexual dress, like neatness and cleanliness, function as protective devices. Let no boss say that poor or nonwhite women smell or "let themselves go"—sexually or in terms of their appearance.

Class and caste differences in life expose conditions that make everyone uneasy—and "uneasiness" among the powerful often leads to some form of reprisal or violence. It is best to hide these differences if possible, cover them up with a good "appearance." Low-salaried women try to look as "pleasing," as invisible, as non-threatening as possible: for their own pride and safety—and in order to put others at ease.

Women who wear the Islamic veil, the Catholic habit, the orthodox Jewish dress, are behaving in a similar way. They are avoiding a bad reputation; they are avoiding rape; they are avoiding being fired —by their husbands or by their priests. Their secular female counterparts follow their example—but in more modern and subtle ways. "Plain"-looking women, soft-spoken women may not advance economically, but they may avoid the boss's arbitrary wrath or the rapist's arbitrary eye.

Women's Voices

"Let your women keep silence in the churches: for it is not permitted unto them to speak; but they are commanded to be under obedience, as also saith the law. And if they will learn any thing let them ask their husbands at home: for it is a shame for women to speak in the church."

—St. Paul, I Cor. 14:34-35

"Leaning against the water cooler, two men—both minor executives—are . . . discussing last Sunday's Giants game. . . .

"A vice-president walks by and hears them talking about sports. Does he stop and send them back to their desks? Does he frown? Probably not. Being a man, he is far more likely to pause on his way and join in the conversation, anxious to prove that he too is 'one of the boys,' feigning an interest in football that he may very well not share at all. . . .

"Now let us assume that two women are standing by the water cooler at 9:45, discussing whatever you please: women's liberation, clothes, work, any subject except football, of course. The vice-president walks by, sees them, and moves off in a fury down the hall, cursing and wondering whether it is worth the trouble to complain—but to whom?—about all those Goddamned bitches standing around gabbing when they should be working. . . .

"What he *cannot* do is join in. Two women talking together, from a man's point of view, represent a closed circle. To enter it is to lose a portion of your power by entering a woman's world, to expose yourself to things that are unfamiliar, vaguely threatening, and frivolous at the very least."[9]

Traditionally, women, like children, were supposed to be seen and not heard. Sometimes they were not supposed to be "seen" by anyone, i.e. by men outside the family. Today, women still tend to remain silent in places *sacred to men*—i.e. public places—if they appear there at all. There are a number of verbal styles women use to offend the least, to reduce potential male discomfort, fearfulness, and hostility whenever they enter public places—especially for money.

Some women remain hauntingly silent. In churches, in synagogues, in schools. Slowly, sometime after puberty, their wildly waving

[9] Michael Korda, *Male Chauvinism: How It Works* (New York, Random House, 1972).

hands, their excited voices are lowered into modest silence. With each other, and in *private* or "family" places, women can shriek, giggle, demand. But not where money is being openly made.

Women are off to a safe start if they occupy subservient positions in public places. But even then women try to speak softly, reasonably, calmly, and deferentially. (Too loud and she's called "hysterical" or "shrill.") In their tone of voice, in their body posture, most women ask for permission to speak. They issue "suggestions" rather than commands—even when they are *in* command. They modify their suggestions into questions. Or a woman carefully "gets" men to say what she thinks. And she usually gets no credit, no recognition for her efforts. (This is why women are being considered as such potentially good middle-management executives: they are so "sensitive," so mediating, so "human service"-oriented—at a time when fringe benefits and "status" are assuming new importance owing to a "shortage" of salary money at middle levels.)

Many women academicians, and women business executives, if they wish to survive professionally, must find ways of communicating —quickly and frequently—that they are on the "men's side," that they are not threats, that they are actually even *more* "feminine" or "maternal" than other women. And so, the token female vice-president may apply her makeup and have her cigarettes lit for her during business conferences; the female professor may "flirt" or behave "maternally" toward her male colleagues. The female jockey, rodeo rider and Olympic swimmer may all verbally claim that they "like" men to hold doors open for them. Often, women within the professions offer "being married" or "having children" as primary credentials of deference—in order to get or keep their jobs.

Women try to smile a lot—in elevators, on the street, in the home, and at their salaried employment. "C'mon, honey, why look so serious? Give us a smile, light up our universe for us, show us you're happy."[10]

Women often cover their faces with smiles so that their anger, fear, or boredom doesn't offend or inconvenience others. Women in professional or executive positions learn to smile at the right time—especially when they have to say something controversial, unpleasant, critical—or commanding.

---

[10] But a genuine female smile of satisfaction, especially self-satisfaction, is threatening. Paradoxically, women are also expected to show proof of "unhappiness" at periodic intervals. Tears, certain kinds of bodily illness, silence are used to communicate helplessness, fear, or despair.

Women's smiling is meant to comfort, to please, to nourish. For this reason, women can sometimes "get away" more easily or at least momentarily than men can with a displeasing or controversial statement. When men see a smiling woman, they often feel on personal, sexual, or family territory. It takes men a while to absorb the shock, or strangeness, of a conflicting message such as: a smiling female informing you that God is dead—or that you have been fired.

This is one of the reasons that both women and men "on the job" often experience a female boss as unnecessarily cruel and devious. The woman as boss, like every other woman, may still use her body, consciously and unconsciously, *deferentially*. She also uses her body—her tone, her eyes, her posture—to deny or modify what she is actually saying, thinking, or doing. When women must say no to a man or to a child, their bodies often find ways to soften or deny their words.

Often, when women say yes but don't really want to, their displeasure is carefully expressed through averted eyes, banging pots and pans, migraine headaches—or "frigidity." (But such protest or rebellion is not usually "heard" by men.) Children hear it clearly—so clearly they never forget it.

Verbally, at salaried and unsalaried employment, women apologize for "going first," for interrupting someone else, for taking up male time. Many men tend to interrupt women *all* the time, to bypass the comments made by a woman—only to use exactly the same words later themselves. Business conferences are traditionally notorious for not "hearing" what women say—and "hearing" the very same remark when made by a man.

Women have learned that most men won't listen to them, suffer their presence, or adopt their viewpoint if they have not cultivated an apologetic, tentative, "humble" presentation of self. When men yell—which to women always signifies either potential violence or economic abandonment—women tend to deal with it by making their voices grow softer, more "understanding," more regretful. This is the only way they will be *heard;* this is the only way women have found to protect themselves and their children economically.

Women who work outside the family, in places sacred to men, attempt to "get by" verbally in some other ways too. Especially when they are salaried *as if they were men.* The dropped voice, to emulate male vocal depths; the flirtatious giggle, to signal girlish inconsequentiality; the Grand Dame Lady voice, to signal the existence of a powerful man behind her. These mannerisms are all ways of apologizing for daring to threaten rather than to put men at their ease. For women who work for money it is safer to sound like a little girl, a "rich" female volunteer—or even a male impersonator—than it is to sound like a financially ambitious adult woman.

A male employer or superior doesn't exactly listen to what a woman subordinate says: he tends to tell her afterward what she "really" meant. (And he saves the best parts for the memos he writes.[11]) Or he can listen, hear, show sympathy, and then—do nothing. (He lacks *other* male support to do more.) He, however, is her best friend. He genuinely wants her to *like* him. He likes to see her smiling and agreeable, not yelling and complaining. (He has enough of that at home.)

Thus, men are reluctant to warn a woman about "conspiracies" against her. Nor do they like to be the first to tell her that her hard-earned promotion is not going to mean much after all: that a new (male) committee to oversee her new job has been formed; or that an individual male has been hired as her superior or her co-equal. Theodora Wells gives an example of the kind of conversation that takes place between a "pushy" woman who wants advancement or a raise and a "helpful" male executive. "Be reasonable," he'll begin— and it is he who defines what is reasonable. (By implication, this means that women have a hard time being "reasonable.")

> "He can say 'Can you prove that?' knowing it can't be done; or 'now let's be fair (by my rules)'; Or 'But you just said . . . and now you say . . .' (how can you be so illogical); Or 'Define your terms' (so I can shift the discussion to show your understanding is inadequate); Or 'It's either this or that . . . which is it now?' (Take a position at one end or the other—I'm cutting out the middle ground); Or 'Be specific, give an example' (so I can shoot down the example and prove you are wrong on the whole subject); Or 'Think about it this way . . .' (and I'll control the choices backed with velvet-gloved authority)."[12]

He can interrupt the woman, correct whatever she is saying or attempting to do; he can divert her attention by so doing. He can accuse her of getting emotional. Wells says that finally, if "all else fails [he'll] try verbal dominance. The male voice has sufficient weight to carry the moment, and sometimes longer."

---

[11] This and other points are made very well by Theodora Wells in an article entitled "The Covert Power of Gender in Organizations," *Journal of Contemporary Business* (Summer, 1973).
[12] *Ibid.*

Of course, women in *families* (at home) are not supposed to be male impersonators or verbally quiet. At home, in a place less sacred to men, or sacred in a very different way, women's "true" female verbal selves may dominate. At home, they can gossip endlessly, on the telephone, in each other's homes, over coffee, over bridge, at country clubs, in parks and playgrounds. "Family" women are *always* talking. And about nothing. (How come they are so silent in public places? What are they up to?) "Family" women are supposed to "tell all": to express themselves fully, to confess. Men are supposed to keep their "cool," hide their secrets, sit in judgment, offer absolution. (How come female executives or physicians are so close-mouthed, so impersonal? What kind of *unnatural* creatures are they?)

Women who work on assembly lines and as telephone operators, typists, domestics, waitresses, and file clerks are more like "family" women on the job. That is why you have to carefully supervise them or they will chatter away an entire day's profits.

Women's Eyes, Women's Touch

Men stare. Often openly. Sometimes rudely. Sometimes in friendship or in curiosity. Women generally do not stare. They keep their eyes lowered—lest their stare be interpreted as sexual "provocation." If a woman looks directly at a man's eyes, it is assumed it is a *direct* invitation.

Women avert their eyes. They dart glances about the world. Women learn to sum up entire situations quickly, through a narrow visual frame. They have to. It is the only way they can get the information or feedback so crucial to their psychoeconomic survival.

Although women do not stare, they *do* gaze. Adoringly or girlishly —but not at *many* men, and/or not in public. Female gazing is usually a one-to-one and mutual affair of the heart.[13]

While men stare—at many different women, at many financial projects simultaneously—they do not generally stare at a woman in public

---

[13] Female gazing may take place in public—but only as an expression of communal female deference to one man as he "holds forth": *many* women may look at one priest in the pulpit, *one* male professor at the blackboard, *one* male actor on the screen. When *many* adult men stare at *one* woman she is usually entertaining them, or performing a culturally *devalued* act (involving sex or female nudity), or an appropriately "feminine" act which is not *financially* valued. (Such as giving a lecture on how to bathe and diaper infants.) Very rarely do men in an all-male *group* stare, with respect, at *one* woman who is preaching the Gospel, teaching physics, or commanding military events.

when she is accompanied by another man. Men tend to respect "accompanied" women as another man's property. Here, male-to-female eye contact is phobically or ritually avoided. On the street, or socially, when a man and a woman order dinner or ask for directions, the waiter, the policeman, the male counter clerk all tend to answer the man, no matter who actually asked the question. When a woman is "with" a man whom she is economically superior to, most other men—and women—find it difficult to establish their usual eye contact with the economically superior one, if that one is a woman.

Such nonverbal patterns signify and perpetuate our culture's refusal to allow women to openly enjoy whatever measure of economic power they have. Even when women have more money than women "should" have, they are not treated as if they do. This discourages women from wanting to make money or encourages them to constantly question the value of the money they have.

Many factors are involved in who stares at whom—and when. But one thing is apparent: the use of eye contact usually reduces tension for men and raises tension for women, puts men more at ease, more in the judge's seat, and puts women more on display, more in the prisoner's dock (or in the go-go dancer's cage). For example, while men avoid staring at another man's female property, women tend to look at men most openly when they are accompanied by another woman. Perhaps women feel somewhat safer about initiating a glance, or even a covert stare, when there is not much the man can do at the moment to put the woman's openness to a test—on his terms. Women also look more at a man who is accompanied by another woman for reasons of curiosity and competition, just as a man would look over another man's account ledger or investment portfolio. But the man would do so discreetly, carefully, or secretly. Women do not always fear, respect, or empathize with another woman enough to develop rituals of putting women at their ease. In fact, women probably stare at women—obsessively, competitively, desperately—more than men dare to allow themselves to do with other men. Women are slightly on edge or at least on display wherever they go. This leaves women with less time to contemplate their mortality, or their financial situation.

Men touch women—and first. "Bosses" put their arms around male or female employees, ask genially, benevolently, how their families are. Employees do not return the action without "stepping out of line," without being considered "crazy."[14] "Touching" is one way of signifying power: economic class power in general, and, if then desired, sexual power, the *droit du seigneur*.

Women have a harder time using "touch" to signify power. The same action in female hands is immediately turned into a purely sexual "wantonness" in order to demean the woman, put her off guard, disallow her the *feeling* of sexual and economic power. (If men touched women *only* because of heterosexual desire, and not as an expression of a power differential, we would expect women to touch men at least as often. But they don't. Also, we would not expect secretaries and factory workers to be touched more often than Real Ladies or boss's wives. But they are. Men recognize class differences and class property very well, and adjust their sexual-class sights, and tactics, accordingly.)

The male touch signifies economic dominance. Men touch in order to initiate the proceedings that will give them pleasure.[15]

"Good Little Losers": Growing Up

"Men have superior strength of body; but were it not for mistaken notions of beauty, women would acquire sufficient to enable them to earn their own subsistence, the true definition of independence; and to bear those bodily inconveniences and exertions that are requisite to strengthen the mind.

"Let us then, by being allowed to take the same exercise as boys, not only during infancy, but youth, arrive at perfection of body, that we may know how far the natural superiority of man extends. For what reason or virtue can be expected from a creature when the seed-time of life is neglected?"

—Mary Wollstonecraft, *A Vindication of the Rights of Women*

"You learn a lot from racing cars. You learn what level of risks you're willing to take, and what skill you have. You learn that the important thing is no sudden motion—and that this holds true in life and in love too. If you lock your wheels suddenly this way, there's

---

[14] I am indebted to Nancy Henley's pioneering work in nonverbal communication, particularly for this section and for the sections on female eyes and voices. Nancy Henley and Jo Freeman. "The Sexual Politics of Interpersonal Behavior," *Women: A Feminist Perspective,* Jo Freeman, ed. (Palo Alto, Calif., Mayfield Publishing Co., 1975).
[15] For example, men pay prostitutes to *actively* arouse and *actively* satisfy them—to put them at their "ease" after a hard "breadwinning" race. It only requires money to enjoy some time-travel backward into male infancy. Female infancy is not often revisited.

going to be an opposite reaction which you'd better be prepared and equipped to handle. It's best to do the thing that will get the least reaction."
—Del Goetz, a former racing car driver, now a California entrepreneur, advising women on how to start their own businesses (personal interview).

Men act and women react. Most of what women do can be understood as a *reaction* to male acts of violence. Women try to tame or avoid male violence in its physically murderous or abusive forms and to use male violence in its economic forms.

Women are physically and economically afraid of men. Nature and civilization have not convinced most men to abandon the use of force or cruelty in their attempts to survive—and to succeed. In such a man-controlled world, women do whatever is necessary to avoid "worse" forms of male disapproval or violence. This is the origin of the general female feeling that, no matter what her economic position may be, things could always be "worse." The "worse" fate women seek to avoid involves the possibility of rape, loneliness, economic poverty, and social ostracism. Social ostracism, for women, may lead to rape or economic poverty. Social ostracism usually means being treated like a prostitute or a "bad" woman. A "bad" woman is someone who is loud, selfish, dirty, sexual, aggressive, crazy, violent, etc.

Physicality is a primary experience of self in the world. As boys learn that physical strength or pleasure is considered a basic way of asserting themselves, they learn almost simultaneously that this is primarily what distinguishes "boys" from "girls." And they learn that the difference is important.[16]

The confidence to learn and risk new spheres of self-assertion probably begins with how and what is learned by children in terms of their body egos. It leads (or doesn't lead) to the confidence necessary for achieving mastery in other areas of power: technological, scientific or economic.

Female body language (and financial behavior) is shaped by the physical and sexual socialization of female children; by the kind of supervision or system of rewards and punishments specific to girls; and by the role rape plays in proscribing all female behavior.

Most female children quickly become "little mothers" or "little la-

[16] We have little respect or even tolerance for those who are physically weaker—or smaller—than ourselves. Parents do not really respect children, older children do not respect younger children, physically powerful men do not respect physically weaker men—no matter what *else* the "weaker" has to offer.

dies." Their body movements dramatically change from rambunctious to self-conscious, from outgoing to inward-folded. Such physical transformations can be understood in cultural and psychological terms.[17]

Both boys and girls are taught that "masculine" is "that which is not feminine." Whatever boys do, wherever their human and pregenital physical curiosity or aggression leads them, by definition, becomes sacred space, or territory, a "clubhouse" where girls don't belong or from which girls should retreat. Eventually, girls are taught to sit with their knees pressed close together, their hands folded in their laps—to take up as little male or prohibited space in the universe as possible.[18]

Activities that stress an extension rather than a contraction of the body, such as spectator sports, have traditionally been tabooed for girls.[19] Girls are neither encouraged nor allowed to physically outdo *themselves* or *others* for the sake of a cheering audience. Most girls have not been allowed to experience, directly, the exhilaration—and solemnity—involved in the older generation's "passing of the torch" to youth. Girls do not learn to develop individual athletic excellence which is then *enhanced* by team bonding. Girls are not allowed to exhibit physical strength or skills, which are *achieved*. Girls are supposed to do what comes "naturally": cheer boys and men on the public playing field. The roar of the crowd is reserved only for female youth exhibiting its "natural" beauty—or nakedness. And even here, girls have already lost half their audience because of their sex. Only adult *men* appreciate female youth exhibiting itself. Adult women do not choose to cheer on their replacements.[20] Mothers and fathers cheer their sons on; only fathers cheer their daughters on—and then only in areas that please them.[21]

---

[17] Biology may certainly be involved. But it is not even required as an explanation, since patriarchal culture has so obviously taken its major cues from its own interpretation of biology.
[18] Nancy Henley has summarized a study by J. Silveira which demonstrates that women tend to get out of men's ways on sidewalks more often than men do when the two approached each other. Nancy Henley, "The Politics of Touch." Unpublished manuscript. Also Henley and Freeman, "The Sexual Politics of Interpersonal Behavior."
[19] Physical exercise to keep a female figure firm is not physically or psychologically equivalent to sports. There has also been a traditional fear that "hymens" could be broken if girls exercised too strenuously. This may be one of the underlying reasons for the exclusion of girls from athletic activity.
[20] Adult men can somehow cheer on male youthful strength, which is *achieved* and which *passes* in time, in a way adult women cannot do when they are so harshly judged for "aging."
[21] See Chapter 6, "Women at the Financial Top," for a discussion of the father-daughter relationship.

Thus, girls traditionally, and in every country in the world today, including America, are not encouraged to develop physical strength and/or team skills. When most girls "play ball" at all in America, they play separately from boys; they play softball, not hardball, and they are forced to follow "easier" rules. They also play alone, i.e. no fiercely adoring parents, coaches, teachers, or audiences "roar" for them. Not even when they are the daughters of wealthy fathers.

The discouragement of female physical strength and body-pleasure has crucial psychological implications. Children (like adults) take physicality very seriously. Like adults, they quickly infuse it with symbolic meaning. A "strong" or physically "happy" child is considered a "bright" or "successful" child. A "successful" child is presumed to be somehow in control of what she does.

Although class and cultural differences do exist, most girls are denied the most basic vocabulary of all: that of aggressively or defensively hitting or being sexually "interested" in others.[22] Women can nurse "grudges" for a lifetime. Their bodies haven't been encouraged, or permitted, to learn the body language of sexuality and aggressiveness.

Boys may, in a technological money culture, translate either childhood "strength" or "weakness" into other activities. Schoolyard bullies may become army generals, as may the boys they bullied. Napoleon might have become politically powerful *because* he was short; a man may become economically powerful through counting money, accounting for himself in this way *because* he was bullied in a schoolyard or because he preferred childhood books to childhood brawn.

Girls do not, and cannot, compensate for their culturally induced or exaggerated physical weakness in similar ways. Compensation is actually forbidden to women: in terms of direct wages for labor or in terms of compensating for weakness in one area by developing strength in another.

Today, in the most technologically advanced countries in the world, most girls remain as removed from the development of bodily excellence as they are removed from an understanding of machines—machines which for the most part can perform all that the male body can and more. This is no coincidence. Machines are supposed to help *men* be more physically and economically powerful. Machines have

---

[22] Those classes, races, or individuals that permit such a breaking of the rules to occur usually are powerless to prevent it and are also powerless to prevent the consequent criminal and psychiatric labeling of "their" women that follows.

not been invented to help women overcome physical inferiority. If machines can help women in the kitchen, that's fine, but of less consequence than the fact that machines can help man make more money, get to the moon, commit genocide—and even reproduce the species without women.[23]

The neat penmanship of girls, the quick and obedient memorizing of schoolbook dates *could* be a first move toward compensatory "mastery" on the part of those with a contracted body-ego.[24]

However, girls in modern Western culture are not rewarded for these early attempts at compensation. On the contrary. They are often discouraged and even punished for attempting to develop skills that will command attention, respect—and money. Girls are not encouraged to become adept at mathematics or science. Their "neatness" in numbers is confined to arithmetic. They are encouraged to become bookkeepers, not accountants or mathematicians.

But why do most girls obey this advice? Boys don't necessarily or easily listen to advice or orders given to them against hitting each other, torturing small animals, being rowdy in classrooms—or coming home late, filthy, bloodied, and happy about it all.

Perhaps girls obey orders because they have already experienced or sense the almost immediate and irretrievable danger of waywardness and the ease with which they can be rewarded for just doing what they are told. Most girls are very closely watched and even more immediately judged. "Where did you go? With whom? What did you do? Exactly? Why are you ten minutes late?" are questions asked harshly, repetitiously, darkly of young girls, and less so or not at all of young boys.

Girls must keep their virginity: it is still of prime economic value. Thus, girls become very "sensitive" to and dependent on the opinion of *others*, very sensitive to being praised ("What a *good* little girl!") or criticized ("Girls don't *do* that!").[25] Paradoxically, precisely because so much guarding goes on, girls are not encouraged to develop inner "checks" or controls: there seem to be so many external con-

---

[23] In baby-blue test tubes.
[24] However, the reportedly quicker maturation of girls than boys—for example, their better school grades at a young age, may be a sign of an almost pathological submissiveness, obedience, or desire to please, rather than of any kind of "intelligence" or "maturity."
[25] Thus, female self-esteem is almost completely bound up with what other people think of them. When women lose approval—or love—they are completely devastated. They have lost self-esteem, as well as an economic source of survival. Often women literally have nothing psychologically or economically to hang onto when men desert them.

trolling agents watching, administering "rewards" and "punishments," it hardly seems necessary. This is probably and partially what Freud meant when he claimed that women have poorly developed "superegos."[26]

Female children are usually rewarded and punished more quickly and more severely than male children for each and every action, or inaction. This means that little boys are often allowed greater risk-taking and greater role-failure than are little girls.[27] For this reason, many adult men are often incapable or genuinely unaware of the consequences of their actions; and many adult women are too painfully obsessed, often with great guilt, about *everything* that they do.

Often, not much is expected of girls. They are only supposed to do what comes "naturally."[28] Thus, parents or adults do not reward girls out of pride or respect for achievement when they begin to behave like "girls": cute, shy, seductive, submissive, flirtatious, maternal, frightened, bitchy. Such behavior is not exactly an *achievement* in a money culture. It is not rewarded.

Its absence, however, is punished. Girls may get severely punished if they persist in "tomboy" activities past a certain age, or if they are too sexually, intellectually, or financially adventurous at any age.

Even if girls were encouraged to become physically strong—and were also rewarded and punished—just as boys are, certain sexual practices alone might still break the female spirit at an early age. I am referring to the institutionalized sexual abuse of female children; the psychosexual model of incest, in which girls are encouraged to

---

[26] What is also interesting here is the fact that girls—and women—have been most often labeled as "field-dependent" by psychologists, i.e. dependent on environmental and/or external cues in reaching decisions or in "perceiving." Also, women are not only "dependent" on external cues—they are *distracted* by them, and tend to "do better" in "achievement" testing when working alone. Boys tend to believe that they can "internally control" the outcome of situations. Girls believe that "external control"— luck, fate, or others—is responsible for what happens to them. One study, of college students, by Silvern and Nakamura (1971) suggests that for women, the belief in "external control" is associated with parental restrictiveness and the discouragement of risk taking. Teachers, as well as parents, prefer their little (white) girls to be "dependent." First- and second-grade teachers preferred "dependent" girls far more than "aggressive" girls. "Dependent" boys were not liked more or less than "aggressive" boys. Levitin and Chananie, "Responses of Female Primary School Teachers to Sex-Typed Behaviors in Male and Female Children," *Child Development*, Vol. 43 (4), 1309–16 (December, 1972).
[27] Girls are sometimes allowed the leeway to be tomboys, but only until a certain crucial age. After menstruation girls tread on dangerous territory if they continue acting like "boys."
[28] If this is really believed, one wonders why so many parents claim it is *harder* to bring up a girl than a boy.

fall in love with fathers and to marry father figures;[29] and the terrorizing reality of sexual rape.

Rape functions to keep women in their unpaid and underpaid places, not just physically but psychologically. Our culture's treatment of rape functions to de-authenticate, de-legitimize, and confuse women about the simplest reality. If a woman is "unsure" about whether she causes her own rape, what can she be sure of in life? Was it her fault she was raped? Did she secretly want it to happen? Hadn't she ever fantasized about rape and reached orgasm that way? Maybe it was her fault because she stayed "out" alone? Or because she lived "in" alone—unguarded by a man? Maybe her dress was too short—or her independent swagger too much of an invitation? Maybe it was her fault for not knowing how to defend herself. Maybe, thinks the eighty-year-old widow, it was her fault for not moving into the welfare nursing home "like they told her to do." Maybe she should have listened to her mother and married a rich man, and then this wouldn't have happened.

If a woman can be made to doubt her own body, can she take "risks" with it—or with her imagination? Can she even "risk" listening to her own body when she will be victimized again by attempting to report the rape of her body and, at analogous levels, of her unpaid or poorly paid *labor?* The policeman, lawyer, judge, husband, factory owner, university administrator, physician, priest, politician, corporate president—each tells her she is lying, crazy, or wrong, or that she doesn't have enough "proof." Each man, and her own mother, usually advise her to "forget" it *for her own good.*

The way in which women often act in order to physically survive the act of rape (acting out the demanded—often verbally—demanded roles of lusty whore and frightened virgin) confuses and short-circuits them further. Is this rapist my murderer or my savior? Is this rapist different from other men? How can I turn him into my protector, so he won't kill me?

Some men may have similar feelings on contemplating a male godhead after a tidal flood has destroyed their homes and families. Is He Mine Enemy—or Mine Saviour? Have I deserved this, have I sinned? Will it be worse for me if I accuse Him, deny Him? Perhaps I had better thank Him for not killing me when He so easily could

---

[29] This has been discussed in *Women and Madness,* Phyllis Chesler (New York, Doubleday, 1972).

have. Some men who have been anally raped by men do not need enlightenment by analogy.

Women are carefully taught to value "forgiveness" (for male others) before "justice" for oneself or for other women. And women are also taught to deny this denial of self.

For women to learn how to "lose" (themselves) in order to "win" (love and economic security), and then to discover they cannot exactly "win" anyway, leads to extraordinary apathy and hopelessness.[30]

A woman is (realistically) afraid of getting fired from her job if she demands more money. A woman is afraid of getting "less" alimony if she is too "pushy" and demands *any* alimony or "more" alimony. The avoidance of something "worse" is still on her mind.

Women wonder if they really deserve a "raise" when most men wouldn't hesitate for a moment. Women traditionally keep down expense-account spending and *ask* for less money at any level than men do. Women wonder, with dismay, whether they are being hired because of affirmative action "quotas," or because they are "pretty," or because they are competent. Women wonder if they are being fired because of a "male backlash" or because of something they did or didn't do. Women wonder if they *really* should ask for alimony if they also have "feminist" sympathies—or sympathy for their underpaid ex-husbands-to-be.

Women hesitate—and remain lost. Their "wondering" does not lead to clear answers, nor does it benefit them in other or secondary ways. In a world that values force, money, selfishness, and assertiveness, women are considered only ignorant, weak, and foolish.

Many women have chosen to deal with this fate by trying even harder to look or to be "good," "nice," and "ladylike." Mothers and grandmothers still insist today that Victorian heterosexual "niceties," Victorian female body language, are more necessary now than ever before—given the loosening up—or failure—of certain restrictions on male violence.

In America, anti-feminists or traditionally "feminine" women fear that if bourgeois or upper-class Victorian family life or female body

---

[30] Apathy, not anger. Women are not supposed to show "anger" to men. Men can physically kill them for this. And being deserted is better than being dead. . . . Psychologically, the suppression of female anger leads to, at worst, prolonged depression, self-hatred, chronic and sudden suicide attempts, and chronic acts of violence toward other women. At best, suppressed or denied anger exhausts vital and creative energies. In other words, by the time most women manage to survive there is not much energy left for economic success or emotional pleasure.

language is legislated out of existence by adherents of single-standard behavior, men in power will strike out at all women—including those of their own class, and of course at all men and women beneath them in class or status.

The body language of female deference and/or of a "beautiful appearance" is what most women are still convinced will save them—or protect them from "worse"—in a world of male violence and male power.

3. I'd Rather Be Dead Than Ugly: The Psychoeconomics of Beauty

Woman's obsessive concern with appearances, and with her own in particular, represents the expenditure of many hours and many dollars: time which is not salaried, money which is not tax-deductible, and labor which is not considered part of the Gross National Product.

Women of all classes and ages spend a great deal of thought and money on trying to look "good": young, beautiful, sexy, or classy—"above suspicion." Their jobs—economically and psychologically—often depend on it. Wage labor employment—jobs ranging from that of domestic and waitress to that of prostitute, model, entertainer, and businesswoman—are acquired, kept, or lost as a function of a woman's appearance. Is she young enough? Are her breasts big enough for our kind of waitress? Are they too big for our kind of receptionist? Does she know "how to dress" for our kind of company wife?

Women *survive* psychoeconomically by looking "beautiful" or "sexy" and by maintaining other essential appearances. (A "good" reputation, or a "spotless" home.) Sometimes some women *succeed* financially, by selling their beauty in beauty contests or by selling beauty products to other women. But the money involved in winning beauty contests is nowhere near the money that male athletes receive in the form of college scholarships and bonuses, which may then be parlayed into professional athletic contracts.

The winner of a Miss America beauty contest may receive about $100,000 and a college scholarship for a year of making chaperoned commercials. If she is very lucky, she may receive some sort of movie or entertainment contract. But most beauty queens still have to marry for money, the boy next door or perhaps his more affluent equivalent. Further, we seem to expect our beauty queens to be sexual virgins. In November, 1974, Helen Morgan, the newly elected Miss World, was deposed as an "unwed mother." Anneline Kriel of South Africa took her place—a blond sexual virgin whose fiancé was widely quoted on his disapproval of sex before marriage.

We never ask whether a male basketball or football star is a virgin, much less "bench" or retire him if he is not. In other words, male athletes get more money and—presumably—more sex than female beauty queens.

Where real or "big" money is involved, beauty can be a liability rather than an asset for women. Men in Wall Street and Washington do not want to mix business with a woman's financial pleasure. Men do not want to be "distracted" by a beautiful woman as they plan military and financial strategies.

Yet most women still pursue beauty: frantically, compulsively, defensively—despite any appeal to common sense, despite any paeans to the importance of "inner" beauty, despite the low economic "payoff" involved. The overwhelming female concern with beauty—or rather, the universal female fear of being ugly—supports several industries.

Mirror, Mirror, on the Wall . . .

In the original story of Cinderella, the two stepsisters are so desperate for a prince that one cuts off her toe, the other her heel in order to fit into the glass slipper. (Their blood gives them away.) The fairy tale has many real-life precedents. Women have had their foot bones broken in China and their feet bound in order to signify their status and to attract and please men.

In ancient Japan and in the West today, women dance, run, or hobble along on shoes with six-inch heels. Women have worn corsets and heavy petticoats that made them faint. They have then consulted physicians who "bled" and "diagnosed" them, prescribing rest instead of exercise. Women have bound their breasts—and chemically expanded them; have worn long dresses that they've tripped over, and miniskirts that do not provide enough warmth in winter. Women have kept their hair long, to have it dreadfully caught in factory machinery, dragging them to mutilation or death.

More recently, women have literally mutilated themselves, surgically, in order to have smaller girlish noses, larger breasts, firmer chins, and a no-wrinkle face and body.[1] They have also starved and exercised, not for health but for beauty. Some women have died, gone blind, or developed cancer after silicone breast injections. They claim they "had" to do it: to get a Las Vegas job or keep a straying husband.[2] Other women have had their face wrinkles or acne scars burned off "chemically" with carbolic or phenol acid. Surgeons charge anywhere from $200 to $1,000 for some variety of this chemosurgery. "Wrinkle farms" with and without medical supervision charge between $1,000 and $4,000 for their miracle cures. Diet pills, diet cures, obesity clinics, health clubs, rest farms exist for women of all classes, all ages and, I might add, for women of all *weights*. (A one-hundred-pound woman is often found dieting as fiercely and as frantically as her two-hundred-pound sister.) There apparently is no such thing as being "too thin" for modern American women.

Women may *feel* like a million dollars when they look good—*but they haven't got a million dollars*. Psychologically, women search for what they lack: not penises, but breasts, buttocks, fine figures, good bones. They search to cover up or change what they have: broad noses, sagging bellies, female smells. Despite—or underlying—the well-known charge of narcissism, women generally have very low body-esteem. Women are insecure about *everything* related to their bodies. Women value their bodies (sex-specific and other body parts) less than men do—but have rarely said so in strictly *financial* terms.

In a 1973 study, however, they did. Female and male college students were asked to "write down the amount of money you would ask in compensation for each part of your body that was lost." Female college students thought their eyes were worth a median dollar

---

[1] Plastic surgery is being used by more and more middle- and upper-class women. Poor women would use it too if they could afford to. Their ideology is no different: only their financial ability to practice it.
[2] Linda Watt, "The Ugly Truth About Silicone," *Today's Health,* April, 1974. Not all women die or become sick because of cosmetic surgery. Many are pleased and claim they got what they wanted. And it is not only women who turn to artificial means of keeping their youth alive. Some men do too—in a culture where youth overthrows age at younger and younger ages.

value of $20,000. Male students thought their eyes were worth a median dollar value of $50,000. Men over sixty-five placed a median dollar value of $25,000 on their eyes; females over sixty-five, a median dollar value of $10,000.[3] It is not surprising that juries and courts tend to award women lower damages than men in cases of body mutilation and accident.[4] Women are already primed to demand less.

What Price Beauty?

Manufacturers and advertisers of female cosmetics and clothing do not force women to buy something they don't want. On the contrary, both ads and products promise to satisfy deep female needs.

Women have long been conditioned—by all organized religions if by nothing else—to feel that they are dirty and need "cleaning up": soap, deodorant, perfume, toilet water, and vaginal sprays can easily be sold to them. Women have long been conditioned to think they are ugly and need to "make up" for this glaring defect: lipstick, face powder, eye makeup, and other cosmetics can be sold to them. Women have been taught that aging makes them useless and even uglier than before: cosmetic surgery, hormone creams, face lifts, and chemical treatments can be sold to them.

Cosmetics and clothing are substantial industries in America.[5] It is difficult to estimate the actual number of dollars or the dollar-*value* equivalent of unsalaried time spent by women on cosmetics and clothing. Some women shop during their lunch hours and on Saturdays, for bargains or for ideas. Some shop three or four times a week and think about how they look for three or four hours every day. Some have neither time nor money to browse for ideas or buy prepackaged solutions. But they read supermarket-stocked magazines in the bathroom or after the children are in bed, sew their own clothes, curl, straighten, tease, or cut their own hair, or exchange such services with their friends or within their families.

These activities, in terms of time and cost, vary from class to class

---

[3] Robert Plutchik, Hope Conte, M. Baker, and U. R. Weiner, "Studies of Body Image to Dollar Values of Body Parts," *Journal of Gerontology*, Vol. XXVII, No. 1 (1973), pp. 89 and 91. In this study, the population was asked the financial value for the loss of a penis—but not for the loss of a vagina, a breast, or a uterus.
[4] Nagel and Weitzman, *Women As Litigants*, 23 Hastings Law Journal 171 (1971), pp. 182–187.
[5] "Consumer Expenditures and Income: Survey Guidelines Bulletin 1684," United States Department of Labor, Bureau of Labor Statistics (1971). Superintendent of Documents, U.S. Government Printing Office, Washington, D.C. 20404.

and from woman to woman. There are no reliable statistics on the actual number of hours involved. However, on the basis of Labor Department surveys, it is clear that women of all income brackets in America spend roughly the same percentage of their budget or net income on beauty care—about 3 percent. If anything, women with incomes under $3,000 spend a *greater* percentage of their reported budget on beauty care (3 percent) than do wealthier women—who reportedly spend 2.4 percent of their $15,000-and-over income on beauty care.[6]

Government and private industry offer various statistical estimates of how much money is made by the beauty industry from consumer sales.[7]

In 1973, the major cosmetic companies all reported growth in a market that has been estimated at between $2.5 billion (1973) and $4.9 billion (1974).[8] More specifically, in 1973, Americans spent $800 million on fragrances, $470 million on facial makeup, and $450 million on facial treatments and face creams.[9]

Avon and Revlon are the two largest cosmetic companies. Between 1964 and 1973, Avon tripled and Revlon doubled their net sales.[10]

In 1972, manufacturers (with more than ten employees) reported to the Department of Commerce that the value of shipped female "outerwear" clothing was nearly $2 billion. They valued their shipment of female underwear at more than $600 million and that of "toilet preparations" at more than $4 billion.[11]

---

[6] *Ibid.*
[7] These sources are: "Consumer Expenditures," U.S. Dept. of Lab., and *Consumer Price Index*, all years; Department of Commerce tables on the "Value of Manufacturers' Shipped Products" including *Survey of Current Business*, Table 2.5; *Personal Consumption Expenditures*, Vol. 54 (July, 1974); Standard and Poor's *Industry Survey*, the "Health Care, Drugs, and Cosmetics" Section (August 15, 1974). Molly Synon, "Scents, Face Treatments Record Biggest Industry Sales Gains: Maxwell," *Ad-Age* (December, 1974), 5c.
[8] Synon in *Ad-Age* estimates a 1973 market of $2.5 billion; Standard and Poor's estimates a 1974 market of $4.9 billion. The major cosmetics companies—Avon, Revlon, Max Factor (Norton Simon), Estée Lauder, Elizabeth Arden (Eli Lilly), Noxell, Helena Rubinstein (Colgate-Palmolive), Chesebrough-Pond's, Lanvin—Charles of the Ritz (Squibb), Coty (Pfizer), and Germaine Monteil and Mary Kay—all reported growth in 1973. Avon owns 40 percent of the estimated $2.5 billion cosmetics retail market and Revlon is reportedly double the size of any domestic competitor.
[9] Synon, *op. cit.*
[10] Standard and Poor's *Industry Survey*, "Health Care, Drugs, and Cosmetics." Avon's 1973 net sales were listed at $1.15 billion; Revlon's net sales were at nearly $509 million. As of 1974, Avon's stock plummeted. Whether inflation-recession factors or Avon's specific marketing procedures caused this still remains to be seen.
[11] Exactly $4,199,400,000. In this case "toilet preparations" include categories such as perfume, face powder, eye makeup, lipstick, and permanent wave solutions *and* toothpaste and deodorants, which presumably are used equally by men. It should be noted

Statistics on expenditures are provided by the Department of Labor. In 1960–1961, families—or "consumer units"—spent nearly $20 billion on personal beauty care (clothing and cosmetics). In 1973, these expenditures jumped to more than $51 billion. Naturally, both price and population increases may account for part of this increase.[12]

A very important fact is implied by the Department of Labor in its Consumer Price Index material. The Consumer Price Index for deodorants in January, 1970, was 104.3—and 105.2 in January, 1974. The Consumer Price Index for "face powder" in January, 1970, was 116.0. This jumped to 150.0 in January, 1974. The Index price for other beauty items, such as perfume, has not jumped like this. Nor has the Index price for toothpaste or shaving cream. Some research revealed the probable reason.

Face powders and creams are oil-based. Mineral oil, a refined petroleum product, is widely used in all cosmetics, including hair preparations, lipstick, body lotions, and facial creams of all kinds.[13]

The multinational and Arab oil cartels—in which no woman has a voice—are deciding how much a woman must pay to look and feel "beautiful." Women have little real say over what they can buy and how much they must pay for it—in those areas that are considered to be intimately "female."

What Do Women Think a Beautiful Woman Looks Like?

Most women are (comparatively) short people who believe that they are "ugly." Several studies and many interviews confirm the

---

that the recent attempt to sell beauty products to men is both recent and unsurveyed. The male consumers of makeup and perfume are probably confined to certain large American cities and are in the male minority, especially when compared to the female consuming public.

[12] I can only speculate about the extent to which this figure reflects an increase in the actual *volume* of consumer expenditure. The figure for 1973 was collected differently from the 1960–1961 figure. For this reason, the increase may not represent a true or exact trend.

[13] Chemists, pharmacists, and authors agree that petroleum-based mineral oil is widely used in cosmetics, mainly because it is easier to reproduce exactly each time. (Animal oils may differ from time to time as a function of environmental or nutritional changes.) Mineral oil is not considered harmful or dangerous to the adult human skin. However, mineral oil-based spray products *do* cause lypoid pneumonias in infants, who cannot assimilate the oil particles in the air. This information is contained in *CTFA Cosmetic Ingredient Dictionary 1973*, First Ed., Norman F. Estrin, Ph.D., ed., CTFA, Inc., Washington, D.C. See also Deborah Chase, *The Medically Based No-Nonsense Beauty Book* (New York, Knopf, 1974). In a personal interview, Dr. John J. Sciarra, Professor of Industrial Science, Brooklyn College, formerly of the Department of Cosmetic Science, St. John's University, also confirmed the above.

greater *concern* that women have about their appearance than men do, but also their greater unhappiness with what nature has wrought. True: ninety-eight-pound male weaklings, bespectacled, nonathletic male youths suffer from what nature has wrought too. But they can sometimes compensate for their lack of physical strength by developing intellectual or economic strength. Fewer women take this route, and even when they do, their "reward" is not as great, either economically or psychologically. No matter how rich or famous or smart a woman may become, she's still "ugly" if she thinks she is. And it counts, especially if others still say she is. Men, especially rich or famous men, are never considered "ugly." Or they never think of themselves in these terms, and never suffer because of it.[14] Men are "rugged." They may have "craggy" or "strong" features. When a woman is described as having "lots of personality"—or a rich father—everyone knows that she is "ugly."

What look makes women feel "like a million dollars"? What do women think is beautiful? A "strong" body? A "healthy" body? A body that "feels good"? Not really. Women seem to be mesmerized by something else. In one study of body attitudes, those women who liked their bodies more than anyone else did, either male or female, were "tall and thin."[15] And yet, aren't we the culture that celebrates large, nonfunctioning breasts? Do women want to be "thin" *and* "big-breasted"? Do women want to be "beautiful" like asexual Ladies, or Virgin Marys—or do they want to be "beautiful" like the sexual Magdalene? Or is the trick to appear to be both at once?

The Meaning of Looking Young, Tall, and Thin

The model, the mannequin in America, and increasingly in world culture, is certainly young, tall, and thin:[16] her pelvic bones thrust forward, to be counted along with ribs and collarbones, positively skeletal, a perfectly dead woman, often in makeup so artificial, she might as well be lying in a casket. Occasionally, high-fashion models

---

[14] Rich men may indeed worry about whether they are *loved* for themselves or for their money. But not whether they are *beautiful* or not.
[15] Richard Kurtz, "Body Image—Male and Female," *Trans-action* (December, 1968).
[16] When men in Brazil, Mexico, Africa, or the Middle East achieve upward class-mobility they seem to start preferring their women "thin." Audrey Topping in a *New York Times* article dated January 14, 1975, quotes an aristocratic Kuwaiti woman as saying, "In the old days, our women were poor and fat and did nothing except care for their families. Now we are rich but thin because we all want to wear the latest fashions."

are made up to look somewhat vampiric: not only a dead but a dangerous woman. But a model gets very good money—*for a woman*, for looking this way. What does this image of woman satisfy?

Woman as "thin" is the most effective way of denying and devaluing woman as "fat": as pregnant, fertile, or sexual. Until recently, middle- and upper-class pregnant women in Europe and America were "confined," or kept hidden, when they began to "show"—show their mortality, their sexuality, and most important, their reproductive power—a power great enough to produce life, but not great enough to confer immortality.

We are also a culture of Protestant and European-originated rulers. Women of African, Indian, or Mediterranean origins are not usually considered "classy." Sexy or motherly, yes; queenly, no.

To be a queen, to be regal, to be a Lady, is above all to show restraint and to be perfectly at ease. Female thinness is *supposed* to be a genetic matter, like having the right bones. The work of trying to become or remain thin is supposed to remain a secret. Women dieting, women shopping—minimize or deny that they have done any "work." To work hard at getting what you are supposed to have at birth is to reveal the fact of lowly birth—a loss of divine protection. Women are supposed to *provide* that divine protection, as Goddesses on earth, in each home and on every billboard.

There is another aspect to female thinness. Sociologically speaking, our culture is a male homosexual one: women who look like men, particularly like beautiful male adolescents, will command the highest price as either models or wives. They are the "classiest" kind of Real Ladies.

In the study of body attitudes cited earlier, the women who were happiest with their bodies were *tall* as well as thin.[17] And models *are* tall as well as thin. Here, being "tall" may relate to passing for male. Men, and therefore women, both value height. Height is somehow associated with strength, competence, and goodness.[18]

Height in our culture is economically and politically rewarded. "Tall" men tend to win American presidential elections—and to earn more money than shorter men. "Tall" women, especially as successful entertainers, tend to earn more money than most women do.[19]

---

[17] Kurtz, *op. cit.*
[18] God is often imagined pictorially and in fantasy as omnipotent, omnipresent, and, of course, as a very tall white man.
[19] See Chapter 6, "Women at the Financial Top," for a discussion of this. Factors such as birth order, class and race are also involved.

Traditionally, women who are financially successful in "male" areas, particularly in finance, whether they are tall or not, tend to minimize culturally devalued aspects of femaleness. Such women speak in deep, firm, male tones. (Financially successful men do not adopt girlish giggles or maternal "concern" as signs of economic power.[20])

Human visualizations of divinity, and replications of it, are not androgynous. The Goddess Aphrodite is essentially female, but she has been turned into a taller, thinner, paler, and somewhat more cruel version of her once fuller bodied and *erotically* maternal self. She has become Mars disguised as a virgin, and we, unicorns all, are quickly seduced and trapped by this (male) image of beauty.

Is Beauty an Economic Asset—or Not?

Once upon a time, beautiful young female virgins were sacrificed to pagan gods or medieval dragons to ensure the triumph of their fathers' armies or to save their village. Today, female youthful beauty is not as dramatically sacrificed. It is sacrificed—or sold more quietly, over and over again, by increasing numbers of women, all of whom prolong their youthful appearance as long as possible.

Most women aren't given financial offers they can't refuse for their beauty. And those who are—often have tragic tales to tell about it.

In the case of Hollywood sex symbols, the tale becomes a suicide fable, a contemporary passion play or miracle drama to be acted out and retold again and again. Marilyn Monroe, Diana Barrymore, Frances Farmer, all tell us such tales about their Hollywood triumphs.[21]

As women age, many grow depressed, suicidal, fanatic about their appearance—beautiful women even more so. In one study, "beautiful" women reported greater unhappiness with aging than did either "beautiful" men or less "beautiful" women.[22]

Marilyn Monroe's suicide is an example writ large of what happens when a woman's sexual beauty is so marketed to the apparent exclusion of all else that it *does* result in the real or feared death of every-

---

[20] This does happen sometimes in patriarchal religious realms—where men wear dresses and often effect "feminine" manners.
[21] Diana Barrymore, *Too Much, Too Soon* (New York, The New American Library, 1957). Frances Farmer, *Will There Really Be a Morning?* (New York, G. P. Putnam's Sons, 1972).
[22] Ellen Berscheid, Elaine Walster and George Bohrnstedt, "Body Image: The Happy American Body," in *Psychology Today* (July, 1974).

thing else. Eventually, with aging,[23] the beautiful woman begins to fear that she is no longer marketable. Confusedly, she experiences her "marketability" as "being loved." She fears the loss of attention, the loss of love, the loss of a saleable identity. Now, she may begin to make impossible demands—*for a woman:* for "love" and reassurance.

The beautiful woman fears that her stupidity, her anxiety, her ugliness, so long and well hidden, are now about to show themselves, betray her, proclaim her an imposter, a has-been. (All women, even beautiful women, think they are really ugly.)

The aging beauty queen may believe she *deserves* to die. She is growing hideously old. She will no longer be able to "get by" as Daddy's or Bluebeard's favorite. She feels useless. She may kill herself. Or repeatedly try to. Or she may embark on a search for youth through chemicals, clothes, and surgery if she is wealthy enough. But she will be nervous all the time. She will not often contemplate other roads to financial, or emotional, wealth.

From an economic point of view, only a *few* women can market their youthful beauty in a financially spectacular or even secure way. Most women quickly lose their youthful beauty, despite attempts to prolong it.

Poor women—the majority of women in the world—bloom but briefly. Poor nutrition, poor medical and dental care, dim and crowded bedrooms, classrooms, and factory rooms, all paint age quickly onto the faces and bodies of the poor. Whatever natural beauty they had cannot save them from their allotted drudgery. Also, poor women have a harder time transforming their beauty into legal or lifetime financial arrangements. Men of all classes, poor or rich, are used to seizing (poor) female beauty and "having" it without paying for it.

Wealthy or royal women do not have to be beautiful in order to receive marriage offers from wealthy men. Their fathers have already "spoken" for them. Economically speaking, wealthy women have the least need to prolong their youthful beauty or to improve on Nature's design. Many make it a point of honor—or status—not to do so. Many other wealthy women purchase the most expensive fresh air, exercise, leisure time, and cosmetic care that money can buy, discreetly, and as a matter of course. But the beauty of a rich man's daughter never

---

[23] A process that begins at age twenty-one in our Lolita-land.

seems to win control of her own inheritance for her—or a deciding voice in the destiny of nations.

Middle-class women and those women who aspire to middle-class comfort are very involved in the beauty-and-marriage sweepstakes contest. However, it is not enough to be beautiful. Even—or especially—beautiful women must be willing to barter sexual, domestic and reproductive services also, for either stock tips or marriage.

The tyranny of beauty is not simple, either in its psychic or economic effects. *All* women are forced into relationship with this impersonal standard of beauty.

Beautiful women, like Hollywood blonds, are supposed to be "dumb." Mass audiences—and a private audience of one rich man—do not enjoy or respect a beautiful woman with too many brains, ideas, or ambitions. Traditionally, we laugh at dumb-but-beautiful typists whose spelling drives their employers crazy. If a woman is beautiful and genuinely wants to be bought for the highest price, she has to hide or minimize her ability to think. Publicly, on television, or in private drama, she has to laugh at herself for having ideas or even for wanting to solve things on her own. (The only "idea" really permitted her is the "desire" to marry a rich man.)

All men seem to want a "dumb" young "thing,"—one who doesn't ask too many questions and is willing to be a good playmate. But all men also want a "smart," responsible, and loyal wife, one who will tend to the business of home and children and even to her *husband's* business. As long as her business dealings are used to help her husband and not to establish any independent financial power of her own. All men may want a "smart" wife *and* a "dumb" girlfriend, but only rich men can economically afford the two.

From a strictly economic point of view, beauty is as much a liability as it is an asset to women. Very beautiful women are generally, and understandably, disliked by most heterosexual women. They, in turn, tend to scorn or at least downplay female friendships: men are their bread and butter, their sun and stars.

"Beautiful" women certainly face economic competition from (beautiful and unbeautiful) men. They are also economically threatened by "ugly" women, who promise to work harder and be more loyal to men as employees and wives than do "beautiful" women. "Ugly" women are thought to be less spoiled, more grateful, more humble, and somehow more resigned *at the start* to putting up with their economic fate. And they often are. It is a clever—and lucky—beauty who can use her asset to become independently wealthy.

In a strange way, "ugliness" is sometimes allowed to work for *some* women. An "ugly" woman's financial, political, or intellectual ambitiousness, especially when she is no longer young, is sometimes understood or forgiven her. Plain, "no-nonsense"-looking women seem to offend other, less ambitious women and to sexually distract equally ambitious men less than beautiful women do.

Paradoxically, those women who presumably get close to powerful men because of their beauty are least likely to succeed them as their economic, political, or intellectual heirs. Female beauty, like female sexuality, has its place and its rewards, but the place is not in the U.S. Congress, and its rewards are not liquid gold.

4. Who Really Controls the Purse Strings?

The search for power and wealth conforms to our imposed sexual roles. The quest for money is often a sexual chase which appears to have no place for women. It is "going a little too far" when the "castrating, aggressive bitch" wants not only into the bedroom but also into the locker room and the boardroom.

The psychosexual aspects of money, wealth, investment are vastly different for each sex. Ask men why they invest their money and you hear: "freedom," "game," "risk," "speculation," "success," "prestige," "excitement," "power." Asking women, one hears "security," "old age," "future," "rainy day."

Men are involved in the hunt, the chase, the conquest, and the quantity of conquered game, be it capital or sex. Men experience money as sexual. "Making a killing" is orgasm in the extreme. Girls and women are not even encouraged or allowed to learn about money, its sources, how money as a means of power, or at least control of one's life, is pursued.

"She Walks, She Talks, She Invests"

" 'I don't really know anything about stocks,' said the bright-eyed pretty thing across the table. 'But I love the market. All the men I know love to talk about the market, and if a girl can listen to them about the market, it makes them feel good. . . .'

" 'You thought of that one all by yourself. . . . And what is the stock you had yourself?'

" 'Comsat,' said the bright-eyed thing. . . . 'I just love it. . . .'

" 'Do you know anything about the prospects for Comsat? What kind of money it's making, or could make?'

" 'No I don't care. I don't understand that anyway. I just love Comsat, and I'll never sell it. I don't care if it goes down.'

" 'You don't care if it goes down?'

" 'No I wouldn't care. I won't ever sell it. Someday it would come back. It's too well behaved to stay down; whenever it goes down it comes back up, anyway. . . .' "[1]

Exceptional—practically unfound (even in Wall Street's better days, when male traders, themselves now on the verge of extinction, were making daily killings)—is the woman who is a trader—who continually buys and sells for quick turnover and profit rather than for long-term investment.

The principal concern of women who own stock through their own efforts is security. Their assets, usually obtained through inheritance or gift, are not acquired in the all-consuming, aggressive speculative chase for money; their concern is with the safety of their capital "investment."

These women feel safer with blue-chip stocks, mutual funds, time-deposit certificates, and corporate bonds.

It is believed on the street (Main Street, not Wall Street) that women own and control America's wealth. This, it is said, results from female ownership of stock in the private corporation. Can the female "tycoons" be the same people who can read a recipe but not a financial report? Who can spend money but not understand it? Who can inherit money but not influence its motion?

The contradiction that women are *said* to control the economic fortunes of America yet are universally presumed to be too incompetent to comprehend anything but "feminine," "household" language—cozy domestic terms—becomes very obvious when examining books on the subject. Women's guides to finance are laced with analogies to love, marriage, engagements, happiness, shopping, cooking, babies, etc., as if women will understand only concepts brought within their domestic frame of reference.

But most writings for men about money assume an inability to read or comprehend anything which is not presented in *sexual* terms.

[1] Adam Smith, *The Money Game* (New York, Random House, 1968).

Books for Men

"The market is like a beautiful woman—endlessly fascinating, endlessly complex, always changing, always mystifying. I have been absorbed and immersed . . ."[2]

". . . the study of women is the best preparation for the market. It ought to be easy to recruit apprentices for a serious study."[4]

"Women have an advantage. The smart people are likely to be men, and sometimes men can be intrigued with more than fees and commissions. The Game Women play is Men, and perhaps that leaves them free to be less involved in this one."[6]

"The robber barons, as the tycoons of the post-Civil War era came to be called, descended upon the investing public much as a swarm of women might descend into a bargain basement on Saturday morning."[8]

Books for Women

"As a woman, you actually have advantages over the male investor. You probably have more leisure time in which to read, learn and make decisions. You have your feminine intuition and your basic knowledge of shopping and bargain hunting."[3]

"There are as many sizes and shapes of bonds as there are of gowns, shoes, and foods."[5]

"If you can envision Wall Street as one gigantic dish and the institutions as a single giant egg beater . . ."[7]

"If you were so inclined, you could nonchalantly walk into your broker's office with a shopping list containing orders for coffee, eggs, cocoa, sugar and corn. He would not consider you unusual nor would he offer you green stamps for your purchase. But neither would he sell you groceries. He would simply sell you a commodity futures contract, a concept far removed from supermarket shopping."[9]

Most people do not own anything. A minority fraction of the population owns corporate stock; women "own" a minute portion, and they control virtually none. What women own is generally in name only. They do not control the money. Women do not make the decisions regarding the buying, selling, or trading of stocks and bonds.

[2] Smith, *op. cit.*
[3] N. Leonard Jarvis, *A Woman's Guide to Wall Street* (Englewood Cliffs, N.J., Prentice-Hall, Inc., 1969).
[4] Smith, *op. cit.*
[5] Jarvis, *op. cit.*
[6] Smith, *op. cit.*
[7] Jarvis, *op. cit.*
[8] C. Wright Mills, *The Power Elite* (New York, Oxford University Press, Inc., 1957).
[9] Lotte Kahn, *Women and Wall Street* (New York, MacFadden-Bartell Corporation, 1963).

Women do not make the decisions of the corporations or governments by which the stocks and bonds are issued. Women are rarely privileged with "insider information"; at best, they are corporate "dummies." Women do not control the banks—even those at which they borrow money or buy time-deposit certificates—nor do women control the governments in whose notes, bills, and bonds they may invest. Money managers are not women. Analysts or researchers are sometimes women, but their job is to make recommendations to men who DO make the decisions, sales, purchases, and the money.[10]

Women may become owners of securities through inheritance (usually from fathers or husbands).[11] The daughters of wealth are "finished off" and become other rich men's domestic and social assets. They may receive presents and trust funds but are not groomed to inherit, manage, and control the family's wealth. That is their brothers' province. As a daughter and then as a wife, the "wealthy" woman may have owned nothing,[12] probably knew nothing, and was taught nothing of the business, assets, or how to manage them. And then the widow of sixty-five may feel she is too old to start unlearning and learning. Upon inheritance a husband-surrogate is found to deal with the portfolio. The daughter, wife, or widow who has a trust fund usually has a male trustee (a bank with male trust officers) parceling out the funds in a mandated effort to control the female beneficiary and, at the same time, save tax dollars. Male lawyers, male accountants, male stockbrokers, male money managers decide how to put "her" money into various corporations, funds, bonds, mortgages—also controlled by men.

Sociologist Cynthia Epstein says, "Women are systematically convinced that they shouldn't try to take over control of money. They are made to feel uncomfortable about it, uneasy about it. They're

---

[10] *The New York Times* (February 4, 1973). The estimated total of 5,000 female registered representatives is considered very high since "So many women who have passed the exams . . . are assistants to men brokers or firm vice-presidents, and they don't actually work themselves on a commission basis."

Muriel Siebert was the first and is the only woman to purchase a seat on the New York Stock Exchange. She purchased her seat in December of 1967, remained an individual member until September, 1969, when she incorporated and became Chairperson and President of Muriel Siebert and Company, Incorporated.

[11] Nelson Rockefeller, at his confirmation hearings for his appointment to the vice-presidency, said of his grandfather, John D. Rockefeller: "He gave to his only son, my father, four hundred and sixty-five million dollars. There were additional substantial gifts to his two daughters, Alta Prentice and Edith McCormick, and to other members of his family but the bulk of his money went to charity and to his son." *The New York Times*, September 24, 1974.

[12] Except as is advantageous for tax purposes.

Who Really Controls the Purse Strings?

very insecure about their decisions. And one thing feeds on the other, and they feel stupid and they ARE stupid, and then because they *are* stupid, they think they have no capacity to learn beyond that."[13]

Serious money is one of America's great secrets. Those who have it decline to talk about it for such diverse reasons as taxes, gentility, fear of kidnappings and subsequent ransom demands. Statistics about wealth and stock ownership are not easily obtained.

The rumor is: "Women own most of the wealth because they own most of the stocks." The truth is that women do *not* own or control wealth or investments.

First, most Americans—male and female—do not own stock. In the last study done by the New York Stock Exchange, 29 million adults in the United States owned stock; 90 million did not.[14] The most affluent 1 percent of U.S. families and individuals accounted for 47 percent of dividend income received and 51 percent of the market value of stock owned by all families, while 10 percent of the wealthiest Americans accounted for 71 percent of dividend income and 71 percent of market value (including stock held by fiduciaries and agents), according to the Survey of Current Business. These figures probably understate the concentration of stock ownership that would be indicated for upper-income groups if families were classified by their normal lifetime income or their average income over a period of years.[15]

Second, individually "owning" assets has very little to do with controlling them, the corporations behind them, the American economy, or anything else. Third, what women "own"—that is, have registered in their names, but do not control—is slightly less than half of the individually owned shares; and individually owned shares are a small portion of America's outstanding assets. The number of shares held in companies with more than 300 shareholders or $1 million in assets is 5,701,000,000 held by women and 9,283,000,000 by men.[16]

---
[13] Personal interview, Easthampton, New York, August, 1974. Author of *A Woman's Place*, Berkeley and Los Angeles, University of California Press, 1970. A member of the President's Advisory Committee on the Economic Role of Women (1972–1974).
[14] *A Detailed Look at the Individual Investor*, Marketing Highlights from the 1970 New York Stock Exchange Shareownership Study (1971).
[15] Marshall E. Blume, Jean Crockett, and Irwin Friend, "Stockownership in the United States: Characteristics and Trends," *Survey of Current Business*, Social and Economic Statistics Administration, Bureau of Economic Analysis, U.S. Dept. of Commerce, Vol. 54, No. 11 (November, 1974).
[16] *Shareownership 1970*, Census of Shareowners, New York Stock Exchange (1970).

Institutionalized Wealth

Women do not control wealth any more than they control institutions.

In the current investment market, very little trading is done by or on behalf of individuals; institutional investors, investment companies, educational institutions, foundations, guardianships, investment clubs, life and other insurance companies, mutual funds, non-bank-administered estates, nonfinancial corporations, nonprofit organizations, partnerships, pension funds, personal holding companies, personal trusts, profit-sharing plans having legal ownership of the shares bought and sold, religious groups, and banks account for over 70 percent of the dollar value of the New York Stock Exchange trading volume, in publicly held shares.[17] The institutions bought and sold an average of 15.9 million shares a day and accounted for 62 percent of public shares and 70 percent of dollar value.[18] And institutions—banks, insurance companies, unions, pension funds,[19] mutual funds—are not controlled, dominated, or seriously participated in by

The Leading Financial Institution Investors (excluding unions and pension funds and governments)	Investment Portfolios (Billions of $)[20] (excluding real estate investments)
Morgan Guaranty Trust	$27.2
Bankers Trust	19.9
Prudential Insurance	18.3
First National City Bank	17.2
U.S. Trust of New York	17.0
Metropolitan Life Insurance	16.5
Manufacturers Hanover Trust	10.9
Mellon National Bank & Trust	10.5
Investors Diversified Services	9.7
Chase Manhattan Bank	9.2

[17] "Are the Institutions Wrecking Wall Street?" *Business Week* (June 2, 1973).
[18] 1971 Public Transaction Study, Research Department, New York Stock Exchange, Inc. (April, 1972).
[19] Pension funds accounted for the largest growth in institutional stockownership. Blume, Crockett, and Friend, *op. cit.*
[20] *Business Week* (June 2, 1973).

Who Really Controls the Purse Strings?

women. Of the institutions listed on the next page, only one woman's name appears among those of the top officers.

In light of the actual figures it is insignificant to say that of the small portion of individually owned stocks, almost one-half are "owned" by women.

The institutions have even greater sex-segregated economic power when one considers the special status of "insiders" and their ability to receive preferential information and treatment.[21] Sidney Homer of Salomon Brothers, investment bankers, has said the "institutions tend to go one way or the other massively and almost in unison. They know what the others are thinking and doing."[22]

Women are not part of the boys' clubs, the locker room, or the poker game; they are not part of the economic incest. As outsiders, women don't get information that could influence important trading decisions. "Three-quarters [75 percent] of the share volume represents investment decisions made by men."[23]

The appearance of approximately equal division of stock registrations[24] results principally from such factors as women's longer life expectancy, transfer of stock to wives to help limit husbands' liability and to avoid probate, and for community property laws, tax, and estate advantages involved in distributing income and assets. But even in individual investment and certainly in non-individual investment, decisions are made by men, as are the before-and-after economic factors.[25]

Women hold 32,008 of the 94,472 positions in the securities industry, but only 621 management positions, which equals 6.5 percent of the management jobs and 54.1 percent of the clerical jobs.

The Securities and Exchange Commission (SEC) has not issued rules requiring brokerage houses to recruit, train, and upgrade women. In May, 1974, a complaint was filed with the SEC alleging

---

[21] "Institutional Investor Study Report of the Securities and Exchange Commission," Summary Volume (March 10, 1971).
[22] *Ibid.*
[23] NYSE, *Public Transactions* (1971).
[24] Of the *individually* [my emphasis] owned, publicly held shares, adult females owned 49.9 percent and adult males 50.1 percent.
[25] Female ownership is decreasing. In 1952 "publicly available stocks registered in the names of individual females amounted to . . . 43 percent of all such stock. By 1970, only 38 percent of the total.

"While females have always been equally represented in terms of shareholder numbers, the male investor apparently controls the wealth. Females in 1970 owned only 42 percent of the dollar value of stocks, compared with 53 percent in 1962." NYSE, *A Detailed Look at the Individual Investor,* Marketing Highlights from the 1970 NYSE Shareownership Study (1971).

that the New York Stock Exchange used a screening test in filling sales positions that was very male-oriented and therefore discriminatory. The NYSE could only defend its position by saying "the test was prepared originally for use of member firms in a much more different climate than today."

The SEC then began to look into charges that the New York Stock Exchange test which screens the backgrounds of prospective registered representatives is biased.[26]

An additional way of emphasizing that women do not own most American assets, and that what they own they do not control, is by further breakdown by investment according to income range. For example, in the household-income range of $10,000 to $25,000 there is considerable investment in mutual funds, which, of course—taking the element of control from the individual stockholder—are largely managed by men.[27] Therefore, even if the wife were going to participate in decision making in an individually managed portfolio, group investing, such as in mutual funds, eliminates this possibility.

It is generally recognized and accepted economic policy that money used for investment purposes, however small in amount, must be "discretionary," or disposable income. "No characteristic is more indicative of potential activity than income. What is considered disposable, discretionary income, i.e. . . . what . . . can . . . be . . . invested really puts the woman earner out of the investment category."[28]

And women, all classes of women, heads of household or not, do not have incomes equivalent to their male counterparts. In fact, the same is true whether the woman works outside the home or not.

> "Among women, whether heads of household or not, family income tends to be lower than that of adult males. The median household income among shareowner women was $12,300 in 1970, compared with $14,600 for men. This difference is probably due to the large proportion of retired or widowed women shareowners and of females in a lower-paid income group."[29]

But since it is well established that women heads of household would have the least available discretionary income, they are not likely to be in the stock market. Therefore, figures showing that male

---
[26] *Women Law Reporter,* Washington, D.C. (October 1, 1974).
[27] NYSE 1970 Shareownership Study.
[28] *Ibid.*
[29] *Ibid.*

Who Really Controls the Purse Strings?

shareowners have more money than female shareowners should take into account that most women were already eliminated from investment categories.[30]

In fact, most women shareowners (remembering, of course, that female stock ownership and control are negligible in any case) are housewives.[81]

One out of every eight individual shareholders is a widow. The probability is that she is at least in her sixties. She acquired her holdings through time and service, neither of which is a liquid asset. Invariably the widow, while a wife, was left out of the process of acquiring economic information and economic assets.

Women are not in the job categories which carry profit sharing, stock, and stock options, and they certainly weren't when such fringe benefits were highly desirable economically.

Women are actually excluded from even being considered "active traders," since the New York Stock Exchange defines active investors as those who make at least six trades a year. The Exchange has found that in addition to his singularly male characteristics, the active investor became a shareowner by purchasing stock through a broker/dealer—and earned over $15,000 a year. We know that women most often acquire stock not through purchase but through inheritance, gift, or company plan, which of course categorizes them as inactive.

In addition, only one-quarter of sales and clerical workers (female jobs) have acquired securities.[82] The two employment groups with the largest stock ownership were the managerial and the retired.[33] Of course, the problem is circular and self-generating because of male and female roles. For example, during the year 1969, 80 percent of stock transactions of $20,000 or more were made by investors who attended college;[34] traditionally, this would mean more men. In fact, "the majority of shareowners who made some transactions in 1969,

[80] Of households owning shares, 85.3 percent have male heads of households, and 14.7 percent have female heads of households. NYSE, *Shareownership 1970*, Census of Shareowners (1970).
[81] "A majority, or 58 percent of adult female shareowners are in uncompensated occupational categories. Not unexpectedly, housewives comprise 70 percent of these 'nonemployed' women. . . . Only 26 percent of the nonemployed women are retired, compared to 90 percent of the men." NYSE, *A Detailed Look at the Individual Investor*, Marketing Highlights from the 1970 NYSE Shareownership Study (1971).
[82] NYSE, *A Detailed Look at the Individual Investor*, Marketing Highlights from the 1970 NYSE Shareownership Study (1971).
[83] Blume, Crockett, and Friend, *op. cit.*
[84] NYSE, *A Detailed Look at the Individual Investor*, Marketing Highlights from the 1970 NYSE Shareownership Study (1971).

irrespective of the market value, at least attended college."[35] And women are still less likely than men to attend college. Thirty-nine percent of women high school graduates, compared to 53 percent of male high school graduates (i.e. class of 1972) were enrolled in college in October, 1973, according to the United States Department of Labor, Bureau of Labor Statistics.[36]

Male college graduates had a median income of $14,350, compared to $9,162 for women. But for men who had completed elementary school only, the median income was $7,840 as compared to $4,400 for women.[37] It has been noted that the difference between male elementary school graduates and female college graduates is only a little over a thousand dollars.

It appears that sexually distinctive patterns of asset acquisition are generated from childhood on. Gifts to children tend to differ along sex lines. While girls are given dolls, boys are given, as they say, "a start in life." For example, male children own 60.6 percent and female children own 39.4 percent of the individually owned stock held by nonadults. Moreover, in its last study, the New York Stock Exchange ascertained that the volume of stock owned by girls was ten times higher than it had been eighteen years before; but for boys the increase was twenty-seven-fold.[38]

[35] *Ibid.*
[36] *On Campus with Women,* Project on the Status and Education of Women, Association of American Colleges, Washington, D.C., No. 9 (June, 1974).
[37] *Ibid.*
[38] NYSE, *A Detailed Look at the Individual Investor,* Marketing Highlights from the 1970 NYSE Shareownership Study (1971).

5. Wealth: A Tale of Two Sexes

"Mrs. [Happy] Rockefeller was interested in writing and apparently wrote well. . . . [She] toyed with the idea of a career in journalism. It was not, however, the sort of thing young women of her station tried unless they had to earn their keep. Instead, she made her debut, did volunteer hospital work and in 1948, married a young scientist, Dr. James Slater Murphy. . . . the price of divorce was yielding custody of her children to Murphy and after months of hesitation and negotiation she paid it."[1]

"John Schiff [Dorothy Schiff's brother] was the sibling chosen to attend Yale and Oxford and to perpetuate the dynasty. John Schiff is senior partner of Kuhn, Loeb, the family investment bank where the young Dorothy was once refused a clerical job."[2]

"To this day the female line is as rigidly kept out of Rothschild affairs as the male line is included. . . . [The very first Rothschild will stipulated clearly that] daughters and sons-in-law and their heirs have no part whatsoever in the existing firm."[3]

Women who are born into wealthy families or who marry wealthy and politically powerful men embody female "success." Other women envy, admire, and "love" them.

In the winter of 1974, Pat Nixon was voted the "most admired

---

[1] Helen Dudar, *McCall's* (November, 1974).
[2] Gail Sheehy, "The Life of New York's Most Powerful Woman," *New York* magazine (December, 1973).
[3] Frederic Morton, *The Rothschilds* (New York, Curtis Publishing, 1961).

woman" by *Good Housekeeping* magazine readers.[4] The ten women most admired by other American women in 1974 were, in order:

1. Pat Nixon
2. Golda Meir
3. Rose Kennedy
4. Julie Nixon Eisenhower
5. Shirley Temple Black
6. Patricia Neal
7. Betty Ford
8. Princess Grace of Monaco
9. Ethel Kennedy
10. Mamie Eisenhower

All of these women have power "by association" with the exception of only Golda Meir, who "placed" second on this female-chosen list; she is known for having an extraordinary and nearly visionary measure of independent power. And even here, Meir's "image" happens to be that of a very domestic and earthy grandmother. Patricia Neal, an actress, is also appealing to women, as a legally married mother who also struggled heroically with a severe illness.

These ten women are presumed—by women—to have it "made." Like good blues singers, they stand by—and a little behind—their husbands.[5] They are appropriately maternal and wifely.

Mamie Eisenhower has been quoted as saying, "I have but one career, and its name is Ike." Lady Bird Johnson said, "Anything that's done here [at the White House], or needs to be done, remember this: my husband comes first, the girls come second, and I will be satisfied with what's left."[6] But women believe that these "top ten" women have money or power—or are otherwise worthy of female admiration. After all, these women wear wonderful clothes, they furnish wonderful homes wonderfully and they have dinner with the world's interesting people.

Few female hearts pause to notice that those interesting *male* people retire to another room after dinner, where, without benefit of womenfolk, they make the decisions that control the world.

---

[4] *Good Housekeeping*'s public relations department reports nearly six million readers during 1972–1973. *The respondents for this survey were all female* and numbered approximately 1,100. Presumably, they represented a cross-section of the general readership.
[5] Or fathers, as in the case of Julie Nixon Eisenhower.
[6] Both quotes are from J. B. West, *Upstairs at the White House: My Life with the First Ladies* (Warner, 1973).

Few admiring women seem to understand that these "top ten" women spend a lot of time waiting.

> *Janie Crawford*
> "i love the way janie crawford
> left her husband   the one who wanted
> to change her into a mule
> and the other who tried to interest her
> in being a queen
> a woman unless she submits is neither mule
> nor a queen
> though like a mule she may suffer
> and like a queen pace
> the floor"
>
> —Alice Walker[7]

Most Great Ladies in America are assumed—by women—to have power. They have the ears and share the beds of presidents and kings. They can destroy another woman's social career or create a political career for a properly charming young man. But they can do only certain limited things for *themselves*.

Great Ladies are said to have power, when what is really meant is that they have a "controlling" part in maintaining the status quo. Their diplomacy is that of a eunuch's: deferential and indirect. Their fate is tied to the rise—or fall—of one man.

The Lady's presentation of feminine helplessness and wifely/maternal competence represents short-range and highly limited *tactics* rather than long-range *strategies*.[8] Such coping mechanisms may benefit one woman, some of the time, in certain ways, and may also gain privileges or protection for her own children and for some of her friends and members of her family. But not always. After all, husbands do die, or retire—voluntarily or against their will. Their widows, or abandoned wives, are not always well taken care of.

Few wives or widows in America inherit their husbands' political thrones: Nellie Tayloe Ross in Wyoming; Margaret Chase Smith in Maine; Lurleen Wallace in Alabama; and Miriam Ferguson in Texas are the exceptions. Even when wives attempt to succeed their husbands politically, they are not given formal political party support.

---

[7] *Aphra, The Feminist Literary Magazine*, Vol. 5, No. 3 (1974), p. 52.
[8] Ti-Grace Atkinson makes this crucial distinction in *Amazon Odyssey* (Links Books, 1974).

When they are, it is only to be used as "rubber stamps"—or "fronts" for their husbands or for their husbands' political cronies.

The tradition of presidential widows assuming the presidency, and even that of daughters succeeding their fathers, as Indira Gandhi did, is not practiced in America. Unlike corporate executives, most wives cannot "move on" to another company that easily. Spiro Agnew can *still* make money after his forced vice-presidential resignation. His wife, without his continued support, would have much less of a chance if he abandoned her or if she were forced to support the two of them financially.

As many women of the Watergate crisis have shown us, Great Ladies are always one man away from "the top"—and one man away "from welfare."

Women who are known for their beauty, their high birth, and/or their brilliant marriages are not disliked in quite the same way that women known for their ideas or their independent accumulation of capital are. In fact, women like Jacqueline Kennedy Onassis and Marilyn Monroe are not disliked at all. As icons of "feminine" success, they are loved—and devoured. Consumed, followed, mobbed by the adoring needy. As, for centuries, the wretched have adored—and needed—the Virgin Mary; as prisoners and beggars have shoved each other aside for a glimpse of the queen's carriage. There is no need to dislike, or hate, these two women who, with their baby-breathy voices and wide-eyed vulnerability, embody America's twin-bodied Queen of Heaven on Earth: the Good Girl and the Bad Girl, the Virgin Lady and the Magdalene—American style.[9]

But Great Ladies, and even queens, are always doomed to some tragedy: their husbands' rumored philandering, the death of their children—or of their husbands. We forgive them their royal life best when tragedy becomes a bond between (their) Heaven and (our) Earth. Widow-queens hold the crowd's trust most of all: a woman of high birth, a mother, a woman who presumably has no sex life—the Mother of Us All. In countries other than America she may even wield formal power. In America, she is given respect, and certain types of *informal* power. The widows of powerful men are "consulted," are asked to "sponsor" legislation or people "behind the scenes," but not stage center.

---

[9] In America, even the Magdalene is "really" an innocent little girl. Lust, eroticism, and fertility in Protestant America are not sacred. They are graphically and savagely disembodied and dehumanized in profane rather than sacred ways, in cinema, literature, and massage parlors.

Wealth: A Tale of Two Sexes

Women admire women who are "wealthy" but who do not work for money. Such women are true Great Ladies. And such Great Ladies also function to keep poor women at home—and in factories. If even the Greatest Lady is essentially a married mother, it would be unseemly, and unwise, to be less. Making money—as a boss or a worker—is really not "Ladylike."

Some women are "wealthy"—and are known to work for money. Such women are not necessarily admired by other women. Until recently, financially successful "working" women received no "press." Even today, hardly as much attention is focused on them as on "nonworking" Great Ladies.

For example, most women do not really identify with the female head of a large company. A small boutique, a real estate business, a candy store—an economic "holding" pattern, yes; an economic "extra," yes; but female economic power—no.

A few women who are known as business executives may be known to women, and their economic power forgiven them, *if* they are also properly married Ladies. Preferably widows. Olive Ann Beech of Beech Aircraft, Katherine Graham of the *Washington Post*, and Joan Crawford of Pepsi-Cola do run financial empires. They are all widows who were married to the "right" husbands. These women, and some few others, are at the *female* financial top.

6. Women at the Financial Top

Nothing Succeeds Like Success—Your Father's or Husband's, That Is

Most men at the financial "top" in America have fathers who are or were also "at the top." C. Wright Mills[1] in 1957, Ferdinand Lundberg[2] in 1968, and G. William Domhoff[3] in 1970 each discussed the existence of a male "ruling class" in America.[4] *Fortune* magazine, in 1970, analyzed America's top five hundred business executives.[5] Of course, they are all men, 80 percent of whom are Protestant. (Ninety-three percent of those in banking and insurance are Protestant.) The article notes that

> ". . . a striking number of the executives started out in their present company at or very near the top—as president, chairman (or) founder. . . . 45 percent of the top corporation male executives had fathers that stood at the very top of the business hierarchy either as founder or chairman of the board or president of the company, or as a self-employed businessman."

---

[1] C. Wright Mills, *The Power Elite* (New York, Oxford University Press, Inc., 1957).
[2] Ferdinand Lundberg, *The Rich and the Super-Rich* (Bantam Books).
[3] G. William Domhoff, *The Higher Circles: The Governing Class in America* (New York, Vintage Books, 1971).
[4] For the moment, we wish to avoid the liberal and conservative criticisms leveled against such theorists and will try to concentrate only on those Americans who control approximately 85 percent of the nation's money.
[5] Robert S. Diamond, "A Self-Portrait of the Chief Executive," *The Fortune 500-Yankelovich Survey* (May, 1970).

Women at the Financial Top

But where have all their sisters gone? And what happened to Horatio Alger?[6]

Fortune magazine believes that Alger still lives, or at least once lived. In their 1970 article they note that "22 percent of the chief executives began as stock boys, trainees, junior clerks or hourly shift workers." They note that 16 percent of the chief executives are "the sons of blue-collar workers or farmers."[7] In a 1973 article on recently self-made multimillionaires, *Fortune* found at least 39 men who made or became "worth" from $50 to $700 million between 1968 and 1973—without benefits of a family fortune.[8]

At top corporate levels, men outnumber women 600 to 1. In 1972, of the 6,500 top officers and directors of America's 1,300 largest corporations, only 11 were women.[9] In both the 1970 and 1973 *Fortune* surveys, there were no women listed at the top corporate levels. In other words, the daughters of wealthy fathers do not inherit the "ships of industry" as do their brothers; and the daughters of poor fathers (for example, blue-collar workers or farmers) do not rise to the "tops" of corporations—as 16 percent of *their* brothers did, at least during one brief period in American history. The daughters of the nation have not recently become multimillionaires—as at least 39 of *their* brothers did from 1968 to 1973.

Certainly, there are some notable female exceptions, but they are very few. And their entrance into the boardroom is not made easy for them. A daughter of wealth, such as Dorothy Schiff, the publisher of the New York *Post,* had to fight for her right to run the newspaper.[10] Marriage, rather than college or a "trade," even at the top, was her supposed destiny, as it was Eleanor Roosevelt's. Roosevelt, another daughter of wealth, also had to fight valiantly to climb up off her pedestal, in order to earn her own money, and her own opinions. However, she neither amassed a financial fortune of her own nor achieved formal, independent, and direct political power for herself.

---

[6] Gone the way of Ichabod Crane perhaps?
[7] However, these data are unclear. Such men could *still* have had fathers and fathers-in-law "at the top" who started them at the "bottom."
[8] Arthur M. Louis, "The New Rich" (September, 1973). However, these data are also unclear: these men may not have inherited *established* fortunes but enough of a fortune to make one. The article notes that individuals who were "worth more than 50 million dollars five years ago or who became wealthy merely by inheriting established fortunes" were excluded from the study.
[9] A 1972 *Fortune* survey, quoted by Wyndham Robertson, "The Ten Highest-Ranking Women in Big Business," *Fortune* (April, 1973).
[10] Gail Sheehy, "The Life of New York's Most Powerful Woman," *New York* magazine (December, 1973).

When we talk about a financially successful woman, we mean that she is successful—for a woman. As Cynthia Epstein has noted:

> "One thing is clear about those women regarded as successful in the United States. Women at the top are at the bottom of the top, just as they are at the bottom of any stratum in which they happened to be represented."[11]

Also, such women are usually the daughters of wealthy fathers. Fewer women than men have risen in Horatio Alger fashion. And those few who have are simply not in the same financial league as men whose careers have been financially "meteoric." Operation Bootstrap is primarily a male preserve. Traditionally, women have "needed" a wealthy father more than men have—in order to succeed financially—although most wealthy daughters did not found or run corporations—or countries. On the contrary. Few women who were born into wealth have struggled heroically or greedily for the "right to work." Those who have are so few in number that they have not, as a group, directly controlled the course of economic history. Most upper-class women try to lead Ladies' lives—after "finishing schools" have finished them off. Like most women, they conform to what is expected of them: they "look" good, they marry, have children, plan dinners, flower arrangements, and horse shows; socialize and gossip with each other; play golf, swim, do charity work, drink, visit psychiatrists—and die. They no more than other women have fought to claim legacies of inherited wealth—or legacies of self.

It is difficult to compare men and women at the financial "top" when we are talking about two different "tops," and when there are so few women who have arrived at the female top by any route. However, in 1973, *Fortune* magazine published an article entitled "The Ten Highest-Ranking Women in Big Business."[12] Eight of the ten were either wealthy through inheritance and/or through going into business with their legal husbands. Recently, a number of women have also been appointed to corporate boards. Most of them are the daughters and wives of upper-class men.[13] While many men dream

---

[11] Cynthia Fuchs Epstein, "Bringing Women In: Rewards, Punishments, and the Structure of Achievement," *Women and Success,* Ruth B. Kundsin, ed. (New York, William Morrow and Co., Inc., 1974).

[12] Robertson, *op. cit.* The women are: Olive Beech, Dorothy Chandler, Catherine Cleary, Katharine Graham, Ruth Handler, Bernice Lavin, Tillie Lewis, Vera Neumann, Mala Rubinstein, and Stella Russell. In 1973, the average age of these ten women was sixty.

[13] For example, the following eight women have been named to corporate boards: Helen Copley is a newly elected Director of Wells Fargo, Incorporated; Helene R.

about and actually do marry the boss's daughter, they don't have to go into business with *her* in order to head the company. Women apparently either "need" wealthy relatives who will allow them to work or a male protector-partner whose presence allows them to work. With some exceptions, the single woman of working-class origin does not—perhaps is not allowed to—"operate" at the female financial top.[14]

For example, while the female entrant into the financial stratosphere is still basically an unwelcome intruder, if she *must* intrude, it is better that she be married than single and better yet that she be married to a wealthy man. It is expected that male executives be married too, but mainly because a wife is needed to perform crucial functions for him and his job, while remaining financially or socially dependent on the corporately dictated status quo. The *wife* doesn't necessarily have to have her own money. A female executive, however, does not have a wife. She needs instead a relatively wealthy husband in order to financially "boost" her to a level where she can hire other women to perform domestic and child care services and, if necessary, wifelike hostessing services for her.

It is always desirable if wives or husbands of executives have financial or social connections of their own. However, in the case of a female executive, it is probably as necessary—psychologically—to know that she feels deference or is maternally protective to some man

---

Foellinger, President of Fort Wayne Newspapers, Incorporated, is on the Board of General Telephone of Indiana; Katharine Graham, publisher of the *Washington Post*, is on the Allied Chemical Company Board; Marilyn (Sulzburger) Heiskell, now on the Board of Consolidated Edison and the Director of the Meikin Company and *The New York Times* Corporation; Martha Peterson, Barnard College President, is on the Boards of Metropolitan Life Insurance and Dry Dock Savings Bank, and has served on the Exxon Corporation Board; Mary G. Roebling, former President and Chairman of the Board of the Trenton Trust Company, is now serving on the Board of the National State Bank of New Jersey; Cecily C. Selby, the Executive Director of the Girl Scouts, now on the Boards of RCA and Avon Products; Marina Von Neumann Whitman, now on the Boards of the Manufacturers Hanover Trust Company and the Westinghouse Electric Corporation.

[14] Of course, there are women who do very well financially—"for women"—who are single and/or of working-class origin. They are not, however, at the female financial top. Many women, including feminists—none of whom are at the female financial top, are *still* forced to base their careers on private relationships with men. Such women must be *better* than men at their jobs, but must "team up" with men for the opportunity to *work*. Older or economically superior men—college presidents, judges, business executives, scientists, and politicians—are beginning to hire their wives and girlfriends as highly skilled assistants to themselves. The male professional-social network is then made available to the woman-wife-mistress-business partner—as long as she is useful to her business-husband. Today, women are still trying to influence state and national policy through the traditionally dubious and indirect means of marrying and/or campaigning for male politicians. This is occurring at the same moment in history that some women are trying to *become* those politicians.

somewhere—if not at the office, then at least at home. But this expectation, when fulfilled, presents another problem: doesn't her family represent a genuine conflict of interest for her?[15]

The idea of a woman executive not being married or a mother is threatening to everyone. It is "unnatural." Thus, traditionally, mothers married to relatively wealthy men were the most likely to be present in boardrooms—if there were any women there at all.

Since most mothers, even if they have been married to wealthy men, have not "intruded" themselves into boardrooms, what, if anything, is different about the women who have? And are they very different, psychologically speaking, from the single women or non-mothers or wives of poor men who have also entered financially rewarding places where women are not wanted? Before we try to answer these questions, it is important to remember that very few women in America (or in the world) make or have much money. Most American women earn no money or very little money—$2,000 to $6,000 a year. Ten thousand dollars a year is a lot of wage—for a woman. Twenty thousand dollars a year is considered "high"—for a woman. Advertising agency owner Mary Wells's self-appointed salary in 1972 of $384,000 is unimaginably high—for a woman. But not for the (male) President of General Motors.[16]

In a world where people, both male and female, can starve to death or live at a malnutrition level of poverty, making such fine distinctions at the financial "top" may seem grotesque. But it is important to make such distinctions in order to understand the way in which economic and psychological discrimination against women cuts across lines of class and merit—so much so that few women of any class origin have "succeeded"—either as salaried workers or decision-making capitalists. In understanding the difficulties or limitations of being at the "female top," we can understand why so few women are there, and how little real power such "successful" women have. It should be very clear that women who are unskilled or who earn under $7,000 a year have even less power.

Fathers and Daughters

Class, race, religion and, for women, marital status are all important correlates of financial "success."[17] For women, one other factor

---

[15] Not if her husband is wealthy enough or if her children are old enough.
[16] Salary doesn't always tell the entire financial story about a person's wealth or power.
[17] Interestingly enough, birth order and height—for both women and men—also seem to be correlated with financial achievement in America. Several unpublished studies

may mediate, depress, or override the influence of class or marital status: the father-daughter relationship.

For example, if a woman is born into the "right" family (in terms of money, race, and religion), and is also well educated, none of this will necessarily lead to anything but financially dependent marriage and motherhood.

In the past, researchers have suggested that female "achievement," particularly in the sciences, is related to having a positive paternal role model, or to being brought up as a father's—or a mother's— "son." Margaret Hennig, in her interviews with twenty-five white female business executives, did find a "close, warm, sharing, and supportive relationship" between these women and their fathers. (Which she characterizes as "atypical.") In general, their mothers were not employed outside the home.

But Hennig correctly rejects the hypothesis that these women were raised like "sons":[18] Most daughters receive a different quality of maternal and paternal nurturance than do sons.[19]

Numerous studies have focused on the mother's role in child rearing. While considered an essential duty and a natural instinct, it has also been held responsible for all human evil. Far fewer studies have looked at the father's role, particularly in relation to his daughter's development. In fact, when fathers are discussed at all, it is mainly in relation to sons, and not to daughters.[20]

Recently, some research has been done on the father-daughter relationship. Dr. Joyce Walstedt demonstrated that paternal influence was crucially involved in forming what she calls the "altruistic other orientation" of most women.[21] According to Walstedt, the father's ability to do this is "out of proportion to the amount of time" he ac-

---

done for this book revealed, for example, that 63 percent of women in the 1974 U.S. Congress were first-born children. Seventy-three percent of the men listed in *Current Biography* (and chosen via a random selection procedure) were first-born children. As a group they were also significantly taller than the average American male. Women similarly chosen from *Current Biography* were also significantly taller than the average American female. Fifty-three percent of these women were also first-born children—a significant number, statistically speaking.

[18] Margaret M. Hennig, "Family Dynamics and the Successful Woman Executive," in *Women and Success*, Kundsin, ed.
[19] This has been discussed theoretically in Phyllis Chesler, *Women and Madness* (New York, Doubleday, 1972).
[20] Joyce Walstedt, in "The Role of the Father in the Socialization of Altruism and 'Otherness' in Women," an unpublished doctoral dissertation, Rutgers University (1974), notes that "the son is at least five times more likely to be researched and theorized about as the daughter. Relations between fathers and daughters were the least studied; mother-daughter relationships came next, and entire books relegate daughters to a single chapter."
[21] An orientation which was related to financial dependence or economic poverty—within a *middle-class* sample.

tually spends with his daughter. She found that women who were very "altruistically other" in orientation had fathers who stressed their *own* importance as patriarch heads of the family. The fathers specifically discouraged "unfeminine" and encouraged "feminine" behavior in childhood and adolescence. They also behaved in a sexually defensive or suspicious manner toward their daughters' heterosexual interests.[22] Walstedt summarized her findings in this way:

> "The father does not create his daughter's feelings of otherness directly by being rejecting and cold, nor does he prevent her otherness and its response in altruism by being warm and accepting, i.e., by Treating her as a One. The Altruistic Other Orientation appears to be far more dependent on the extent to which the father socializes the daughter into a typically feminine and nonintellectual role than it is upon the emotional quality of the relationship."

This last point is important. Fathers of all classes, trades, and professions, who *could,* theoretically, be excellent role models or mentors for their daughters simply aren't. Upper-class fathers (and mothers) are as eager to socialize their daughters into the "keepers" of the feminine status quo as are parents of other classes. Politicians, professors, plumbers, and priests; stockholders, salesmen, and soldiers—most do not usually apprentice their daughters to themselves.

In another study, Dr. Betsy Belote found that extremely "masochistic" women reported positive relationships with their fathers, whom they characterized as

> ". . . more gentle . . . and more nurturing than their mothers. It is possible to feel close to a father but not learn from him anything other than how to be a 'good girl.' "[23]

Belote concludes that

> "fathers are the principal transmitters of social expectations of masculinity and femininity within the white American family."[24]

What Walstedt and Belote are suggesting can be expressed at its

---

[22] This supports Chesler's hypothesis of the basically incestual model of psychosexual development for women (Father-Gods impregnating Daughter-Virgins). Chesler, *op. cit.*
[23] Betsy Belote, "Sexual Intimacy Between Female Clients and Male Psychotherapists: Masochistic Sabotage," unpublished doctoral dissertation, California School of Professional Psychology (1974).
[24] A number of earlier studies have suggested this also. For example, H. B. Biller, "Fathering and Female Sexual Development," *Medical Aspects of Human Sexual Development* 5:11 (1971).

most extreme in this way: the mother's role in creating a "successful" child, male or female, is a relatively negligible one, or at least is very vulnerable to paternal attitudes and actions. A father can rescue a daughter from *impotent* "femininity." Or he can more strongly enforce "femininity." Fathers can more easily offset a mother's attempt to either break or make a child's "will to succeed." A father who is, for example, a mathematician himself has the power to either encourage his daughter to follow a similar path or teach her to be a "woman" to him.

The more "successful" a father is *objectively* in terms of money or recognized accomplishments, the *harder* it might be for his daughter to become autonomously powerful—if *it is against his wishes*. We do not have many autonomously powerful or rebellious women among the upper classes in America.[25] Perhaps they were both "rewarded" too powerfully by benevolently protective and conservative fathers at too young an age, and faced with punishment for nonconformity that would have meant a total fall—from pedestal to gutter.

"Successful" women tend to ward off the evil eye of male—and female—dis-ease and jealousy by denying that they were ever ambitious and by attributing their success to luck. (They are not then responsible for what they have done and shouldn't be blamed for success.) For example, Katharine Graham of the *Washington Post* was quoted some time ago as saying:

> "I still don't believe I have it [the newspaper], it's luck. . . . I know it sounds girlish to say that."[26]

Similar comments have often been attributed to other women. Jane Trahey, the President of Trahey Advertising, believes that "luck" and "help" were very important to her—although she very energetically and clear-mindedly underlines the importance of "homework, chutzpah, and the setting of priorities" (personal interview). Jean Nidetch, of Weight Watchers, Incorporated, claimed that she knew nothing about money, that the idea for incorporating or marketing the plan was not her own, that "the money end" was all handled by men for her—and that the entire venture was just a "lucky accident" (personal interview). All of which may be true. There may be room at

---

[25] Although other things being equal, the women of more privileged classes have, in point of historical fact, been able to earn more money and "pay" for more revolutions, repressions, or reforms than have less economically privileged women. But they have not been as well represented in history as their upper-class brothers have.
[26] Robertson, *op. cit.*

"the female top" for even fewer women than there is room for men at the "male top." And luck may be a deciding factor even more for women than for men.

Some studies suggest that women, more than men, tend to attribute their "success" to accident rather than to effort; to the intervention of external forces rather than to the pressure brought to bear by themselves on external events. A verbal or psychological style of passivity or innocent surprise may be more acceptable in women than is a verbal style of ambitiousness or pleasure in one's own achievement.[27]

[27] It is difficult to decide to what extent women who have worked hard actually believe that "luck" or "accident" is important to them—or whether they have learned to say what people expect to hear. (Psychologically, it is always more comfortable to believe what you say.)

7. Women and the Internal Revenue Conspiracy

It is no secret that those in the highest income brackets may pay little or no tax.[1] Though tax laws, like other laws of the United States, pretend to treat all citizens equally, the laws are inequitable and uneven as they are written and as they are applied. The original concept of a graduated personal income tax has been thoroughly destroyed by advantages to those with money and special interests. We are not here focusing on *all* the inequities of the Code, but just those which assault women.

The Internal Revenue Code caters to many special but related interest groups, such as investors, owners of commercial real estate and other businesses. However, there is no recognition given to the special needs, problems, and expenses of women, *as* women.

Tax return forms do not directly question sex but are nevertheless completely male-oriented. Women don't receive institutionalized tax protection as last hired, first fired, lowest paid; women are given child care responsibilities, but little tax relief. Jobs almost always occupied by women may be excluded from the employee tax system. For example, deduction of wages to "domestics":

> "To fail to deduct those wages is in itself sexist discrimination. What the gentleman really is saying is what that woman does in a home is of no worth."[2]

---

[1] E.g. Richard M. Nixon, Nelson A. Rockefeller.
[2] Rep. Martha Griffiths, as quoted in Susan and Martin Tolchin, *Clout: Woman-power and Politics* (New York, Coward, McCann, and Geoghegan, Inc., 1974).

Representative Griffiths underscored these tax inequities privately, commenting that while wages for domestics could not be deducted beyond a certain income level, the loopholes of tax law allowed businessmen routinely to deduct money spent on prostitutes by including these sums in their "entertainment" expenses.

Paradoxically, among the Tax Code's many built-in incentives and what is known in Internal Revenue language as "disincentives," is the *disincentive* to marry or, for women, if married, the disincentive to earn money. In terms of tax as well as other pressures, our country would have women do *only* one or the other.

Marriage and motherhood and beauty, youth, and sex are, we are told, the business of women. But then the system changes its mind. For tax purposes, women's work loses all business aspects.

The Internal Revenue Code encourages and perpetuates traditional husband-wife roles by reflecting the attitude of society toward married women's working outside the home; this labor is treated as secondary, supplemental, and optional. The Code, out of capitalist, patriarchal necessity, can see to it that it does not "pay" for the wife to work—at least not if she's going to earn "real" money. This is another way of assuring that her work and, therefore, to a degree she *herself* are not taken seriously. A married woman may work as an interim measure, an aide to her husband, a hobby, or as a way of accumulating "pin" money. Actually, more than 35 million[8] women work; usually because they have to. But tax obstacles are set up at every turn.

Mothers and married women are victims of special economic inequities including tax disincentives which keep them from working outside the home (except at the lowest paying jobs), overcharge them when they do, and give no relief or reward for working *inside* the home.

A mother can't get adequate child care, can't get adequate income, can't get adequate tax deductions; if she does get a job, she will be paid less, she will get no business deductions for her costs of child care, much less for the generally disadvantaged position of being female in a traditionally sexist society. As for *free* volunteer work outside the home, which she does in addition to her free work inside the home, she is an Internal Revenue nonentity. Unlike the person who can give *money* to charity, the woman who gives her volunteer labor,

---

[8] 35,320,000. *Marital and Family Characteristics of Workers,* Bureau of Labor Statistics, U.S. Dept. of Labor, Special Labor Force Report No. 173 (March, 1974).

her human capital, usually the only asset she has, can get no tax credit, since labor and time are not tax deductible.

The tax advantages that are supposedly gained by married couples benefit the man whose wife is, at best, marginally employed.

As Philip Stern has written,

> "Since the advantages of income splitting are greatest when the wife's income is zero, if she wishes to keep her cash value at a minimum she must at all costs avoid remunerative activity. . . . This information [cash value of the wife] should be used with the utmost discretion and selectivity. Clearly, it should at all costs be concealed from one's wife. . . ."[4]

In fact, as Stuart Filler, professor of tax law, says,

> "[We have] a system of federal income taxation which places a discriminatory tax burden on families in which husband and wife work. The discrimination or disincentive to work is directed at the wife. . . . a husband and wife's incomes are exaggerated, and thus, the wife's income is taxed at rates of tax which begin at the husband's highest marginal rate of tax. The couple obtain no benefit from filing separate returns because the rate of tax applied to the separate incomes of married couples filing separately is substantially higher than the rate of tax that would be applied to their separate income if they were not married."[5]

Tax laws reflect social judgments about life-styles, and taxpayers are penalized or rewarded according to their conformance to traditional roles. Before determining income, income bracket, and deductions, taxpayers are classified as to life-style (single, head of household, married), and the appropriate classification will determine the tax table which will apply to the particular tax return.

Despite general belief to the contrary, married couples *with two similar incomes* can be taxed at higher rates than single persons.

Generally, two single working people pay less than two-earner families, as long as the lower-income spouse (usually the wife) earns at least 25 percent of the total income of the couple. Most married people file jointly, but any tax advantage is lost where there are two earners unless they have extremely disparate incomes.

There is a Tax Cost of Marriage at almost any level of income be-

---

[4] In the well-titled book, *The Rape of the Taxpayer*, Philip M. Stern (New York, Vintage Books, 1973).
[5] Assistant Dean, Hofstra University School of Law, Hempstead, N.Y. Personal interview and private correspondence.

tween $8,000 and $40,000 if the wife earns at least 25 percent of the total income earned by the couple.

Professor Filler concludes that

> ". . . The TCM is so substantial, and thus the work disincentive for the wife is so great, that the family is probably breaking even or earning very little as a result of the wife's employment (this conclusion is based on the increased tax cost and other costs that must be incurred for the wife to be employed), or the TCM is so substantial that the couple would be financially better off [if] they were not married but lived together."[6]

And, in fact, the Tax Cost of Marriage is even greater than the figures alone would indicate. Though it *seems* paradoxical to say that the Code both rewards and punishes marriage, the penalties don't arise unless the nonworking spouse begins to earn money, and money in excess of about 25 percent of the couple's combined earnings. However, a single woman would have a standard deduction which she essentially loses on marriage, along with the child care deduction she would have had as a single parent; by presumably being put into a higher tax bracket (of which she will probably not reap any direct benefits), she may lose the child care deduction entirely.

The Internal Revenue Code is filled with examples of discrimination against women; often, despite the realities of the offices, factories, shops, schools, and hospitals, these are in the form of reinforcing America's conception that a woman's place is in the home.

There is a significant, substantive tax discrimination against women, particularly married working women, although, on the surface, all persons with similar life-styles and similar incomes are treated the same, male or female. For example, all taxpayers are eligible for certain tax deductions.

Nevertheless, there are benefits more often realized by men than women. There are, at every level, opportunities of which men are more able to avail themselves than are women. For instance, men utilize business deductions which theoretically women could, too, except for the fact that women rarely have businesses. And even though not all men have business deductions, women *rarely* do regardless of their class or family income.

For example, Dr. Phillips, a physician, takes his winter vacation by attending a medical convention in Palm Beach, making the trip tax deductible.

[6] *Ibid.*

Ms. Fredericks, his medical secretary, gets the same week off, but wherever she goes, whatever she does, it is not likely to be tax deductible.

Or, Mr. Jones is President of Acme, Incorporated, a small business corporation. The company leases a car for Mr. Jones personally. The car is "written off" by Acme as a business expense.

Ms. Green, a schoolteacher, rents a car for her vacation at a summer resort. The expense is not tax deductible.

Business expenses are subtracted from gross income; the result determines the adjusted gross income, the tax bracket, and therefore the tax liability. The businessman who takes his client out for drinks subtracts the cost from his gross income before determining adjusted gross income and the appropriate tax bracket; he is redistributing his costs so they are shared by the public. Business deductions are unlimited and need not be measured against income or cut off at a maximum figure.

But the working mother who pays a babysitter so that she may go to work and earn taxable—and taxed—money may not deduct the cost from her gross income as a *business deduction*. However, if a woman could deduct child care as a business expense, she would not lose money by taking standard deductions, which would be preferable to her unless she has other significant deductions. Business deductions are generally unavailable to working women; the obvious business expense of child care is not allowed as a business deduction. This item is considered to be a "personal expense," meaning less tax advantage, if any, than a valid business-related one. It costs women more to work. The courts have refused to find, thus far, that child care is a necessary expense for the production of income and employment by working mothers; instead they say childbearing is voluntary (notwithstanding that abortion and birth control have not long been available, much less legal) and that the married woman's decision to work is discretionary. But most married women work because they must.

After subtracting all *business* expenses from gross income, the taxpayer is left with a figure known as the adjusted gross income. She may then subtract an automatic standard deduction of 15 percent of adjusted gross income or $2,000, whichever is less;[7] the deductible expenses do not have to be proven. Or, the taxpayer may itemize all deductions. The maximum which a married couple or two married

[7] 1974.

individuals may deduct without itemizing is the same amount a single individual gets. Through marriage one person, in effect, loses her standard deduction. For a married person to elect the standard deduction, her spouse must also opt to use it. Since women say, and probably quite honestly, that they know nothing about tax, it would appear that in most situations the husband's decisions control.

After *business* expenses are deducted, decreasing the general revenue, and therefore leaving more liabilities to be absorbed by the non-tax-deducting public, only then may personal expenses, those which women will most likely have, be deducted. But even then the deductions may be denied.

Child care expenses, even though they enable the mother to work, even to the extent that they are deductible, are deducted as personal expenses from the adjusted gross income; they are not treated as business expenses.

The "child care deduction" is available to married persons, non-married widows (and widowers), divorced and separated men and women who are gainfully employed.[8]

For married couples to qualify they must file *joint returns,* both must be gainfully employed substantially full-time (unmarried taxpayers qualify even if employed part-time). A divorced person is eligible for the deduction only if she is both the custodial parent and the one treating the child as a dependent for tax purposes. The deduction is available only for those who itemize their taxes and would be lost to those taking a standard deduction, who are generally those with less income.

The maximum deductible amount is $400 per month for child care in the home. For care at centers outside the home, there is a scale of:

$200 a month for 1 child
$300 a month for 2 children
$400 a month for 3 or more children.[9]

There are no additional deductions for larger families.

In addition, severe income limitations are imposed, once the combined annual adjusted gross income exceeds $18,000[10] (50 percent on money over $18,000 child care expenses are deductible only to the

---

[8] The services covered must be care, not education (except for preschool children), of children under fifteen, and also, despite the fact that the section is known as "child care deduction," other dependents including parents or spouses who are physically or mentally disabled.
[9] 1974. These figures were increased in 1975.
[10] 1974. The allowable maximums have been raised.

extent of 50 cents on the dollar to the maximum of $4,800). And if the combined income reaches $27,600, no child care deduction is allowed. None. As soon as the wife's income brings the family over the allowable maximum, or even if the husband reaches that on his own, the child care deduction is lost and, accordingly, the wife's net income reduced. The usual argument to defend the limitation is that it isn't fair to benefit high-income families at the expense of other taxpayers. In other words, to avoid subsidizing the work "hobby" of a woman whose husband has some money. Yet this rationale is not applied to her husband's stock market fun and games to eliminate capital gains incentives, for example, which are for the benefit of upper-class *taxpayers* who are frequently *nontaxpayers*.

Incomes of husbands and wives are combined for purposes of determining the limitation on the amount of the child care deductions but combining incomes would not be required if the couple were not married. If not married, either party whose working income was under the limitation would be entitled to the deduction.

As noted, a family taking the standard deduction loses child care deductions, which are available only to tax deduction itemizers and not to people who take the standard, statutory deduction and file the short-form return. The effect is to deny the deduction to those with less complex returns and less accounting expertise—the very ones whose incomes fit within the "Guidelines."

There is also built into the child care deduction a deduction up to the same amount for household domestic services, even where they are not exclusively for the care of the child. They are partially deductible if they allow both spouses to be employed full-time. These are not available to otherwise eligible working persons who have no children. As a matter of fact, as long as there is a qualifying individual, e.g. a child, "amounts paid solely for household help and NOT for the care of the qualifying individual are fully deductible."[11]

Unlike business expenses or even investments, which may be purely speculative, costs of medical care must be directly related to the existing needs of the patient. Therefore, the courts have said that a sick mother who is unable to care for children and does so only at risk to her life cannot deduct as a medical expense the cost of a nurse

---

[11] Carol Faye Simpkin, *Child Care and Household Expense Tax Deduction Under the New Section 214: Is This Really the Reform We Were Waiting For?* The Women's Rights Law Reporter, Rutgers University, N.J. (Fall/Winter 1972–73).
See also: Alan L. Feld, *Deductibility of Expenses for Child Care and Household Services, New Section 214,* 27 Tax Law Review 415, 441.

to care for her children, since it is not sufficiently related to the mother's health![12] Or, when a mother had throat cancer, and sent her children to boarding school, the tax court reasoned that since the mother had cared for the children in the past, if she was incapacitated—or if she died—some substitute had to be found. It was a nondeductible expense; since the children's absence benefited only the mother's throat and not her general well-being, the costs were not a deductible medical expense.[13]

According to the Internal Revenue Service, the cost of care for children by other than the biological mother is always of a substitute nature and therefore not tax deductible. On the same theory, you cannot substitute one type of food for another (e.g., special health diet) and treat it as tax deductible, or an old-age home instead of an apartment, since you would have to have some food and some home anyway; and when a young child must be cared for by a third person, it is not done for reasons of health—the child's or the mother's—but for the mother's "convenience."

Why is it that when a businessman calls in a temporary person to *substitute* for his secretary who is out sick, the salaries he pays are tax deductible to him?

Joint Return, Joint Liability

Joint income tax returns mean, at the very least, that both signatures appear. Yet the woman who is asked by her divorce lawyer, or banker, or rental agent: "What was your taxable income last year? What were your husband's earnings? What accountant prepared the tax return?" usually has no idea. Out of embarrassment, ignorance, intimidation or past involvement, she simply, obediently, and annually signed the documents put before her.

Lack of information may be the least of the problems facing the wife who ignorantly signs a joint tax return. Even worse, she may be liable to the government for monies due or for fraud. Though predictably she doesn't think her own signature stands for much, she is nevertheless assuming responsibility for the truth and accuracy of the tax return.[14]

---

[12] But see Riech v. Frank 302 F. 2d 374 9th. Cir. (1962).
[13] Ochs v. Commissioner, 195 F. 2d 692 2nd Cir. (1952) (344 U.S. 827 *Cert. denied*).
[14] If there is a valid separation agreement, in which the husband agrees to assume past tax debts but then doesn't, though she has contractual rights against her husband, the wife can't stop the government from proceeding to collect monies from her.

Women face a definite danger when they sign joint tax returns they don't read or which the husband may have falsified or when the husband has defaulted on tax payments, leaving the wife equally liable.

The Internal Revenue Service is not generally impressed with the fact that a wife just signed whatever her husband told her to.[15] There are, however, "innocent spouse" exceptions.

For example, if the husband omits gross income *solely* attributable to him (IRS disregards community property laws in making this determination) which is more than 25 percent of the amount filed and the wife can prove she did not know and had no reason to know of the omission, she is relieved of liability. *But* IRS can take into account whether or not she directly or indirectly benefited from omitted money and then use that against her.

Or, when there is a showing of *fraud,* underpayment of tax is punished by adding 50 percent of the underpayment to the tax bill. But the innocent spouse on a joint return is not liable unless some part of the underpayment is due to her fraud.

Luxury Problems

Manipulation of tax and capital for the advantage of each other are "luxury problems." They become problems of the general public which is subsidizing the affluent. These luxury problems involve tax discrimination in statutes which, though not directly legislated against a woman, surely reflect what her place is. These may go beyond such "female concerns" as child care and health, and appear in sections of the Code in which, for example, tax benefits are allocated to married persons as only one-half each, since no matter how married couples file (jointly or separately), in law, they are one person.

Before marriage, each party is entitled to deductions which one of them loses. And the one who loses is likely to be the woman. She has nothing to invest, presumably wouldn't know what to do with investments, stays out of financial decision. When a husband decides to open a new business, get out of the market, cut his losses, and so on, he usually doesn't act—even in a community property state—as if the assets and deductions are one-half his wife's.

---

[15] In the case of *Aylesworth v. Commission of Internal Revenue,* 24 Tax Court of United States Reports 127 (1955), Caroline Aylesworth testified that her husband "told me if I did not sign it, that I would be very, very sorry. He told me that he would destroy my father. He told me that he would mutilate my face."

People with money to invest, whether they win or lose (it is sometimes more advantageous to "take a loss"), get tax breaks unavailable to those who gain income only through working. For example, capital gains, and sheltered income being taxed less than earned money. But among those with discretionary income to invest, married investors are less equal than others. There should be *no* advantage or special tax treatment for capital gains and losses (despite the debatable theory that it encourages investment of capital), but since there is, why should its application be different, based on life-style and whether the taxpayer is a "couple"? Nevertheless, a single taxpayer pays lower taxes on the first $50,000 of capital gain than other types of income, but married persons have a *total* of $50,000 of capital gains advantage. Also tax deductible is the noncorporate payment of interest on loans, mortgages, installment purchases, etc. Women have a harder time getting credit, establishing business, etc., and are less likely to be (1) tax itemizers and (2) deducting interest. The limitations on the deductible amount are $25,000 on a joint return *or* for a single taxpayer, or $12,500 for each of two married taxpayers filing separately.

In other words, two married persons, whichever way they file, can deduct a maximum of $25,000, whereas two single individuals can deduct $50,000.

For tax purposes certain interspousal transactions are not allowed preferential treatment, though the same or similar transactions, gains, and losses would be beneficially treated between individuals with business relationships, even associations which may exist for the exclusive purpose of tax avoidance, and for which poorer people, including those in "Mom and Pop" businesses, would not have the know-how or the resources. For example, business people establish and dissolve layers of partnerships, corporations, and other incestuous entities which may indeed be closer than the husband-wife relationship. Real estate deeds, for example, are known to trade hands from individual to corporation to partnership and back again even within a twenty-four-hour period, depending on the financial—tax—advantages to property owners.

Real estate can be depreciated (an artificial, paper expense which the property owner is credited with having absorbed whether or not the building is declining because of use, and therefore depreciating in value) if it produces income, but not if a lessor and lessee are married. While this may be correct and appropriate, the result would be different if, instead of (or as well as being) husband and wife, they were Corporation A and Corporation B.

Tax shelters (including accelerated depreciation on real property and depletion allowances on oil wells) are schemes whereby persons with large incomes can use long-term "losses" to offset their gains and lower their taxes. Although tax shelters are totally inequitable to the population at large, husbands and wives must share the advantage rather than each being a separate entity.

Taxation Without Representation

Considering the total lack of female "input" into tax law—there has been *even less* involvement here than in some other areas—perhaps it should not be surprising that the economics of taxation, welfare, and Social Security are so sexist. The Internal Revenue Code is written jointly by the two houses of Congress, in the House of Representatives by the Ways and Means Committee and in the Senate by the Committee on Finance; there is also a joint Committee on Internal Revenue Taxation (Joint Finance Committee). There are no women in the entire United States Senate, of course, so naturally there are none on the Senate or Joint Finance Committee. In fact, from its inception in 1815[16] there has been exactly one woman on the Senate Finance Committee and she was appointed for a term of two days! She was Hazel Abel, a Republican from Nebraska, who replaced a deceased colleague on November 30, 1954. The session of Congress (the 83rd) terminated on December 2, 1954.[17]

Not to be outdone by the upper branch of Congress, the House of Representatives has also had a woman on Ways and Means, its parallel committee. Martha W. Griffiths, Democrat of Michigan, served on the Committee from 1961 until her retirement in 1974.[18] There

[16] Then known as the Select Committee on Finance and Uniform National Currency.
[17] The Library of Congress publication "Women in the United States Congress" lists a Mrs. Veronica Boland as a member of the House Ways and Means Committee in the 77th Congress, and Mrs. Irene Baker as a member of the Ways and Means and the Joint Committee on Internal Revenue Taxation in the 88th Congress. My research indicated that this was in error. Subsequent correspondence with the Library of Congress and the House Committee on Ways and Means established that neither of these women was on the committee mentioned. Both women had been elected to fill the unexpired terms of their deceased husbands. While both men were on the tax committees, neither wife was. In reply to my inquiries the Chief of the Reference Department of the Library of Congress informed me by letter, ". . . it now appears that there is doubt about the accuracy of some of the assignments listed in the Congressional Research Service Reports."—E.J.G.
[18] In the term commencing January, 1975, Martha Keys (D.-Kans.) was appointed.

have been *no* women on the Joint Committee of Ways and Means and the Senate Committee on Finance.

Needless to say, there were no women drafters of the Constitution, or female members of Congress when direct income tax was first introduced via a constitutional amendment in 1913. The American woman had not yet won the right to vote, much less a place in the Senate, much less on the Senate Finance Committee! Nor have there been women Presidents, Cabinet officers, or judges who might have had any major effect on tax (or any other) law.

Should a dispute between taxpayers and government ever reach the courts, the chances of having the facts heard by, and the law interpreted by, a woman judge are negligible.

As terrifying as this condition would be if the two committees did nothing but write tax laws, it is even worse than it seems, since their jurisdiction goes beyond tax laws. It is so broad that it includes Social Security and Medicare, Medicaid, welfare, unemployment compensation, maternal and child care, revenue sharing, and other matters, all of which have greater impact on the lives of women than do most other federal programs.

Assuming that proposed pieces of tax legislation get out of the House Ways and Means and Senate Finance Committees, they then have to face floor votes under a Closed Rule, meaning a yes or no vote without amendment. So passage or defeat is by bodies in which, in the case of the Senate, there are zero female members, and in the House, eighteen,[19] who have essentially nothing to say about tax legislation, Social Security, welfare, Medicaid, etc.

Yet no American revolution has ever been fought because of *this* "taxation without representation."

Tax Package

Proposals

Legislative change cannot necessarily be counted on to attack root problems, much less cure them. However, there is often room for reform, provided that reform is recognized as just minor change along the way and does not seduce people into being satisfied too quickly.

---

[19] As of the 1974 election.

Our tax system is equitable in its original conception only; in practice, it is extremely unjust. However, working "within the system," using the system's own rationales, suggests modifications in the laws which could be used to give some relief to women. In fact, since women are not fully participating citizens in American society, or at least in society's benefits, it can be argued that they should not be subject to the same laws as other people. In tax, one of our few *directly* economic bodies of law, women should probably be subject to special legislation.

Marriage and children and beauty and youth and sex are the business of women. The system in power says this and does everything possible to make it true. But men can't have it *both* ways. A woman who carries out the functions expected of her should get some of the advantages a man gets.

Men have created our economic system, including the structure of income tax. And women, of course, receive the fewest benefits.

The first thing which will change men's attitudes is a shifting of weight in the economic balance. Because the one constant place where men feel pleasure and power is in their pockets.

Following are tax "reforms" to be effectuated while our present laws and social institutions—including income tax—are in effect.

Proposal

> "She gets her living by getting a husband. He gets his wife by getting a living. It is to her individual economic advantage to secure a mate. It is to his individual sex-advantage to secure economic gain. The sex-functions to her have become economic functions."[20]

While marriage is a woman's work (in addition to any other jobs she may have), her expenses in connection with securing husband and marriage shall be tax deductible as income-producing business expenses.

All beauty products and treatments, clothing beyond minimum needs, subscriptions to relevant guides and reading matter, and anything which tends to facilitate a woman's job of finding and keeping a man and a marriage shall be deductible to her.

[20] Charlotte Perkins Gilman, *Women and Economics,* Carl N. Degler, ed. (New York, Harper and Row, 1966).

Proposal

Alimony shall be treated as the divorced wife's earned business income. Accordingly, the expenses entailed in earning such income shall be tax deductible. It shall be recognized that alimony is payment to the formerly married woman for the performance of her profession and as a reflection of her economic dependency.

Support, maintenance, or alimony to the wife shall not be deductible by the husband or taxable to the wife.

Proposal

Since women are valued by their bodies and reproduction, tax credit shall be given to the woman who cannot have children, whether through involuntary surgery (hysterectomy) or other biological factors, and to every woman who suffers loss of one or both breasts or other disfigurement, severely impairing her "value."[21]

Proposal

"Subsidies," for the benefit of poor persons, are "welfare." When the wealthy get them, the euphemisms are "depreciation" or "depletion allowances."

One of the favorite tax shelters of those eligible for them is oil depletion allowances. Briefly, and simply, one of the attractions of oil is that persons who need to appear to reduce their income so that there is less to pay tax on can get the first 22 percent of income tax-free, being taxed according to their bracket on the next 78 percent.[22]

One of the favored rationales of oil depletion allowances is that ultimately one's investment will dry up because, say the beneficiaries of this thinking, "every time you remove a bucket of oil from the ground, that's one less bucket remaining."

Likewise, there is a certain finite number of times the human female (not male) can reproduce. Every time a woman delivers a child, that's one less she is capable of delivering. Her value, as seen by society, may thereby decrease.

Therefore, women shall be granted a body depletion allowance for

---

[21] Tax benefits are now given for loss of sight or limb.
[22] 1974.

each and every child delivered. This shall be apart from and in addition to the tax exemption for the child, and shall have the effect of reducing her income tax group to the next lowest bracket.

Proposal

On the other hand, women who do not have children, and men who have vasectomies, shall be given a tax credit.

Through the harvest of the 1973 crops, under the Agricultural Adjustment Act, there existed a system of subsidizing farmers: they were paid *not* to grow certain crops.

Though the United States may have no official, domestic policy on birth control, except making it difficult, we are certainly involved with population control in other, perhaps more secular, countries of the world, especially for the purposes of experimentation. Legislation, through tax or other forms of subsidy, the result of which would be to offset some of the discrimination suffered by persons who refrain from having children, would not necessarily involve establishing a national policy. But in recognition of the fact that there is a population explosion and that the cost to the government and the taxpayers of supporting each child is X, we can return to the people who do *not* add to that population explosion permanently, or within any year, a certain amount of money in terms of tax relief each year.

Under the "farm price support soil bank program," for example, acreage was reserved by farmers to rent to the United States Government, which then "retired" the land, removed it from production, and allowed it to lie fallow; the farmers, including corporate farmers, were compensated.

If it is true that the beneficiary of farm subsidy programs is the public and not the individual farmer or individual farming corporation, the individual parent is not necessarily the beneficiary of tax incentives for not having children, but rather the public at large would be.

Proposal

After three months of pregnancy, tax exemptions shall be available retroactively to time of conception.

Under present law a woman conceiving April 1 and giving birth the following January 1 cannot get any exemption for the nine months of pregnancy, notwithstanding that people on both sides of the abortion battle agree that at some point a human fetus is being carried.

Tax-sheltered investments in cattle, for example, provide valued losses through immediate deductibility of feed and grain, even though the particular investment yields no income from which to make the deduction.

Proposal

Human labor is at least as valuable as dollar capital. And most volunteer work is done by women. Therefore, volunteer work done in the interests of any social, cultural, educational, political, scientific, religious, or charitable organization shall be tax deductible to the same extent that direct monetary contributions would be.[23]

Proposal

All taxpayers shall have an absolute right to accounting advice and assistance provided free at any time of year to any individual who cannot afford to procure such services privately.

If an individual is indicted on charges of tax fraud, for example, and cannot afford to retain counsel, a court-appointed attorney will be provided. But even without the case of a criminal situation, only people with the money to hire advisors know all the tax laws, schemes, "loopholes," special benefits, preferential treatment.

Furthermore, deductions which are only available to itemizers may be lost on the person who must either file her own standard deduction return or pay a small fee to have the simple return prepared.

Proposal

Before being eligible to use income splitting, married couples shall sign an oath stating that "both parties do in fact have equal ownership, management, and control of the income, assets, and liabilities of

---

[23] Congressman Stewart B. McKinney (R.-Conn.) introduced HR 13586, a bill to grant such credit for persons doing volunteer work with the mentally or physically ill. However, the maximum credit value in the bill was $750 per year per taxpayer, and the value of the volunteer services was to be computed at $2 per hour, or the minimum wage.

the marriage partnership, with penalties for perjury and fraud inhering to the oath."[24]

Proposal

In recognition of their inferior economic position in our society, women shall be taxed at lower rates than men.

[24] Recommended as "Bonnie Plan" by Virginia Cowan, Esq., in testimony before House Ways and Means Committee. *Congressional Record,* April 11, 1973. Introduced into Congress by Richard Fulton, Tennessee. HR 9325 (1973).

8. Marriage and Motherhood: The Psychology of Total Commitment

"I know that somewhere, just to give me the lie, lives a beautiful (got to be beautiful) intellectual, gracious, cultivated, charming woman who has eight children, bakes her own bread, cakes and pies, takes care of her own house, does her own cooking, brings up her own children, holds down a demanding nine-to-five job at the top decision-making level in a man's field, and is adored by her equally successful husband because although a hard-driving, aggressive business executive with eye of eagle, heart of lion, tongue of adder, and muscles of gorilla (she looks just like Kirk Douglas), she comes home at night, slips into a flimsy negligee and a wig, and turns instantly into a *Playboy* dimwit, thus laughingly dispelling the canard that you cannot be eight people simultaneously with two different sets of values. She has not lost her femininity.

"And I'm Marie of Rumania."

—Joanna Russ, *The Female Man*

HE: Darling, why must you work part-time as a rug salesman?
SHE: Because I wish to enter the marketplace and prove that in spite of my sex I can take a fruitful part in the life of the community and earn what our culture proposes as the sign and symbol of adult independence—namely money.
HE: But darling, by the time we deduct the cost of a babysitter and nursery school, a higher tax bracket, and your box lunches from your pay, it actually costs us money for you to work. So you see,

you aren't making money at all. You can't make money. Only I can make money. Stop working.

SHE: I won't. And I hate you.

HE: But darling, why be irrational? It doesn't matter that you can't make money because *I* can make money. And after I've made it, I give it to you, because I love you. So you don't *have* to make money. Aren't you glad?

SHE: No. Why can't you stay home and take care of the baby? Why can't we deduct all those things from your pay? Why should I be glad because I can't earn a living? Why—

HE: (*with dignity*) This argument is becoming degraded and ridiculous. I will leave you alone until loneliness, dependence, and a consciousness that I am very much displeased once again turn you into the sweet girl I married. There is no use in arguing with a woman.

—Joanna Russ, *The Female Man*

The industrial money-culture is completely dependent on the human labor of wives and mothers. And yet, both psychologically and economically, these women are completely excluded from and penalized by this culture. Mothers in America are so many millions of Biblical enclaves in the modern world—a world which reserves financial rewards for what it values most. Our culture needs and values specialized, professional expertise, preferably expertise that can be turned into money. The ability to turn everything (and anything) into money is what we call success or power.

From century to century, women have performed diffuse, nonlinear, nonvertical, repetitive labor—by "instinct."

Mothers are not licensed; they do not belong to medieval guilds or to twentieth-century unions. They learn whatever it is they have to learn from *their* mothers, who learned it from their mothers. As Charlotte Perkins Gilman wrote in 1898, "No mother knows more than her mother knew: no mother ever learned her business; and our children pass under the well-meaning experiments of an endless succession of amateurs."[1]

Modern occupations are contractually defined, involve specific tasks, and take place during specific hours. Since this is the case,

---

[1] Charlotte Perkins Gilman, *Women and Economics*, Carl N. Degler, ed. (New York, Harper and Row, 1966). For the last century, some women have had access to higher education outside their fathers' houses. However, most educational institutions reinforce original family ideology, armed with the even greater authority of scientific truth—a truth not far removed from what our grandmothers taught our mothers. If *this* authority should fail, more overt barriers of economic exclusion persuade women into eagerness for marriage and motherhood.

limiting the time sold and rationally quantifying the money earned is an enormous improvement over labor conditions in feudal Europe and sweatshop America. Traditionally, and through the eighteenth and nineteenth centuries, master-servant and master-slave relationships involved the performance of *many* tasks at *all* hours. Today, only very highly paid corporate executives, self-employed entrepreneurs—and mothers—are expected to be totally loyal, skillful and "on call" at all hours.

However, unlike corporate and private businessmen, wives and mothers cannot convert their skills and time into experience that "counts" in some other job—nor can they convert their labor into liquid capital. Mothers cannot leave their present jobs for "better" positions, nor are they automatically promoted to other positions after they have completed the job of child raising. ("Dropping out" of the job market to *have* children usually means a permanent crippling of direct money-making capacities.) Wives and mothers can't even leave the job of house care and mothering after an eight hour day. In a country where male workers have fought bitterly for—and won—the eight hour day and five day work week, wives and mothers still work like nineteenth century domestic servants or "house slaves," round the clock, seven days a week. *And* their "private" lives are far more open to view and control by their husbands—or male legislators—than are the "private" lives of their husbands visible to *their* male employers, or even to their wives. Men in factories or corporations don't have to tell the boss what they do, exactly, and with whom, when they are away from the job. The average wife must account for her time and how she spends it to her husband. If she is sexually "unfaithful" she can be beaten or economically abandoned, in much the same way as the Victorian parlormaid could be dismissed when she became pregnant or "took on airs." And as the "welfare mother" can be denied even minimal funds if she has a man hiding under her bed.

While the *emotional* commitment of wives and mothers to their work-lives might seem equivalent to the commitment and hours put in by ambitious businessmen or politicians, their payoff in terms of money and power is so much less, there is hardly grounds for comparison. The hours worked by a wife and mother are in no way related to the benefits she receives. Her payoff (economically and psychologically) is totally unrelated to the quality and quantity of her work. Her "pay" is always indirect and is completely dependent on either the goodwill or the income of her husband, or on male legislators who decide what welfare levels and other economic benefits will be. For wives, there is no direct or definite relation between what they put in and what they get out.[2] They are like ignorant primitive farmers at the mercy of unknown natural disasters: they can plant, pray, and even reap, but none of these acts will ensure their own physical safety or material security.

For those who honestly believe that mothers have "true" power—*especially* because they stand outside of the money culture—it is important to realize how very little that culture values the job of wives or mothers. And how much control it has over the destinies of mothers. As we shall see, women are supposed to perform such labor for no wages, no financial security, and no guaranteed emotional "happiness." (Which many women expect and demand, in a way that few men do in relation to either marriage or their wage labor.)

If motherhood were truly powerful and respected, there would be no male wars without mothers involved in the decisions that directly kill the fruits of female labor (people); nor would mothers on welfare be considered "lazy cheats" for whom even pitiful amounts of money are "too much."[3] Mothers would be paid good salaries for doing honorable work. And when this work no longer existed, mothers would certainly appear on the unemployment casualty list—thereby swelling it to such proportions that the unemployment figures might be closer to 60 or 70 percent than the already unmanageable 6 to 25 percent admitted to. And "mothers" (if motherhood were powerful) would never have to live alone or in mental asylums, nursing institutions, and dangerous welfare hotels, after they were over forty-five or sixty-five: men who become senators, Presidents or bishops do not. When a "mother" dies, this fact alone would entitle her to an obituary in *The New York Times* (mothers and wives of *rich* or *important men* do appear there from time to time).

The actual job description of a wife and mother is difficult to describe: assigning a dollar value to it can, at best, be only speculative. Such a dollar value is difficult to calculate and even more difficult to legislate or unionize into existence. Perhaps, from a politi-

---

[2] Who knows how a healthy or happy or creative child is "made"? Or what the cash value for her is?

[3] Rape, prostitution, and war are the three great methods men have of spitting into their mothers' wombs. Prostitution, because men have contempt for and condemn prostitutes; rape, because this is clearly a politically violent act of terror, intimidation, and punishment, used specifically against women; war, because it is the most genocidal method men have of killing—outright—the fruits of female labor.

cal and moral point of view, the unionization of *multiskilled* mother-laborers might prove as disappointing as the unionization of *single-skilled* laborers in America. Such unions have clarified and frozen the boss-worker relationship rather than eliminated it. But unions are better for workers than no unions—as long as boss-worker conditions exist anyway.

"I Don't Work—I'm a Housewife"

Most full-time, middle-class wives in twentieth-century America have absorbed the jobs formerly performed by domestic servants, and of course have continued the job of reproducing and rearing the human species. Wives and mothers (the majority of women in America) do all this—and also work outside the home for minimum wages. They shoulder two other burdens—those of guilt and bitterness: guilt for not being home all the time and bitterness for not being able to materially provide well enough for their children.

Recently the following want ad appeared in *Ms.* magazine:

> **HELP WANTED**
>
> REQUIREMENTS. Intelligence, good health, energy, patience, sociability. Skills: at least 12 different occupations. HOURS. 99.6 per week. SALARY. None. HOLIDAYS. None. (will be required to remain on stand-by 24 hours a day, 7 days a week). OPPORTUNITIES FOR ADVANCEMENT. None (limited transferability of skills acquired on the job). JOB SECURITY. None (trend is toward more layoffs, particularly as employee approaches middle age. Severance pay will depend on the discretion of the employer). FRINGE BENEFITS. Food, clothing, and shelter generally provided, but any additional bonuses will depend on financial standing and good nature of the employer. No health, medical, or accident insurance; no Social Security or pension plan.

Absurd? But true. This is a fairly accurate summary of the job of a full-time housewife. More labor is required when there are children or many children and, of course, when the father, if he is present and employed outside the house, cannot earn enough money and the mother must also work outside the home.

Various attempts have been made to translate the job of wife and mother into financial terms. In 1972, the Chase Manhattan Bank, for example, computed "woman's work" in the home to be "worth"

$257.53 a week or $13,391.56 a year. They calculated that women work 99.6 hours per week at the following twelve jobs: nursemaid, dietician, food buyer, cook, dishwasher, housekeeper, laundress, seamstress, practical nurse, maintenance "man," gardener and chauffeur. At least six other jobs can be added to these twelve: for example, that of educational counselor or teacher, child and marriage counselor, bookkeeper, secretary, social director and hostess, and wifely companion (sexually and emotionally).[4]

In 1974, telephone requests of several state and private employment agencies on the Eastern seaboard for a wife-mother to perform all of the above work were, understandably, met with disbelief and/or laughter. *Each* of these jobs could be filled for different amounts of money. For example, an (unskilled) babysitter could be hired for $2.25 an hour or for $90 a week on a nine-to-five basis, for five days a week. Cooking, ironing, phone answering, and chauffeuring would naturally require more skills, cost more money, and ultimately would be at the worker's discretion. (If she's poor and desperate she will agree to do all these things, until she finds a better deal.) Weekends and evenings would constitute "overtime" and would cost more money. Only the very wealthy can afford to hire "housekeepers" with a high level of managerial efficiency; only the very wealthy can afford a *staff* of domestic servants. Most women *are* that staff, and cannot afford to hire a staff of their own.

There are three major problems with computations, such as the previous Chase Manhattan estimates. First, the figures are not and cannot be reliable. If such services existed on the open market and if all women (or men) were to be paid for these services, the cost per hour or per year would change considerably. Theoretically, it might be higher—or lower—than the Chase Manhattan figures.[5] Also, the cost of benefits such as pensions, health care, and Social Security would have to be included in any honest modernization of the wife-mother service. The kind of managerial efficiency and loyalty demanded of wives and mothers might cost a great deal if performed by "strangers" for "strangers."

[4] Some of these tasks, such as secretary, are more likely to be required in the middle and upper class than in the lower classes. However, family socializing and "cementing" good relationships among a kinship structure is primarily the woman's job—in all classes. Some of these tasks are also, presumably, shared by fathers, such as helping children with homework or visiting classrooms.
[5] Economist Carolyn Shaw Bell made this point in an article, "Definitions and Data for Economic Analysis," *Women and Success,* Ruth B. Kundsin, ed. (New York, William Morrow and Company, Inc., 1974), and again in a personal interview.

This brings us to the second point. Women's attempts, and successes, at creating a "family" atmosphere or an emotionally supportive and stable haven for men and children in a cruel and violent world are, from one point of view, the most "productive" labor there is. Such labor is also composed of a series of very tangible chores: house cleaning, diaper changing, food cooking, etc. However, such work is *not* considered "productive" by the economists who compute the Gross National Product; nor is it necessarily considered "productive" by those who consume this product—children and men. Often, it is not considered "productive"—in the modern sense—by those women who work at it and who say, "I don't work; I'm a housewife and mother." From another point of view, the female willingness to "produce" homes without receiving direct wages and without having the necessary operating expenses to do so maintains the technocratic-capitalistic status quo. Most male laborers could not perform their jobs—in factories, corporations or universities—without a woman producing the intangible and the tangible for them. Employers do not financially recognize the essential nature of "woman's work" on their payrolls.[6]

In times of war our national government has taken over the products of private industry and paid well for doing so. But mothers are not paid money for rearing male children whom the male government then sends into war to kill and die. Nor, for that matter, are women who are sent into the "war" of motherhood entitled to disability and medical benefits, or home and educational loans, as are the (mostly) male veterans of wars. Have you ever heard of a mother being sent to college on a government loan because she had done her "service" in producing and rearing a citizen? Or, have you heard of a private corporation routinely paying a bonus and offering other financial advantages to the *mothers* of the men or women they hire?

The third point to be made is this: Paying women for doing "women's work" would keep women where they already are: primarily at home. However, they are at home now—but with no real security, appropriate financial reward, or any financial liquidity. Labor unions did not do away with capitalist-worker relationships in America. If anything, they cemented them further. But unions did improve the worker's material fate and, to some extent, gave him

---

[6] For example, married men and/or fathers do not often receive higher salaries than single men or male non-parents. When men abandon their families, their employers rarely reduce their salaries. In other words, the labor of mothers and wives is not really reflected in a man's paycheck.

some more control over the kind or level of abuse he suffered. Housewives need a union to do the same for them—*as long as they are doing the work anyway.*

I Gave at the House: The Psychology of Motherhood

Women become wives and mothers without "thinking" about it. They don't have to. Most women have been allowed to think of nothing else from the time they could think at all. Three- or four-year-old girls are congratulated for acting like "little mothers"—pushing doll carriages, playing house, dressing "up," flirting with Daddy. (It is no wonder that girls are said to mature faster than boys—they aren't expected to mature very much.)

The dominant female role model in Western culture is that of the Virgin Mary—an asexual girl who gives birth to a divine male redeemer-child and who is then powerless to save him from crucifixion by other men. It is not surprising that women traditionally have been sexual virgins at marriage, and intellectual and economic virgins throughout marriage; it is not surprising that they seek to marry godlike men, in order to produce a male child. Daughters are "all right," or even "desirable," but only after sons are produced.

Virginity or naïveté, innocence, ignorance: such traits are necessary in order for a woman to be marriage-marketable. Dowries, of course, are highly desirable, as long as the money involved is inherited and not earned by the bride. Women are not supposed to ask questions or know about money or power. At least, not "nice" women. They must do everything for "love." The mystique of love shields them from simple reality: "I am not marrying for money, but for love; I am not controlling my children because they are all I *can* control, and just for a short while, but because I love them."

Altruism, self-sacrifice, idealism, the giving of oneself to others—these traits are equally necessary for the role of wife and mother. The woman must be willing, no, maniacally eager, to be swallowed up whole, in terms of primary identity, by the institution of the family.[7] Women are conditioned to invest more affection, more "self" into relationships in general, and into the primary family relationship in particular.

The wife-mother woman must prefer, indeed enjoy, vicarious rather than real rewards or experiences. Her husband's paycheck and

[7] Lewis Coser, in *Greedy Institutions* (New York, Free Press, 1974), makes this point.

professional identity are supposedly real enough for her; her children's achievements are supposedly real enough for her; male sexual pleasure traditionally has been more real than her own (lack of) pleasure, and could, indeed, make up for it.

When the wife-woman or mother-woman expresses her "altruistic-other" orientation and is satisfied with the social, psychological, or economic rewards it elicits, she feels happy or fulfilled. When she is in conflict with her altruism, or when it doesn't "pay off" as it is supposed to, she is "unhappy."

At such a time, she looks for "help." She tells friends, clergymen, psychiatrists—anyone who will listen—that "something is terribly wrong." At this time, rather than state what *exactly* is wrong, she tends to express her anger or discontent indirectly, through physical symptoms. Headaches and backaches are far more socially acceptable than are angry words or un-Ladylike actions. In general, women "somatize" as much as possible. They suffer postpartum depressions, develop skin diseases, obesity, and gynecological problems rather than analyze or face whatever they think is "worse" than what is making them unhappy now.

Much of what women do, and feel, stems from a need to avoid something "worse" rather than to achieve something "better."[8] Much of female altruism and pacifism is based on low self-esteem and physical cowardice or inexperience.

For Love or Money

Women are geared to making "total" commitments for which they expect total returns. Covert and overt female expectations are highly unrealistic, and are dealt the usual death blows by reality. But women are also taught to be "unprepared" for unmet expectations. Women who do what they are told to do, do not expect truly "bad" things to happen to them as a *matter of course*.[9] Women think: maybe they won't have money but they will be happy—they'll have a loving family; or, maybe there won't be enough time for "understanding" but at least they will all be healthy and materially comfortable; or, if a hus-

---

[8] How such behavior is formed has been discussed elsewhere. Briefly, it includes the incestuous relationship promoted by fathers, usually to enforce a daughter's "femininity," rather than to promote her humanity; the mother's essentially powerless and therefore contributing role to this developmental process; the close supervision of or the many external controls placed on daughters. See Chapter 2.

[9] Female expectations vary from class to class and perhaps race to race.

band dies or abandons the family, the children will "make up" for his absence. However, most of these adjusted expectations are not met—for most women. And their capacity, psychologically, to accept or minimize these disappointments is less than heroic.[10] In general, when "bad" things happen to them or to their families, women are prepared to adopt the strategies of denial and self-blame rather than those of perception or struggle.

Today, in America, women are paid less money or not hired at all because they either are or potentially can become mothers. Pregnancy is viewed with alarm. It is treated as a disaster or a disease and not as a natural or desirable event.

Further, the gynecological and obstetrical procedures reserved for the mothers of our race have come under increasingly negative scrutiny, e.g. pregnancy is treated, *when* it is treated, as a "disease"—one that male doctors in forbiddingly antiseptic hospitals "cure" at their own convenience, and for high fees.[11] Many women do not remember their hospital confinements as something they really "expected."

Wives and mothers, like other victims, psychologically deal with misfortune by blaming themselves, attributing it to God, or simply by hiding it from others, if not from themselves. For example, women do not, traditionally, talk about being slapped or beaten up by their (middle-class) husbands. They do not talk about being raped or left sexually unsatisfied by their husbands. They do not talk about being sadistically belittled or left quite alone with small children—with or without money—for years at a time, or for a lifetime. They do not talk about the "death of love" or the loneliness of the Married Lady. They do not talk about resenting or hating their children. And when they do, they are consumed with guilt. They do not talk about the injustice of being primarily and totally responsible for children, as almost all mothers are.[12] Nor do most women "complain" about having

---

[10] Of course, men doomed to unemployment and/or imprisonment do not often turn the tragedy into poetry, politics, or philosophy. But again: if the above point is also true for men in "their" area, that doesn't make it untrue for women in "their" area.

[11] This criticism should not be mistaken for a criticism of genuine and necessary medical advances that have lowered the infant and maternal death rate, decreased pain, and increased the probabilities of a normal, healthy infant. It is important, however, to also note that too few medical investigations and diagnostic-treatment programs have been planned for problems that negatively affect women but that do not interfere with actual childbearing or male sexual pleasure. For example, chronic vaginal infections, the negative side effects of the female birth control pill and other devices, menopause, postpartum depression, premenstrual and menstrual pain—all have not been well studied.

[12] Most fathers do not perform as parents. Those who do try to spend more time with their children do so because they can economically afford to and because they have decided it is good for *them*, not necessarily for their wives.

to work at many jobs—that of wife, that of mother (jobs which consist of many sub-jobs), and that of worker outside the home. For a sex that supposedly does nothing but "talk," wives are remarkably silent about crucial matters. (As if to name the discontent or injustice is to admit its existence; as if psychological denial can somehow make reality disappear.)

The intrinsic importance of parenting is not being questioned here. The abysmally low level of financial and psychological reward is. The importance and difficulty of "successful" parenting is not being questioned; our society's refusal to admit and deal with the problem is. Motherhood is not being questioned; motherhood as forced labor is. Mothers, like many other forced laborers, are not given the proper tools with which to do their jobs. Most mothers do not have an adequate amount of money, education, housing, and leisure to insure healthy child or family development according to anybody's standards. But mothers are the first to be blamed when their poverty produces children who are self-destructive and socially dangerous. Their children blame them; they blame themselves; and psychiatrists, psychologists, judges, teachers, and husbands blame the mothers as a matter of guiding principle.

In all fairness, women have as great a right to mediocrity and failure as men do. (If only *mothers* really believed this!) But women as mothers compare themselves to ideals, not to reality. They are—or feel they should be—mirror versions of the Virgin Mary as Earth Goddess. They are "revolted" by the idea that they are workers in the industrial vineyards. Remember: American women are told they are supposed to marry for love and for God and not for economic survival. It is psychologically difficult for mothers to accept the grim realities of economic exploitation, of being used, and of using others in turn.

Children are treated as their mothers' total responsibility: They are what she "produces" in the world. And yet, she is far more exploited economically than the assembly line worker or the physician and also far more involved with her product than they are. Poorly assembled machines, money lost, lives lost—all "happen" to the best of men, but do not often plague and follow them to the grave or keep them awake nights. As mothers are kept awake. Women who have no other property—or even who *do* have other property—tend to treat their children as property.[18] As Juliet Mitchell has noted in *Woman's Estate*, maternity in capitalist society often attempts a "sad mimicry" of alienated production. Motherhood becomes a substitute for "work," the child is seen as an "object," but "there are few more precarious ventures on which to base a life." Workers on the assembly line, mothers on the reproductive assembly line—both are fated to part with half-finished "products" that can never really be owned or controlled by them.

Women are thoroughly conditioned to *want* to be good to and to sacrifice themselves for male children and for adult men. (Not for other women.) This inhuman sacrifice of self has a dangerously shortsighted altruism at its core; an altruism that ensures the female's eager complicity with the status quo. And the status quo is one in which marriage and motherhood do *not* "pay off," economically and psychologically, as we think they *should*. Nevertheless, women feel even more threatened when marriage and motherhood as basic female survival mechanisms are taken away from them. They fear, as usual, that something "worse" will happen, if they leave an abusive husband or abandon their children. And they are right. The nonpayoffs of divorce and of marketplace employment do, in all reality, match many women's nightmare expectations.

---

[18] Children tend to "own" their mothers as much as, if not more than, they are owned by them. Mothers *feel* "owned" by their children.

9. Survival Tactics: Marriage and Divorce

Americans marry. They also divorce.[1] And remarry. Marriage is a popular female survival technique. So is divorce.

People marry for different reasons. One major reason women marry: it is the most available, if not the only, survival option in a world which has narrowly defined a woman's place. Marriage may be another way of saying "nothing left to do." Marriage looks good, is glorified, compared with the kinds of jobs women traditionally get. Actually, wives also work in the offices, stores, factories they thought they were escaping. Not only have women been allowed fewer options, but they are also programmed to anticipate, seek out or await, and then gratefully accept the marital condition.

Men, despite their projected antimonogamy posture, seem to welcome marriage.[2] It gives them, of course, the best of all worlds. It is not one life *or* the other. A man can easily have a profession, wife, children, home without choosing. His power and control over the purse strings have been secure in the work place and in the home. Men display and demand the same economic dominance in the home as they do in industry, commerce, investment.

---

[1] From August, 1973, to August, 1974, there were 2,233,000 marriages and 948,000 divorces. From January to August, 1974, there were 1,490,000 marriages and 639,000 divorces. (The United States Department of Health, Education, and Welfare Public Health Services, Health Resources Administration, *Monthly Vital Statistics Report*, October 24, 1974.)

[2] George Gilder in *Naked Nomads* (New York, Quadrangle, The New York Times Book Company, 1974) asserts, "Our major social problems come from single men." Cf. Jessie Bernard, *The Future of Marriage* (New York, World Publishing, 1972).

Survival Tactics: Marriage and Divorce

No person can afford to be economically dependent on another. That includes wife upon husband. But control through the dollar is mandated by capitalism and sexual economics. And the other side of the dependence coin is domination and power and contempt.

The "traditional" marriage quid pro quo, the arrangement, the exchange, the trade, the contract, if you will, is one in which the husband economically supports his partner and she performs her wifely duties, which are domestic and sexual. Support is not seen as payment, but as a husband's contribution for ongoing services rendered by a dependent female who is incapable of supporting herself.[3] It is also assumed that women *want* to devote themselves to their husbands' needs. It is not unusual, however, for people to do what they *must* do, convincing themselves and others that it is what they *want* to do. It is only when people have genuine choices that they can be said to be doing what they want.

Men have established and maintained the economic imbalance which has kept women financially dependent. The individual husband who disclaims any liability for the problem is still part of the ruling sex. He is the same person who says, "No wife of mine is going to work." Or, "I won't have my children raised by a stranger." Or, "Our clients won't accept women handling their accounts."

Women have never been able to "compete" with their brothers. They may have escaped literal femicide[4] but historically the very definition of being female excluded them from financial competition, such as for the inheritance that traditionally fell to the oldest son of a family. Woman's inescapable lot was economic dependence on father, husband, or brother.

But, as long as she did not marry, a woman had certain legal if not property rights: the right to sue and to own and control her own property, which, as daughter, she might inherit if there were no competing male offspring. However, "spinsterhood," despite or perhaps because of its possible economic advantages, was never considered a desirable female state.

Up until the nineteenth century, *married* women, however, had no such rights. Female rights and identity ceased to exist upon marriage.

---

[3] A Tennessee court said: ". . . the husband is still head of the house and the wife is still in duty bound to render services for the protection of its comfort and happiness and which the law presumes to be gratuitous." Hull v. Hull 208 SW ^{2} 28, 186 Tenn. 53 (1948).

[4] *femicide:* "The killing of a woman." *Oxford English Dictionary*. It is noteworthy that there is no equivalent word for the killing of a man, specifically. *Homicide* refers more generally to human killing.

As Blackstone wrote, "By marriage, the husband and wife are one person. . . ." And that one person, the law was not ashamed to say, was the husband. The husband had no duty to account to his other half for the income and profits on her property; he had exclusive rights to maintain, manage, and control. Her personal property became her husband's; her real estate could be conveyed by her husband only. The wife could not contract, sue, or be sued. The husband, then as now, acquired the "obligation" of supporting his wife.

In nineteenth-century England and America, married women's property acts were enacted, which, on paper, gave married women some of the "rights" of the unwed, including the right to earn and keep money and to manage and control their own property.

Actually, however, as Leo Kanowitz has noted,

> "Some states continue to limit the wife's contractual capacity with regard to contracts to convey, encumber, or lease her separate real property. Generally, these states require that a deed, encumbrance or lease of the wife's real property must be executed by the husband as well as the wife in order to be valid. As for the husband's conveyance, etc., of his own real property, the wife's joinder is not a condition of validity."[5]

Each of the United States has its own laws regarding marriage and divorce; the laws for divorce and support vary from state to state. They are not federal or uniform, though there are controversial moves in that direction.

More than 99 percent of legislators and judges in the United States are men. Men write, interpret, and enforce laws on the city, state, and federal levels.

When challenged—and defeated—in their protestations that women control the investments, the wealth of America, or that joint title to a mortgaged suburban house has the same economic influence as a commercial real estate syndicate, or that making the choice between two detergents has the same significance as controlling the shopping center (and, more particularly, shopping center real estate), those who attribute such power to women, without risk of being corrected, then argue, "But women do control the most important institution in our society: the family."

However important the role of the "homemaker" or the influence

---

[5] Leo Kanowitz, *Women and the Law* (Albuquerque, University of New Mexico Press, 1969). Presumably, this type of distinction would be a violation of the Equal Rights Amendment, if adopted.

of motherhood, it is a *personal* power, one that is used to illustrate the smallest particle of power.

"[Power] may be as tiny as that exercised by a mother over her children or as great as that wielded by a despotic emperor, or any measure in between," wrote A. A. Berle in *Power*.[6] "Religious, educational, and family institutions are not autonomous centers of national power; on the contrary these decentralized areas are increasingly shaped by the big three [i.e. the major institutional hierarchies—economic, political, and military]," wrote C. Wright Mills.[7]

Even if women have a kind of power within the home, it is not a power transferable from one institution to another. Men, however— diplomats, statesmen, army generals, executives—are somewhat interchangeable. All are much sought after to become corporate leaders or figureheads. But what mother is congratulated on her extraordinary administrative abilities and competence in the home and then asked to serve on the Board of Bendix?

Women's lives are one-to-one relationships. The family is not a power base. One-to-one power has nothing to do with making broad changes or achieving access to either power or the sources of change. Even if Henry Ford "lets" his wife tell him what dinner jacket to wear, it has nothing to do with how the Ford Motor Company affects the people of the United States and, indeed, the world.

Rarely do wives participate, much less counsel their husbands in placement of capital, the money that is going to be used to make money. The "female partner" is not often involved with investment of personal or business funds or policy decisions, much less decisions which have wide implications. She does not tell her husband how to spend "his" money.

Housewives, no matter how many years of loyal service they perform, do not retire; they certainly do not retire with pensions.

> "You can be young without money but you can't be old without it . . . you've got to be one or the other, either *young* or *with money*, you can't be old and *without* it."
> —Tennessee Williams, *Cat on a Hot Tin Roof*

Legislation was introduced in the United States Congress[8] to per-

---
[6] A. A. Berle, *Power* (New York, Harcourt Brace Jovanovich, Inc., 1969).
[7] *The Power Elite* (New York, Oxford University Press, Inc., 1957).
[8] HR 14605, 92nd Congress, then-Rep. Bertram Podell (D.-N.Y.).

mit any married person or head of household who is not covered by an employer's pension plan to establish a self-employed person's pension plan. An eligible person would be treated as the "sole proprietor of the business of managing a household and as having earned income from such business." A housewife would deposit in a bank a sum of money up to $25 per week, until retirement at age fifty-nine,[9] at which time she would draw on this sum as a pension until her death.

One flaw was the theory that "the housewife could use a percentage of the money that she received for the weekly management of her household to create a retirement fund for herself." However, if a woman could deposit money in her own account for her own future, she wouldn't really need to do so under an *organized* pension plan. But as another flaw, even getting back the maximum of $25 per week, even with interest and even without considering inflation, would amount to a meaningless sum.

The concept is not really different from what is known as the Keogh Plan, under which self-employed people (and others without pension plans) can defer income and income tax to a time when their income, and therefore their tax rates, will be lower. The individual takes a specified sum of money annually, subtracts it from gross income—before any taxes—and deposits it with a bank or insurance company which uses the money until retirement age, when payments are made.[10]

However, the tax advantage, which is the main incentive for "self-employed" persons to establish pension plans, is illusory when based on a woman's household income; the taxes would probably be negligible considering the small income she has, if any.

Similarly, Social Security is not extended to homemakers for their work contributions. A woman may receive benefits (delayed income) for her work outside the home, or derivative benefits as the wife of a workingman. The latter, however, are vested only after twenty years of marriage.[11]

---

[9] What housewife "retires" at fifty-nine or any age?
[10] Tennessee attorney Virginia Cowan testified before the House Ways and Means Committee, April 11, 1973, that the Keogh Plan itself should be applicable to housewives.

A Canadian proposal, on the other hand, would have enabled housewives to take part in the Canadian Pension Plan by establishing that when one spouse works, 50 percent of her or his contributions will go toward the other's pension—50 percent is contributed in her name. Kate Blackwell and Karen Ferguson, "Pensions: Are There Holes in Your Security Blanket?", *Ms.* magazine (October, 1973).
[11] Rep. Bella Abzug (D.-N.Y.) introduced HR 159 in the 93rd Congress, a bill to reduce the requisite length of marriage to five years.

Like tax, Social Security discriminates against two-earner families. The benefits of a married woman who has also worked outside the home are her own direct benefits, the difference between that and what she would be entitled to as a spouse if she hadn't worked.

If Mr. and Mrs. Kelly survive to retirement age and her benefits are lower, which invariably they will be (she has probably not worked for the same number of years because of social pressures, maternity leave, and child care, and statistically has—even if she matched her husband's work time day for day—earned less and accrued fewer Social Security credits), she may then take her own benefits *or* derivative credit she would get as a worker's wife, thereby losing her own contributions to Social Security.[12]

After reaching the qualifying age, Mrs. Kelly, as the spouse of a beneficiary (assuming she is not receiving her own benefits): 1) receives 50 percent of the primary insurance amount (PIA). Mr. Kelly, the beneficiary, receives 100 percent. Living together, Mr. and Mrs. Kelly receive 150 percent of the PIA.[13] 2) If Mr. Kelly dies and is survived by Mrs. Kelly, she will receive his 100 percent of the benefits. (If the couple had been divorced prior to Mr. Kelly's death, Mrs. Kelly will still receive the benefits, provided they had been married for twenty years.)

Common Law and Community Property

The vast majority of states are under a "common law" rather than a "community property" system.

> "Equitable ownership, constructive or resulting trusts, and gifts, may be difficult to establish and usually the one who has legal title prevails when a dispute arises. This is so even though the placing of title may have been fortuitous or due to cupidity . . ."[14]

In common law states, the property jointly *used* but not owned by parties may actually belong to one of them, usually the one who made the payments; since it is the husband who has the money to make the purchase, the personal property may well belong to him.[15] Judges may award possession, though not ownership, of the home for

---
[12] American Civil Liberties Union Women's Rights Project Report of July 17, 1974, on Social Security and Sex Discrimination.
[13] *Ibid.*
[14] Malbouf v. Malbouf N.H. 88A2d 308 (1952).
[15] New Jersey, a common law state, decided in the case of Panter v. Panter 65 N.J. 196, 320A² 484 (1974), that property acquired during the marriage could be equitably distributed.

shelter of the wife and children. In other words, a wife may derive the right to *use,* but not *own.*[16]

In the case of *Fischer* v. *Wirth,*[17] for example, the husband and wife had pooled their earnings for twenty-two years but then decided to use the wife's earnings for family support while the husband's salary would be invested "for the two of us" and set aside "for our latter days." The husband took title in his own name to all investments and the family home.

When a divorce occurred, the wife claimed that the husband was able to acquire the house because his legal obligation to support wife and children was fulfilled out of *her* earnings.

The court decided:

". . . a wife who uses her own money to pay household expenses may obtain reimbursement from her husband only when her husband either impliedly or expressly has promised he would *repay* her" (author's emphasis).

"Community property" refers generally to all property acquired *during the marriage* by the "industry and labor" of either spouse or both; all property which is not expressly exempt belongs to both during the marriage. In community property states, the spouse at home is in a theoretical sense attributed with one-half of the family income; and, accordingly, she has right to one-half. As Karen DeCrow has written:

". . . in the . . . common law states she has *no* right to any of the property of the marriage; she all too often is deprived of what is hers. While the marriage was in effect, she had no right to money for household services; upon divorce she has no right to collect back pay."[18]

But as Leo Kanowitz wrote, generally community property *excludes*

"property each owned before marriage, property acquired after marriage by gift, bequest, or device or descent and, in California, the rents, issues and profits of separate property. All other property

---

[16] In the New York case of Manheim v. Manheim 60 Misc.², 88 (1969) a wife was sued by her estranged husband for possession of household goods and furnishings. Mrs. Manheim claimed the articles were gifts to her—because, otherwise, under common law, she would have no rights to them. But the court decided they were not gifts, or jointly owned property, and the wife had right to use, but not ownership.
[17] 326 NYS² 308 (1971).
[18] *Sexist Justice* (New York, Random House, 1974).

acquired after marriage by either husband or wife (with some exceptions) is community property."[19]

Kanowitz and others[20] have pointed out that under traditional community property concepts, management and control of community property has been vested in the husband. The husband's power to sell community property may extend to all property that is not exclusively the wife's. But, depending on the individual state law, the wife may not be able to sell or convey community property without authorization from the husband—unless he has abandoned her or is insane. Or the husband may have "absolute power" to convey any community property except the homestead; he may even have absolute power over his wife's earnings.

Mr. and Mrs. Rosan lived in California, a community property state. They had two children, fifteen and seventeen. For three years before the divorce, Mr. Rosan had earned $25,400; $25,600; and $22,400, exclusive of expense account and after taxes. The family lived in a $56,000 house, traveled, and generally lived well.

Mrs. Rosan had never been employed on a paid basis except for a very brief period, which was terminated because of the emotional problems of one child. However, she had taken courses in real estate in preparation for employment.

The trial court divided, approximately equally, what it considered to be the community property assets. Specifically, the total assets of the husband and wife equaled $53,897. Mr. Rosan received $26,948 and Mrs. Rosan received $26,949. The husband initially received $30,711 (full value of the company stocks he owned) and $500 from insurance proceeds, and he was ordered to deliver to the wife a promissory note in the sum of $4,263, to make approximately equal the amount each received. Mrs. Rosan got everything else from the remaining community property, including: $1,000 equity in the car; $6,790 in cash from sale of the family home; $412 from a trust account; furniture worth $3,000; other stock worth $1,304; an undivided one-half interest in several rental properties valued at $8,000; and an undivided one-half interest in two second deeds of trust valued at $2,180, all in addition to the promissory note from Mr. Rosan.[21]

---

[19] Kanowitz, *op. cit.*
[20] Kenneth M. Davidson, Ruth B. Ginsburg, Herma H. Kay, *Sex-Biased Discrimination* (St. Paul, Minn., West Publishing Co., 1974). *Law and Social Order* 1972:163. "Community Property: Male Management and Women's Rights."
[21] See 60 California Law Review 1683; book review of Kay, *Making Marriage and Divorce Safe for Women.*

The court awarded as support $150 a month for the fifteen-year-old in the wife's custody, $400 a month to the wife for the first year, $300 a month to the wife for the second year, and $200 a month to the wife for the third year. Then spousal support would terminate.

The appellate court noted that in most cases a declining award is not necessary because the incentive for a woman to find employment is usually supplied by the husband's inability to adequately support the family.[22] But, said the court, if this incentive be deemed "insufficient" there would be no impropriety in the downward modification of support should she (the wife) unreasonably delay or refuse to seek employment. When evidence exists as to such unreasonable delay, that factor may be taken into consideration by the trial court in fixing the amount in the first instance or in modification proceedings.

The appellate court found there had been no unreasonable delay. The wife has

". . . no particular training or experience to qualify for any employment that would produce an income anywhere comparable to her half of the community income during the marriage. . . . We find nothing . . . indicating any legislative intent that a wife of a marriage of long standing whose attentions have been devoted during the marriage to wifely and parental duties and whose earning capacity has therefore not been developed should be, at a time when the husband is reaching his peak of earning capacity, relegated to a standard of living substantially below that enjoyed by the parties during the marriage or to subsistence from public welfare . . . the wife has not only failed to develop her own earning capacity, she has presumably contributed to the development of the husband's earning capacity. In many, if not in most, cases the established employment or earning capacity of the husband constitutes the most valuable economic assets of the parties. While this economic attribute is not of such a character as will permit its division as property, it is not to be ignored in considering the problem of continuing support."[23]

A Florida court wrote

"In this era of women's liberation movements and enlightened thinking, we have almost universally come to appreciate the fallacy of treating the feminine members of our society on anything but a

---

[22] "Prior to the decision of the California Court of Appeals in Marriage of Rosan, observers had noted that awards of spousal support were becoming smaller in amount and shorter in duration." Davidson, Ginsburg, and Kay, *op. cit.*
[23] *In re:* Marriage of Rosan 24 Cal. App. 3d 885, 101 Cal. Rptr. 295 (1972).

basis of complete equality with the opposite sex. Any contrary view would be completely anachronistic. In this day and time, women are as well educated and trained in the arts, sciences, and professions as are their male counterparts. The law properly protects them in their right to independently acquire, encumber, accumulate, and alienate property at will. They now occupy a position of equal partners in the family relationship, resulting from marriage, and more often than not contribute a full measure to the economic well-being of the family unit. Whether the marriage continues to exist or is severed through the device of judicial decree, the woman continues to be as fully equipped as the man to earn a living and provide for the essential needs. The fortuitous circumstances created by recitation of the marriage vows neither diminishes her capacity for self-support nor does it give her a vested right in her husband's earnings for the remainder of her life."[24]

Uniform Marriage and Divorce Act

Having fifty different sets of laws on the same subject has become cumbersome and uneven in an era when people move and relocate rapidly and frequently. Consideration has been given to the needs of business, for example, through the Uniform Commercial Code, in which, despite each state's having its own exceptions and variations, the basic articles are similar and have been adopted by forty-nine states. Similarly, there is a Uniform Support of Dependents Act, Uniform Reciprocal Enforcement of Support Act, and a Uniform Marriage and Divorce Act (UMDA).

The UMDA, in its pure no-fault form, means that if one party to a marriage sees an "irretrievable breakdown," there is little left for the other to say or do. She or he may contest the dissolution but has the almost impossible burden of proving there is no irretrievable breakdown. Divorce can, in that sense, become unilateral. Such "freedom" and mobility can be considered valid only if the wife is not left in a seriously damaged position. Right now, she would be, since she is not her husband's economic equal.

The problem of no-fault divorce, then, is where it leaves the wife financially, and therefore psychologically and emotionally. Essentially, a wife of eighteen years, for example, can wake up one day and be divorced. What are the provisions for support?

[24] Beard v. Beard 262 So. 2d 269 (Fla. App.) (1972).

The Uniform Marriage and Divorce Act contains two alternate sets of economic provisions:[25]

One alternative is for the property and assets of the parties to be "equitably apportioned without regard to marital misconduct" and without being bound by the time and means of acquisition or who has the title. Consideration would be given to the duration of the marriage; any prior marriage of either party; any antenuptial agreement between the parties; the age, health, station, occupation, amount and sources of income; vocational skills, employability, estate, liabilities; needs of each party; custodian provisions; whether this division is in lieu of or in addition to maintenance; the opportunity of each for future acquisition of capital assets and income; the contribution or dissipation of each party in the acquisition, preservation, depreciation, or appreciation in value of the respective estates; the contribution of a spouse as a homemaker. In addition, the court may set aside assets for the protection of the children.

The other proposal relates primarily to community property states, apportions property without regard to fault, and gives consideration to: contribution of each to the acquisition of the property (including housework), value of the property set apart to each spouse, duration of the marriage, economic circumstances of each spouse when division is to become effective including the desirability of awarding the marital home or the right to live there for a reasonable period to the spouse with custody. Each spouse's separate property is assigned to her/him.

In addition to the division of property, a court may grant "maintenance" to either spouse upon dissolution or separation, but only if the spouse is to be supported, lacks sufficient property to provide for her/his reasonable needs and is unable to support her/himself through appropriate employment or is the custodian of a child which makes employment out of the home inappropriate.

The court determines the amount and duration of support without regard to fault. The circumstances the court is to consider include: the resources of the supported spouse, her/his ability to support her/himself independently; any property apportioned to her/him; extent of child support; time necessary to get training or education for an appropriate job; standard of living of the marriage; duration of

---

[25] Only Colorado has adopted all of the economic provisions of the Uniform Marriage and Divorce Act. Kentucky, Missouri, Washington, and Arizona have adopted most of the economic provisions.

the marriage; age and physical and emotional condition of the supported spouse; ability of supporting spouse to meet her/his own needs while providing for the supported spouse.

Again, the court may order either or both parents having a duty to support a child to pay a reasonable amount for support without regard to marital misconduct, fault, or guilt.

Significantly, the court can order the money to be paid to the clerk of the court, who will keep records of the payment. If payment isn't made within ten days after notice of any arrearage, the clerk will notify the prosecuting attorney, who will initiate contempt proceedings. The supported spouse may also initiate the proceedings. Also, the court can order wage assignments or an income trust for the payment of support. If the supporting spouse has left the jurisdiction, the prosecuting attorney may institute such proceedings as are necessary to make collection of the arrearage.

Maintenance is terminated on death or remarriage of the supported spouse, unless otherwise provided for in writing or in the decree.[26]

The Typical Case

Arlene is forty. She and Michael have been married almost twenty years. They dated throughout college; when Michael graduated, Arlene, finishing her junior year, dropped out ("temporarily") and worked as a secretary to help finance Michael's graduate education.

When he finished his master's degree, Michael wanted to start raising a family. In her third month of pregnancy, Arlene quit her job. Her doctor, her husband, and her boss agreed it would be better (for her) not to continue working; she could not be a housewife "and also work." Instead, Arlene became a full-time housewife—and a full-time secretary, mother, maid, nurse, chauffeur, hostess. And Michael became a Certified Public Accountant.

Arlene was given an "allowance" to cover household expenses, food, laundry, cleaning. Any "pin" money she could put away was hers.

She became active in community groups and did some volunteer charity work. A second and then a third child was born. Arlene never did return to college.

The couple lived in a state under common law, owned a house not

[26] Presumably support also terminates on death of supporting spouse and it is unclear what happens to the supported spouse.

too far from Michael's office; actually there was a bank mortgage, and the deed was in Michael's name. "Their" other assets were a few stocks (also in Michael's name), some jewelry, and two cars.

Around the time of their nineteenth anniversary, Michael told his wife he thought they should have a trial separation: nothing formal, but just that they should each think more clearly about what they wanted to do. Arlene thought she *was* doing exactly what she wanted to do.

Michael was tired of the marriage. Nevertheless, he said he was prepared to support Arlene and the children in the same way he had done during the course of the marriage (since *she* had stopped supporting *him*). She could have the house and custody of the children.

A day or two later Michael asked Arlene if she had seen her lawyer yet, because he had seen his. Arlene didn't even *know*, much less *have*, a lawyer; Michael retained several in business.

Michael's lawyer told him he was being too generous. "That house is in *your name*, in this state that makes it yours! Why should you just give her all that?"

When Arlene did get sufficiently panicky to see a lawyer, she tried the one who had represented her and Michael when they bought "their" house. He properly told Arlene he thought he might have a conflict since he knew both parties. Then Arlene searched out people who had gone through divorces and saw the first available lawyer.

One of the first subjects to come up at the consultation meeting was legal costs. When the attorney asked for a retainer fee, Arlene asked, "Isn't the husband supposed to pay all that?" The lawyer said if Arlene could raise through savings, or a loan, a retainer fee, Michael might be held responsible for the rest.[27]

Once ready to proceed, Arlene was given this advice: You don't think about a thing; I'll do all the thinking for you. I don't think what you need is money from your husband; what you need is to hook some other guy.[28]

Arlene had been out of the job market for about seventeen years; she had only a high school diploma, no training, and just rusty secretarial skills. She was unprepared to compete with young students or recent graduates.

[27] Women who don't have independent monies—meaning most women—may be in a vulnerable, precarious, and unwholesome position in having their legal fees paid by their adversaries. See Proposals.
[28] "To hook some other guy" is one of the commonly reported euphemisms newly separated women hear from those who suggest her problem is not lack of money, but lack of sex.

Survival Tactics: Marriage and Divorce

She was plagued with questions: Even if I get the house, how can I afford the upkeep? Who would even give me a job? Without one, I can never match my husband's income, I have no pension or Social Security. What about the children? The cost of living keeps rising, Michael's income too. What about my support? What if he dies? What if he remarries or moves away?

Before anything was resolved, Michael moved out of the house. But he continued to "drop in" about four times a week to see the children and stayed for dinner. Invariably he would bring the children gifts—things their mother could no longer afford. Michael would also leave some money. The amount varied and Arlene really never knew how much to expect. Most weeks he left about a hundred dollars.

Arlene didn't really know her husband's income or even the family expenses. Like many women she had never been involved in financial affairs,[29] and he was, after all, an accountant. She believed he was earning about $30,000.

Michael was not eager to sign a separation agreement. He said no one could tell him what his obligations were. He said he might even move out of the country; he might even take the children.

Arlene did not want to go to court; she wanted them to work things out themselves. She hated conflict, hostility. Especially with her husband. She "knew" he couldn't be serious.

But "support payments" became smaller, then erratic, and then almost nonexistent. Arlene felt she had no choice but to go to court.

Finally, Arlene charged Michael with adultery, cruelty, abandonment, and sought counsel fees and court-ordered support of $300 a week for herself and the three children.

On, as lawyers poetically say, the eve of trial, Michael and Arlene came to an agreement.

Agreement	Some Problems
Michael to pay $200 a week to Arlene and children; $100 as child support, $100 as alimony.	⅓ of Michael's *admitted* gross income for his 3 dependents; ⅔ for himself. $100 alimony is tax-deductible for Michael, taxable to Arlene. The child support stops as each child reaches majority.

[29] Even now there is readily available sex therapy for married (and divorcing) couples, but not financial "therapy."

Agreement	Some Problems
Arlene and children continue to live in family home.	Arlene cannot afford upkeep nor can she afford rent elsewhere. Michael gets tax deduction for local real estate taxes, and interest on mortgage, if any; he still owns the house.
Michael to maintain existing health insurance for family.	Children's coverage will terminate at age nineteen, Arlene's on divorce. And in the meantime, medical bills not covered by insurance will come out of the $200 a week.
Arlene to be beneficiary of Michael's life insurance.	Michael can change beneficiary, since agreement doesn't say *irrevocable*. Or he can let payments lapse; Arlene can't afford them.
Arlene and Michael are to divide bank accounts and stocks.	There may be assets Arlene doesn't even know about. And at least partly as a result of all her contributions in the past, *Michael* will continue to acquire assets in the future.

Michael's income and the cost of living are both rising; Arlene's support is not.

Arlene does not get Social Security as a divorced wife unless they have been married twenty years.

Michael gets a pension when he retires; Arlene gets none.

If Arlene is able to find a job, perhaps it will be as a bookkeeper. How come *she* is not a Certified Public Accountant?

Sex and Money

Women's sexual needs and desires are continually frustrated and exploited. First there is the traditional double standard regarding premarital sex. Then there is another double standard for the "straying husband," as contrasted with the "adulterous wife," which continues and intensifies when the marriage breaks down. The wife who is found guilty of adultery may lose any claim to alimony and support even though she has, for years, carried out all the conditions and services of the marriage, sexual and household. In New York, for example, the court *cannot* award alimony to such a guilty wife.[30]

During negotiations or court proceedings, the wife, as a practical legal matter, must abstain from sex.[31] The husband, on the other hand, has little to lose by his sexual activity. As one divorced woman put it, "You have to be faithful to the man you're divorcing—that's insane, absolutely insane! My phone was tapped. I was followed. My doorman was paid by my husband to report on what I was doing. I was a nervous wreck."

A commercially published guide for men advises:

> "The laws of nature still take occasional precedence over the laws of the state, even all fifty states, and the longer she goes without that warm body beside her in bed the more chances she may take. . . .
>
> "Something that may work in your favor is her collecting 'temporary' alimony, sitting comfortably in her lonely house with the rent or mortgage paid for her, luxuriating in her independence. Neither she nor her lawyer are likely to be in a hurry to get the thing over with. And this exasperating situation may give Bloodhound [private detective] that much more time and opportunity to do its work."[32]

One woman was presented with an agreement which said that if she lived with another man, her support would be terminated. This, the lawyer said, was designed to give the woman "moral protection." "If you lived with another man," he reasoned, "and still accepted your husband's money, you'd be worse than the lowest whore, and I'm protecting you from that."

A mother, even once divorced, can *never* really be her own person. Sexually, she is always under the inhibiting threat of being charged with being an unfit mother.[33] Some men insist that their ex-wives be chaperoned at all times! However, a recent New York case, in which

---

[30] In Hessen v. Hessen 33 NY²406 (1974), a husband was denied his divorce on the grounds of cruelty, with New York's highest court saying the necessary result of finding this fifty-one-year-old woman guilty would be to terminate her support and possession of the marital home. Cf. Hammer v. Hammer 34 NY²546 (1974).
[31] Michigan has recently added to its statute: ". . . in a suit to annul a marriage or for divorce the court may, on petition of wife, prohibit the husband from imposing any restraint on her personal liberty during the pendency of the suit."
[32] John S. Rodell, *How to Avoid Alimony* (New York, Stein and Day, 1969).
[33] Long before the divorce, many husbands start out by saying they want custody of the children. In most cases they would probably collapse if the wives agreed. But husbands use the *threat* as leverage in negotiating with their wives, who, if they think they are going to lose their children, will give up an awful lot. Or the husband doing this in court proceedings may think that he is impressing the judge.

a husband established "sexual misconduct" on the part of his ex-wife and had their children removed from her custody, was reversed, the appeals court deciding that the divorced woman's sexual activities which do not affect her minor children are in the area of privacy mandated by the Bill of Rights.[34]

Divorce

"The Best Years of Her Life

"No-fault divorce"[35] has been used to refer to a broad class of legislation, including "irretrievable breakdown," "breakdown of the marriage," "incompatibility," as grounds for marital dissolution, or divorce. Actually, there are few states remaining which allow divorce only on grounds of the fault of a party.[36]

Also included under the umbrella term of *no fault* are the "incompatibility" statutes adopted in some states,[37] in addition to whatever grounds may exist in the state. "Breakdown of marriage" is virtually the exclusive ground in other states.[38] "Breakdown of marriage," regardless of fault, exists as ground for divorce in addition to other grounds in another group of states.[39] Still other states have developed, as a ground for divorce, living apart for a specified period.[40]

No-fault divorce does not necessarily mean that fault is eliminated for all purposes. For example, Arkansas, Idaho, West Virginia, Texas, Florida—no-fault states—permit consideration of adultery in awarding alimony and making property divisions. California's statute eliminates fault and now bases its determination of support solely on the need and ability of the parties to pay. Iowa, by judicial interpretation, has said the admission of fault in connection with alimony or property division would necessarily reintroduce the entire issue of

[34] In the matter of Feldman v. Feldman 45 A.D. 2nd 320, 358 NYS2 507 (A.D. 2nd 1974).
[35] Unrelated to "do-it-yourself" divorce. The total number of states adds up to more than fifty since a state may have several grounds.
[36] Illinois, Massachusetts, Mississippi, Pennsylvania, South Dakota; of these reform is soon expected in Illinois and Pennsylvania.
[37] As of September, 1974, Alabama, Alaska, Connecticut, Kansas, Nevada, New Mexico, Oklahoma.
[38] California, Colorado, Delaware, Florida, Iowa, Kentucky, Michigan, Minnesota, Missouri, Nebraska, Oregon, Virgin Islands, Washington.
[39] Alabama, Connecticut, Georgia, Hawaii, Indiana, Maine, Montana, New Hampshire, North Dakota, Texas.
[40] These include Hawaii, Idaho, Louisiana, Maryland, Nevada, New Jersey, New York (which still involves consent), North Carolina, Ohio, Puerto Rico, South Carolina, Vermont, Virginia, Washington, West Virginia, and Wisconsin.

relative fault of the parties and thus defeat the objective of no-fault divorce. (See Chapter 10.)

Despite no-fault divorce, fault still exists for economic purposes, and may still be considered in the awarding of alimony, maintenance, or support. No-fault concepts, then, make it easier to get divorced, but not to get support.

> "Where divorce is not to be had for the asking, the economic interests and claims of the wife are ordinarily a major facet in negotiation, settlement and the processing of the case."[41]

> ". . . where divorce can be granted for only specified derelictions on the part of one spouse or the other, a dependent spouse has some leverage in securing better economic arrangements than the very inadequate arrangements usually made by courts. This leverage may be lost or seriously eroded by legislation providing for 'no fault' divorce at the option of one party."[42]

> ". . . in [no-fault] states that take fault into account in setting the award, the provisions have more frequently been used to deny alimony to women."[43]

Most women are no more involved with the economics of their marriage than they are with the economics of the nation or the world. They have been kept ignorant about financial matters, even—perhaps *especially*—those that affect them most directly. Being a "dutiful wife" seems to require sentiment and loyalty that are somehow projected as being inconsistent with concern with the woman's own financial protection. Unfortunately, most wives do not recognize this problem until they are drowning in it; women are trained and willing to think about "us," about "together," about "I and thou," but not about I, and certainly not "I-need-to-have-and-understand-money-because-it's-what-runs-the-country-and-our-lives."

A woman coming out of a marriage without the ability to adequately support herself, and without back pay, begins to realize that she has devoted her life to who would be *needing* her, and has paid very little attention to who would be *feeding* her.

The economics of being female are not really improving. Nor is the

---

[41] Henry H. Foster, Jr., and Doris Jonas Freed, "Law and the Family," *New York Law Journal* (February 22, 1974), p. 1.
[42] Henry H. Foster, Jr., and Doris Jonas Freed, "Law and the Family," *New York Law Journal* (October 26, 1973), p. 1.
[43] Homer H. Clark, Jr., *The Law of Domestic Relations in the United States* (St. Paul, Minn., West Publishing Co., 1968).

condition of wifedom. Most divorce reform hurts women more than it helps them; or at least it does nothing to improve their position. It is interesting—and predictable—that in the area of marriage and divorce, it is easier to get a divorce than it is to get economic freedom.

No-fault divorce places wives in even more vulnerable economic positions than they would find themselves in otherwise. The divorce becomes easy to obtain. The means of self-support does not.

People do not want to see themselves as oppressed. But people can never really organize without recognizing themselves as oppressed, without defining common denominators, including their enemies, and without minimizing conflicts of interest, including class and race.

Women have not seen an identity of interests with others similarly situated, so traditionally they have not organized, joined together, gone on strike.

> ". . . the quality of 'organizability' is stronger in men than in women; their economic interests force them into retaliation, while the isolated and even antagonistic economic interests of women keep them from it."[44]

Even now, more female organizing energy goes into job discrimination and related problems than into marriage and divorce, which directly affects almost *all* women! All classes marry, women of all classes become wives.

Women's work is not valued. It is not traded, is not considered productive labor, is not counted in the Gross National Product. "Women's work" in the home, once the setting for productive labor or volunteers, is not in the capitalist mainstream.

However, the circle is such that radical change is *not* going to be visited first upon the home. In this area, for most people, *reform* will have to come first.

New Developments and Modest Proposals

Marriage and the family as now known in America are oppressive institutions. The argument that the state has no right to interfere with people's private lives and that official intervention should be unnecessary in matters of marriage, divorce, and support is one usually made

[44] Charlotte Perkins Gilman, *Women and Economics,* Carl N. Degler, ed. (New York, Harper and Row, 1966).

in the first blush of "romance." In the case of divorce, it is also assumed by the party with the least to lose in the dissolution. But serious reform is needed if the institution, which seems bent on survival, is to survive and allow the dignity of women to do the same.

Proposal

At the time of marriage, both parties shall file with the marriage license bureau copies of their tax returns for the preceding five years and any employment or income-producing contracts they may have with third parties.

There are many tricks such a filing would not prevent, but the wife would at least have some idea of the husband's financial situation. New contracts or employment agreements would be filed on coming into existence. The wife will know if the husband has some way of deferring income or having income diverted into future college tuition payments for children, for example.

Proposal

Prior to marriage,[45] and again, prior to marital dissolution, couples shall be required to attend publicly funded courses in the legal and economic ramifications of marriage and divorce. These courses would in no way be dedicated to preserving the marriage.

If possible, such classes should be structured so that women meet with other women, and men with other men, for a lessening of fear, tension, inhibitions, embarrassment.

Proposal

Bills have been introduced into Congress (usually by female representatives) to amend Social Security to provide that an individual maintaining a household for other persons shall be credited for Social Security benefit purposes and shall be deemed to have performed employment and to have been paid wages (even if not actually received). The amount of wages deemed to have been paid for householder service shall be an amount equal to the national average

---

[45] New York State Senator Karen Burstein and then-Assemblyman Tony Olivieri introduced a bill in 1974 to distribute details of the rights and obligations of the partner in marriage and divorce. Similarly, five years before, feminists had stationed themselves at New York's City Hall to do the same.

monthly wage for employment in service occupations in such month.[46]

A bill has been introduced to provide direct old age, survivor's, and disability insurance and Medicare benefits for homemakers. The "wages" contemplate figures which no one but a wife would work for.[47]

Proposal

Whether through "divorce insurance,"[48] "Judicaid," "Judicare" (free counsel), court orders of advance funds for representation, or the requirement that the husband set up a trust fund for his wife's legal fees (husbands complain about having to pay double sets of fees; actually, from the wife's point of view, it is undesirable for her to be dependent on her husband in this connection, but she may have no choice), wives in adversary proceedings with their husbands must be provided with the ability to engage their own lawyers. In other words, there must be a recognition of an absolute right to an attorney. It is true that this right, where established, has already been used to guarantee a husband's representation in, for example, contempt proceedings for non-support!

Proposal

Legal counsel shall not be waivable when a wife is in litigation against her husband. There shall be guaranteed representation.

However, since rights are generally considered to be waivable, the existence of an alleged waiver must be shown by standards as high as those governing a defendant's waiver of counsel in a police interro-

---

[46] Abzug (D.-N.Y.), HR 3217. Actually nobody would voluntarily work for that pay.
[47] Barbara Jordan (D.-Tex.) for herself and Martha Griffiths, HR 12645; reintroduced, Barbara Jordan and James Burke (D.-Mass.).
[48] The concept of child support insurance (often and erroneously believed to be *divorce* insurance) was introduced in the New York Legislature by State Senator Donald Halperin and Assemblyman Richard Gottfried, by way of proposing a commission to study the *feasibility* of such insurance.
As described by Senator Halperin, "It's designed to insure the minor children of broken families due to divorce receive the necessary money so that they can live at somewhat of a reasonable level."
In the language of the bill, it is "insurance to cover child support and rehabilitation payments for a spouse in the event of a divorce, with provision therein for converting any sums not used for alimony and child support for education and retirement funds when the children reach college age and/or the spouses reach retirement age."
Insurance-industry investigations, however, decided the profits to them were questionable and they were not prepared to underwrite the risk.

gation room. There shall be protection analogous to "Miranda warnings" given to arrested persons. That is, before a wife's waiver of counsel would be enforceable, the husband and his attorney would have to prove that the wife had been informed of her rights, and of what she might be giving up, and that the stipulation or agreement she was about to sign might be used against her; that she was knowingly and intentionally waiving independent counsel, support, child custody (or whatever is relevant); that she realized that her decision was final and might not be subject to modification at a later date. The circumstances of the waiver would have to show intent, comprehension, and free choice.

Proposal

Certain "family" matters shall be removed from the exclusive jurisdiction of existing professional judges (99 percent of whom are white males).

Where divorces are truly uncontested in all their parts, divorce registration should be adequate. But even where the divorce itself is uncontested or where there is some sort of no-fault divorce and therefore virtually no question of law to be tried, the remaining collateral matters should, if undecided by the parties themselves, be heard and adjudicated by their peers, or by feminist tribunals, for example.

Where the issues involved are support, child custody, visitation, and other matters in which there are no legal questions, as such, peers of the couple are in a much better position than—or at least certainly in as good a position as—a professional judge who, in addition to having no particular training in being a judge, also has no special skill or knowledge to evaluate the input and needs of the parties.

Nor need the substitute "judges" be lawyers or psychologists or social workers. The decision makers should be the people directly involved and laypersons in the community. The parties would, very likely, not need legal counsel, but they would have a right to such representation. Or they could ask the tribunal to appoint a lawyer or nonlawyer to assist them, or they could represent themselves or even elect to be represented by a lay advocate of their choice. If a husband has retained paid counsel, at the proceedings (though this would be discouraged) the wife should have an automatic right to the same, paid for by the state but chosen by her, unless it can be shown either that she personally has insurance that will pay for such coverage or that she personally has the funds to pay for it. Her husband's wealth should not be charged to/against her in evaluating her eligibility for free legal services, nor should she and counsel be exposed to the dangers implicit in being paid for by their adversaries.

A sister body of the tribunal would have enforcement powers and would be the forum to bring on nonpayment proceedings.

The purpose of the tribunal would not be to try to save the marriage, since that is no one's concern but the people directly involved; nor should they be sacrificed because it appears to anyone else that the continuation of the marriage would be in the best interests of the children.

Proposal

Deductions of alimony and child support shall be made directly from a husband's paycheck, similar to union dues "check-off" or tax withholding.[49]

Proposal

No divorced party shall remarry who is in default of any support payments to prior spouse and for children.[50] (Of course, following remarriage the default may resume again.)

Proposal

There are numerous suggestions that women be paid for working as housewives. Studies have been done to compute the amount of time women devote to their "chores" and to then attempt to translate that into some hourly or weekly salary, or at least some percentage of the husband's income which should belong to the wife (perhaps being paid directly to her).

---

[49] Advanced by National Organization for Women (NOW). Adopted in some states with regard to child support. California has enacted a law (AB 1946 of 1974, introduced by Assemblyman McAlister) requiring the deduction of child support from the parents' wages in cases of default over certain periods.

Missouri has added that upon motion of either party the court can require payment of maintenance or support to be made of the circuit clerk. If payment is not made within ten days the clerk will notify the prosecuting attorney who, with consent of obligee, will initiate contempt proceedings.

Nebraska: All support orders include direction that money will be paid to the clerk in the district court, who will disburse it to the recipient.

[50] Wisconsin has already enacted such legislation. Wisc. Stats 245.10 Marriage.

As long as woman's relationship to the home exists as it now does, there is merit to such a position. However, as long as women are viewed as belonging in the home and as long as the family or the home is the core institution, it would be preferable to pay the person who is in the home full-time and is the true head of the family, rather than the person who spends some small portion of his time there. Thus, if the woman is at home, the husband, instead of leaving, working, and bringing his wife an allowance, or even salary, should be viewed as *her* employee or agent, who leaves the home, the family, the "core social institution," goes out to hunt, and brings back his catch. She is the principal.

10. The Myth of Alimony: Why Is It the Husband Gets the Stocks and Bonds, and the Wife Gets the Children?

Have you heard the one about the beautiful divorcée sitting home on her chaise lounge, wrapped in a boa and nibbling at bonbons while her ex-husband is struggling to meet his weekly alimony payments?

Who is she? Does she exist? Is she a myth? Isn't it easier to find women all over America who are not being supported or, if they are lucky, have support orders or agreements which their husbands simply ignore?

Most men and women are filled with misconceptions on the subject of alimony—support or maintenance for separated or divorced wives. People believe:

> Where there's divorce, there's alimony;
> All ex-wives are living like the Shah of Iran's discarded empress;
> Judges always favor "the little woman";
> Husbands are forced to make alimony payments so that women can spend their money on drugs, drink, other men, other women, or on a variety of luxuries or crimes;
> The only purpose of alimony is to punish husbands;

Alimony is not really needed because even some *women* are saying they're economically equal to men;
Feminists oppose alimony;
Wives hire high-priced lawyers, and husbands pay the legal bills;
Women prefer alimony to other forms of income and would never voluntarily break away from it.

Women's Voices

"My alimony is due on the first of the month, but it never arrives on time. What's today?"

"The sixteenth."

"Maybe it'll be in the mail today. It is coming, isn't it? It's horrible. Horrible. It makes you feel completely dependent. I know now it's a game—but then maybe it isn't. Is it a game to just make me suffer? I remember the first year, it was Christmas. A time when I could have used it—it didn't come till the first of the year. It makes you very dependent and very resentful. At first I thought, well, alimony is immoral. How can you be a feminist and ask for alimony?

"My divorce took two and a half years. And I was advised not to get a job, because if I got a job then I wouldn't get any alimony. And so for two and a half years I was doing nothing, just getting older. I then discovered that I *couldn't* get a job.

"Well, I'm not that young, and if I could get a job and be self-supporting, I guess there's nothing I'd like better than to say, 'You know, David, you know what you can do with that check.' But I think my children can earn more money than I can; it's not a good feeling at all. My whole life is dependent on it, rent, food. . . .

"I have no other sustenance except that. What can I earn? I did some writing, some research. I've been doing some free-lance jobs. My last job paid absolutely the most miserable . . . it sounded glamorous. Everybody said, 'Ah! You're an administrative assistant! Isn't that great!' But the wages were outrageous. So I feel absolutely . . . but what worries me more is if he dies tomorrow, I have no insurance and no rights to the estate, which I would have in negotiations had we not fought over things like furniture, and pots and pans. That's what terrifies me even more than the fact that I'm dependent on him—the fact that I'm dependent on him living! If he dies . . . I guess you can say that of a married woman, but she has some insurance and at least she has the right to inheritance.

"I was brought up with this idea that some great knight would come along and not only marry me but put me on this great pedestal and hand me service and hand me—I wasn't going to have to do anything. And that's unrealistic, I know now. It's absurd.

"I felt so guilty because I instituted the divorce . . . and my own lawyer made me feel avaricious, greedy, materialistic. That alimony is something I shouldn't have. Then my lawyer said, 'Look, after two years, most men don't pay alimony anyway.' But I was offered a lump sum to remarry!

"They know that wives can't earn anything. They must have some feeling about some kind of obligation. You know, I think a man in a profession would be worried about his reputation, but I guess nobody knows. Because a wife isn't necessarily going to go around and tell on him. We've threatened to picket some of these men's offices, but we've never done it. We've never done it. At the last minute, it always fell through. Some woman said, he didn't pay for such-and-such amount of time and suddenly the check came through. I don't think I want to antagonize him. It'll be worse. So it's a double bind. If you keep after him, you might not get anything at all, and if you don't, you might not get anything at all. And my lawyer always says: You're lucky you get it. I wouldn't even think of writing a letter. Just don't even bug him. Don't do it.

"I have felt mortified and guilty about this whole thing . . . it's having to ask for something. It's asking for money from someone that you're not performing services for. . . . When you're home and you're cooking the meals and sleeping with him, you're performing the wifely duties. But even when we were together I had the kind of husband that made me ask. I don't think you should have to ask. That was partly what led to the divorce. He would say to me, 'If you need a brassiere, or you need a pair of gloves, go find out how much it is and let me know, and I'll give you the money.' I mean, now who wants to be treated—that's like a child getting your allowance from your father."

Betty Berry, who was divorced after twenty-three years of marriage and is NOW's Advisor to the National Task Force on Marriage and Divorce, says:

"He said I was being liquidated like a no-longer profitable business asset.

"I know that my former husband has to sit down and write this check . . . twice a month. He certainly has a lot of unpleasant mem-

The Myth of Alimony

ories and it's—I just don't think it's a very good idea. . . . A few times he does write it a few days late, then all of a sudden I realize how dependent I am on receiving this and it makes me stop and think that this is a very precarious situation. I have suggested to him that this be transferred automatically through his bank to my account, but he has not wanted to do this.

"The alimony I get is not enough to support me. There has been a forty-two percent increase in the cost of living since my settlement was made.

"The whole agreement was dreadful. It was an example of pure economic coercion and I have a letter from my attorney stating that this was the tactic that would be used against me at the onset of the discussions of the divorce if I did not agree to the terms that were offered. The only bargaining power that I had was my signature. At what point would I give in and sign?

"In my naïveté I thought we owned things jointly. I didn't realize that was not the case and almost nothing was in my name. . . . Throughout our marriage, it now seems incredible, I was given so many dollars a week according to a budget that was put in envelopes —three dollars for the beauty parlor, shoe repair, etc. So I had no opportunity to amass any funds of my own. I had some money, though, because from time to time I did work in our marriage and my husband had insisted that I put this money in my own account, so I had just a few thousand dollars which I drew upon heavily during my divorce and which were never given back to me.

"Now my husband is remarried and as in other cases, the second wife[1] has a much higher standard of living than the old wife. This may very well be because at middle age our husbands are successful. We were with them in the years they were making their money. Now they've made it and we're a very convenient tax deduction and now they really begin to spend their money. The few times I am troubled is when I realize I can't take the kind of vacation that my husband will be taking or I will see some social event in the paper, usually I don't think about this, but every once in a while . . . I see pictures of the kind of event I used to attend and which is now out of my life.

". . . and the psychological impact of going to look for a job, at age forty-five, not having worked much, is devastating. It's so frightening. Believe me, you sure are obsolete. It's a whole way of think-

---

[1] Predictably, the most vocal enemies of alimony are men. Second wives, prior to seeing themselves in the position of their predecessors, are hostile, if not as vocal.

ing, not only about skills, but everything. You have to be recycled. Actually, if you can find out what to be recycled *as,* it's fun. The worst is getting over the very realistic fear about what's going to happen to me. But, also, finding a job is not easy. Deciding what kind of work you'll even look for is very hard. . . . you've been so isolated."[2]

There is considerable controversy about "the alimony question." Some people have formulated, and many others have been lulled into accepting, the view that liberation begins with giving up what little one has or hopes to get. So they say women who want to be "liberated" should not accept money from their husbands or ex-husbands. But isn't that a little like saying Vietnam Veterans Against the War should not accept their disability checks?

No person should be economically dependent on another—not even a spouse or ex-spouse. However, most women have been taught to want—and, even worse, to be equipped for—nothing more than acceptance and support by a man. That 35 million American women *are* employed, and constitute 40 percent of the work force, in no way indicates that they are not still economically subservient.

Typically, women have married, cared for children and home. In addition, they may have had some paid employment. But most women's lives outside the home have always had to accommodate themselves to the demands inside the home. Consequently, the arguments available for use *against* job-seeking women are that their responsibilities to their husbands and children are primary, that they will be leaving the work force for maternity-related reasons, that they are entering the work force too late in life, that they don't have the necessary degrees, skills, training, experience. And to acquire the credentials demanded in the work place involves an entirely different life experience—one which most men have not supported for their wives or daughters.

If, when a divorce occurs, the wife is told she's now financially responsible for herself, or even that she will receive "separate maintenance" for a year, there is an assumption that she can come out of the home environment and simply start a new financial life. In reality, the many skills and talents she has mastered will be conspicuously unmarketable. But, even if she can get a job, invariably it will be at lower pay than men—including her husband—receive. She will get no

[2] Personal interview. New York City.

The Myth of Alimony

credit for her life's work, and all that she put into her husband's career, job, life,[3] and for which she has received no compensation. Divorce will not affect a workingman's retirement pension; but the woman will get nothing from her employer-husband, who didn't provide very good "fringe benefits." The same is true of the medical insurance the wife will be losing on dissolution of the marriage. In addition, she may never have accumulated individual Social Security credits, and depending on the duration of the marriage, may not even be entitled to dependent spouse credits.

In fact, even if on divorce, a long-time husband equally divided his income with his ex-wife, she could still be losing. Which is why feminists view alimony as "reparations," "back pay." For women to give up their means of support before the social framework has changed radically is destructive of the individual woman, and of any "movement," since hungry people think of food before the abstractions of "liberation."

Only 3.5 percent of women in the United States receive income through alimony, private pensions, and annuities.[4]

The public generally views alimony as an institution for the benefit of women; actually it is for the benefit of men, or at least for the preservation of the system men enjoy. While the individual man may see no benefit to himself in paying alimony (if he does), it is still to the advantage of the sexual aristocracy. Support keeps women dependent, subservient, and at home.

And as an even more transparent benefit to men, twenty-nine states have laws allowing alimony to husbands.[5] But this "equalization" assumes the virtually nonexistent situation where the wife can earn enough to support not only herself but her husband, too.

Even if it appears equitable to say that either party can get alimony and that it can also be denied to either because of guilt, the wife—"guilty" or "innocent"—is still the one more likely to be unable to support herself.

But the "laws equalizing the obligation of marital support and awarding alimony to both husbands and wives assume the existence of an employment market that does not discriminate against women

---

[3] See Judy Syfers, "I Want a Wife," *Ms.* magazine, Preview Issue (Spring, 1972).
[4] *Consumer Income,* Bureau of the Census, U.S. Dept. of Commerce, Series P-60, No. 90 (1973 based on 1972 data).
[5] Four more don't allow alimony to wives at all, or else only on a statutorily limited basis.

on the basis of hiring, pay, opportunity for advancement or seniority."[6]

And, as a class, divorced women, even including divorced women with children under three, had the highest employment rate of all women.[7]

Among women, divorcées had the highest labor force rate, 70 percent in March of 1972. And even those divorcées with preschool children—in other words, those who did not wait to get divorced till after their children were in school—their employment rate was 62 percent, which is about double the corresponding rate for wives who are living with their husbands, "indicating that many divorcées *had* to work because they received inadequate support payments or none at all."[8]

> "A newspaper which reports that a movie star has had to pay his former wife 'a million dollars in alimony' is usually speaking of a one-shot division of marital assets, not ongoing payments of support."[9]

When media accounts about alimony appear, they are mainly cases of divorce or separation among those in the higher economic groups; newspapers report the unusual divorce or alimony case, not the ordinary one; little is reported about the nonpayment. Alimony is hardly a way of life "in those groups where the wife seldom adds more to the economic aspect of the marriage partnership than her own wage-earning ability,"[10] meaning that the self-supporting woman is penalized twice: she is working for less, but even that will be used against her if she does seek support from her husband.

Husbands, wives, lawyers, news-people are always talking about "alimony jail." In New York, this continues even though the place no longer exists! It did exist once, but at the time it was shut down most of the "inmates" were incarcerated for civil disobedience other than denial of alimony. And those few men there as a result of nonsupport had *refused* to make payments despite the court's findings that they could afford to.

---

[6] Kay, *Making Marriage and Divorce Safe for Women,* book review in 60 California Law Review 1683 (1972).
[7] Carolyn J. Jacobson, "Women Workers: Profile of a Growing Force," AFL-CIO *American Federationist* (July, 1974).
[8] *Monthly Labor Review,* Bureau of Vital Statistics, U.S. Dept. of Labor (April, 1973).
[9] Michael Wheeler, *No-Fault Divorce* (Boston, Beacon Press, 1974).
[10] Catherine Groves Peele, *Social and Psychological Effects of the Availability and the Granting of Alimony on the Spouses,* 6 Law and Contemporary Problems 483 (1939).

The Myth of Alimony

Women are caught in a double bind: They are not economically independent but also cannot count on what they have always been led to believe in—the marital right of support from their husbands.

The monetary control over sexual and household services becomes even more transparent when there is a divorce or a separation. There is no clearer example of the relationship between sex and money than the wife who, after years of "service (household and sexual loyalty),"[11] is in a divorce situation. She gets no back pay, no pension. And little of anything else.

It has been said that every woman is just one man away from welfare. Support by the husband during marriage is almost voluntary, since it may be even more difficult to sue for and collect support *during* the marriage than it is upon the marriage's dissolution. Court-awarded alimony and separation agreements are dangerous, insecure, and unreliable. The "bottom line" is the husband's willingness to comply with his support obligations and the wife's ability to enforce them.

"Alimony" or "separate maintenance" refer to payments made on perhaps a weekly or monthly basis, as distinguished from property or lump-sum settlements involving a one-time division of marital property or payment to a wife in exchange for her release of all future support. (In general, we are discussing here support of a wife, and not dependent children unless specified.)

Alimony traditionally refers to support of the estranged or divorced wife and with increasing frequency to support of the husband.

Alimony is supposed to ensure that it is the husband and not the public that supports an ex-wife. Along the way, "standards" of support are applied which may be ambiguous and arbitrary, but which allegedly relate to the wife's needs, the husband's ability to pay, the couple's standard of living, and the relative fault of the parties. Once fault is considered, there is an element of breach of contract, and punishment.

The more enlightened, nonjudicial view is that alimony is back pay, reparations, payment for past services, and should not terminate on the wife's remarriage, any more than a retired employee who receives a private pension for past consideration and for time and work and money already invested should lose the pension if the worker obtains a new job—a new dependency.

---

[11] One sexual indiscretion by a wife means, under New York law, that a court *cannot* award her alimony if she is found "guilty."

Alimony must be distinguished from child support, although for tax purposes the husband may prefer to label child support as alimony, since only alimony is tax deductible for the husband. The wife often agrees to this because she is in a lower tax bracket than the man, and the income thereafter is taxable to her at a lower rate.

Psychologically, the husband may prefer to call all payments "alimony" so he can justify his fury and belligerence at paying it, overlooking that it is for the support of his children. Also, alimony generally terminates upon the wife's marriage. The wife, for similar reasons, may prefer to have the payments called child support; but these payments may be structured so that the wife is without income once the children reach their majority or are otherwise "emancipated."

The husband undoubtedly realizes that most often, and unless an agreement stipulates otherwise, alimony terminates on the wife's remarriage, whereas child support does not.

Alimony may be set by court decree or agreement between the parties. In the contract known as a separation agreement, the parties and their attorneys negotiate terms which, if in accord with "public policy," are binding and permanent. They may, under certain circumstances, be modified, but should be entered into with a very long-term view.

If there is a separation agreement between the parties, they have entered into a contract between them. When the husband defaults, the wife theoretically has a contract to sue on and is not dependent on the court's deciding to award her support.

"Nice Women Stay Bought"

Money as support during the marriage or as "separate maintenance," alimony, or child support is a tool easily used against children, wives, and ex-wives. During the marriage, the wife, if she is working outside the home, is "supplementing" the husband's income; he's still the "breadwinner." And after divorce or marital dissolution, the man is able to retain both connection to and control of the family unit through money: its absence or presence. A man often describes support as guilt money or as buying his freedom. He proudly, if furiously, proclaims, "I'm supporting my family." The ex-husband can use the payment of money to remove himself or impose himself.

The Myth of Alimony

What has the ex-wife bought? If she's lucky, her financial status quo.

> ". . . to some men the paying of alimony means that they have the right to refuse to concern themselves further about former wives. On the other hand, to others, the making of alimony payments has an opposite meaning, and constitutes for them a reason for maintaining to some extent their former relationships with their families. A man who thinks of money as power and has no sense of guilt in connection with the marital break, may want to pay alimony as a means of retaining his authority in his former home. He may feel that as long as he is contributing regularly to his former wife's support he has the right to demand that he be given a voice in the management of the household of which he formerly was a part."[12]

There is constant talk about anger and resentment on the part of men who must pay alimony. There is little mention of the anger generated in a woman who, after years of marriage, is left with nothing but the hope that her alimony checks will arrive in time to pay the rent, that her ex-husband will enjoy good health and long life, that he is keeping up his life-insurance payments, that she can get some job, that he will pay the children's medical bills.

The ex-wife is constantly trying to placate her adversary. Even if she believes she has "rights," she often decides to "just forget it." Many women swallow their anger and say, "Well, he did sue me for child custody, but I know it was a negotiating ruse. I don't have any hostility towards him, I don't have any ill feeling."

The Reality

By design or neglect, there are almost no statistics available on the subject of alimony—its existence, its nonexistence, its enforcement, its nonenforcement.[13] But the available statistics on alimony indicate

---

[12] Peele, *op. cit.*

[13] For example, in the course of researching this book, I selected Brooklyn, New York, for a study of alimony payments. Attempts were made to ascertain through the Supreme Court of that county the number of divorced women who were to receive alimony and/or child support, the number who did, and for how long it continued. The Supreme Court agreed that *some* of the information I sought was a matter of public record on the "Certificate of Dissolution" which HEW requires the couple or their attorney to file at the time of divorce; in order to see those portions of the form which are public, the author might see some answers which are not—even though it is all available to the federal government. However, the author was denied access to all this statistical information. At the time of this writing, the author is studying the feasibility of a lawsuit against the Supreme Court for denying access to public information.

that it is both sought and awarded less frequently than is generally believed. And it is paid less often, too.

A survey by the American Bar Association[14] of five hundred domestic relations judges revealed hostility to working mothers, hostility to dependent women, hostility to independent women. In the same study one judge said, "Marriage is a woman's business. When the marriage is bankrupt the woman is bankrupt."

Antialimony arguments begin on the false premise that a wife is her husband's equal before the law. "She may own property, bring lawsuits—even against her husband[15]—and is politically his equal."[16] The argument continues that a wife is "economically independent, or potentially so, with ample opportunities to make her way in the business and professional world."[17] According to Justice Hofstadter, "It [alimony] should not be suffered to convert a host of physically and mentally competent young women into an army of alimony drones who neither toil nor spin, and become a drain on society and a menace to themselves."[18]

Or, as an idealistic New York court has put it, women have "practically unlimited opportunities . . . in the business world of today."[19]

Support is an illusory *right,* because a right does not exist without being enforceable.

> ". . . the data available, although scant, indicated that . . . alimony is granted in only a very small percentage of cases; that fathers, by and large, are contributing less than half the support of the children in divided families; and that alimony and child support awards are very difficult to collect."[20]

The American Bar Association Study[21] showed that "permanent alimony is granted in only 2 percent of all divorces and then only where the marriage is of long duration and the wife is too old or too ill to be employable, and particularly if the husband's behavior was a

---

[14] Quenstedt and Winkler, "What Are Our Domestic Relations Judges Thinking?" Section on Family Law, American Bar Association (1965).
[15] An automobile accident, for example.
[16] Hofstadter and Levittan, *Alimony—A Reformulation,* 7 Journal of Family Law 51 (1967).
[17] *Ibid.*
[18] *Ibid.*
[19] Phillips vs. Phillips 1 AD 2d 393 at 395 (1956); reaffirmed in Koren v. Koren 29 N.Y. 2d 408 (1972).
[20] *Recognition of Economic Contribution of Homemakers and Protection of Children in Divorce Law and Practice,* Citizens' Advisory Council on the Status of Women, U.S. Dept. of Labor (1974).
[21] Quenstedt and Winkler, *op. cit.*

The Myth of Alimony

contributing cause of the divorce. Temporary alimony is available in less than 10 percent of all divorces chiefly to give the wife an opportunity to obtain employment."[22]

". . . Alimony in and of itself is not too great a problem as nearly 90 percent of the petitioners waive it."[23]

In 1900, alimony was requested in 13.4 percent of all divorces and awarded in 9.3 percent. In 1922, alimony was granted in 14.7 percent of all cases. According to one estimate, alimony *or* a property settlement is granted in about one-quarter of all American divorces.[24] The percentage of cases in which alimony or a property settlement was awarded in 1950 varied from 7.2 percent of the cases in Florida to 48.4 percent in Kansas.

A Kansas study reveals that from 1956 to 1961, alimony or property settlement was available in about half of the divorce cases. However, in 1942–1943—the only time that the statistics differentiated between alimony awards and property settlements—alimony was awarded in 1 percent of the cases and a property settlement was granted in 10 percent. That ratio, if applied to the 1956–1961 data, would mean that in those cases where alimony or property settlement was had, 5 percent of the wives would have had alimony awards and 45 percent property settlements.[25] Only 2½ percent would then be receiving alimony. The more popular property settlements would really be available only to the wealthy or those with property. Hopson's study found the no-alimony rationale to be, "Since alimony is impossible to collect, there's no reason to grant it."

A study of 12,000 Chicago divorces heard by Judge E. A. Robson in 1951 showed that women waived alimony in 93 percent of all cases, even including out-of-court settlements. While property settlements existed in these cases, Judge Robson concluded that the percentage of waiver was sufficiently high to establish that in the majority of the group studied, women elected to rely on their own efforts for support.[26]

---

[22] Although this is the statistic of one California judge who is referring to his county, and the sampling was small, but presumably accurate—there is very little else known about the economics of alimony, and this figure can probably be more broadly projected.
[23] Quenstedt and Winkler, *op. cit.*
[24] Paul Jacobson, *American Marriage and Divorce*, 1959 Bureau of the Census Statistical Report on Alimony.
[25] Hopson, *The Economics of a Divorce: A Pilot Empirical Study at the Trial Court Level*, 11 Kansas Law Review 107 (1962).
[26] Maxine Virtue, *Family Cases in Court* (Durham, N.C., Duke University Press, 1956).

Joseph Epstein, whose book *Divorced in America* can hardly be described as feminist, writes:

> "Left as a matter of honor, as most personal debts are, it is exceedingly likely that most men who are made to pay alimony would eventually default on it. As things stand now, there is already a long history of financial finagling on the part of divorced men to avoid alimony payments. Alimony-paying ex-husbands have been known to take jobs that pay only room and board, to sign assets over to brothers or friends, to emerge from the vault rooms of obscure neighborhood banks at odd hours, to depart their home states, to leave false (and vastly understated) income tax forms lying around the house, to attempt to extinguish their identities by going into hiding—all to avoid alimony."[27]

Moreover, there are states[28] which, as a matter of law, do not allow permanent alimony.[29] (This does not mean that, on divorce, there cannot be a settlement or division of property.) Pennsylvania has allowed temporary alimony to continue

> *"until a reconciliation shall take place or until the husband shall, by his petition, offer to receive and cohabit with her again and to use her as a good husband ought to do; and in case of her refusal to return and cohabit . . .* [the court may] *discharge and annul the same"* (emphasis added).

And in New Hampshire alimony is allowable, but where there are no children the award can be made for a three-year period only. (It may be modified, terminated, or extended for another three years.)

Many women cannot even get legal representation in seeking financial support. The problem arises where a wife has no money of her own, i.e. most women. First there is the situation of the poor family whose members would be eligible for free legal services (such as the Legal Aid Society), but there are either no such services locally available for matrimonial cases, or there is, perhaps, an eighteen-month waiting list. Equally hard hit is the woman who, although personally without funds, cannot get free legal services because her husband has some money—which she has no access to. The next problem is the woman whose husband can afford to pay legal fees but is unwilling to pay hers; she has great difficulty because lawyers expect to be paid

---

[27] *Divorced In America* (New York, E. P. Dutton and Co., 1974).
[28] Notably Texas and Pennsylvania.
[29] In Pennsylvania unless the wife is "insane."

fees. And having her legal fees paid by her adversary is not satisfactory to the woman in a divorce situation.

Moves by women to secure guaranteed representation despite their poverty has been a double-edged sword. In New York, for example, the ironic effect of that effort has been to guarantee legal representation to the husbands facing contempt of court for nonsupport.[30]

Typically, a husband negotiating a separation agreement or being sued for support threatens to leave the state. His alternating threat is to seek child custody. He assumes, often quite correctly, that the wife is not going to have the strength, stamina, support, resources, or law to really go after him or, finding him, to enforce judgments against him.

And the woman, hearing threats of losing support and losing her children, takes the threats seriously and thinks she is the first wife to be blackmailed by the father of her children.

Elaine Livingston of the Marriage and Divorce Committee, of the National Organization for Women (New York City), says:

> "If you take a man of means, however, they have much trickier ways of avoiding alimony. First of all, in the beginning they hide their assets.
>
> "Without complete and compulsory financial disclosure the original award could be based on the wrong sum to begin with. Or he claims he is almost in poverty. Suddenly he has no job, or he sold his business—and he's put it under another name and so on.
>
> "I was married to a man who apparently was worth considerably more than I ever knew he was worth. I just knew here was a man of means, that he had money. My lawyer said to me, 'Find out where it is.' What do you mean, find out; I don't know where it is and his income tax will only show certain things. Now I understand that you can get private investigators, but my lawyer never told me about that, and I don't know anything about them. But yes, it's true that most women don't ask their husbands what they have, except if it's stocks or something so obvious you would know it. But a man could have property, here, in other states, or somewhere, or he could have tax-free bonds or other things that don't appear on income tax returns.
>
> "Some women aren't getting support because they can't find their husbands, or were married to men who didn't have too much money to begin with so they're all saying they can't afford it."[31]

---
[30] Vanderpool v. Vanderpool 43 AD2d 716, 350 NYS 2d 435 (1973, as amended 1974).
[31] Personal interview. New York City.

Enforcement

Women are uncomfortable in unknown, male-dominated arenas. Although women don't *want* court intervention in their lives, the social-legal-judicial institutions impose themselves wherever we turn: scarlet-letter judgments, child illegitimacy, marriage, divorce, custody, support, attempts to collect support and to enforce agreements and orders.

Some women are reluctant to sue for enforcement of alimony because they know it will be frustrating and expensive, in time, energy—and money. Others avoid the battle for fear it will anger the husband and say, "It's better not to start anything."

Though the state injects itself as a third party in the marriage, it walks away from the issues of support and enforcement.

In every state the husband has an obligation to support his wife during marriage; in virtually every state the wife is liable for support of a husband who is unable to support himself; and in every state both the mother and father are liable for support of minor children.

The Uniform Reciprocal Enforcement of Support Act (URESA), for example, is designed to enforce support orders of dependents across state lines from persons legally responsible for support. As a practical matter, although URESA *may* cover both alimony and child support, it is next to useless as far as alimony goes; slightly less so as to child support. And, despite the so-called Uniformity, the provisions may vary from state to state. The problems of the dependents are serious enough if the family members are in one state. They become overwhelming when one party (usually the male) leaves the jurisdiction.

URESA established a civil support obligation in a "simplified" proceeding which begins with a petition being filed in State 1—the state the husband-father has presumably deserted. If the judge finds that there has been a duty to support, the wife sends to State 2, to which the husband-father has fled or in which he has property. State 2 may order the man to furnish support and send a copy of the order to the first state, along with any payment it receives.

But first, the wife needs to know where the husband is. The respondent (usually the husband) is not required to appear in the petitioner's (usually the wife's) state or the state of marital residence. Then, she is dependent now on two sets of courts, and possibly sev-

The Myth of Alimony

eral sets of lawyers. In the meantime, the husband has the choice of states, can appear in State 2's court without the wife being present, may give testimony and even have the case dismissed without giving the wife a chance to reply.

At the 1973 annual meeting of the National Conference on Uniform Reciprocal Enforcement of Support attended by representatives of every state, participants concerned themselves with *child support only,* and at that, only with monies owed by welfare fathers, or families which, without the father's support, go on welfare. The evidence indicated that states really had no interest in the whole matter except when the state is otherwise absorbing the bill. Thus, the only men really sought after are the poor and those who—though not poor —force their families onto welfare. The conference reported nothing on the subject of *alimony,* whether for welfare recipients or otherwise. The *entire* concern was with the children or, more correctly, with relieving the state of having to support children.

Where it is really a contest between the husband and the state supporting children, the state will move to enforce support payments. Otherwise, the state's formidable powers are not applied.

The conference studied possible "techniques to be used in locating absent parents," including California's suggestion of securing data from the National Drivers' License Data Bank; Washington's suggestion of securing, from postmasters, forwarding addresses, addresses for post office box numbers; from Oregon, expertise on "Military Location" and Indian location; Maryland's representative offered expertise in securing Social Security numbers and employers from the Social Security Administration in Baltimore; while Michigan developed information on securing Social Security numbers from large corporate employers. "Other techniques included Internal Revenue Service, telephone directories, credit bureaus, criminal records, and field investigations."

In a survey[32] of the success, if any, of the various states in enforcing support orders, these are typical of the replies:

ARKANSAS: "Enforcing the act is another story, however. The prosecuting attorneys are charged with the primary responsibility for enforcing the act and, if they refuse or neglect to do so, then the welfare department may do so. Very few prosecuting attorneys have the time or personnel with which to discharge

---

[32] In a letter sent by the author to the URESA enforcement agencies of every state.

this duty so whatever action is taken is usually by the welfare department attorneys. The few attorneys in that department are usually snowed under with other department business which has priority over URESA matters. Consequently, Arkansas is not providing the service to the other states nor its own obligees that the situation deserves.

"Our courts award alimony only in exceptional cases, i.e. where the wife is totally incapable of supporting herself. This attitude, I am sure, spills over into the judges' decision when adjudicating URESA cases when we are the receiving state."

IOWA: ". . . relating to the enforceability of alimony decrees. I do not know where you could obtain the materials you desire."

ILLINOIS: "The Act in Illinois is not generally used to enforce alimony decrees although I think the Illinois Statute is broad enough to include such enforcement. . . . I admit to absolute frustration. . . . The state's Attorneys are not interested in acquiring more cases and becoming involved in family affairs even at the expense of public aid and public aid fraud. . . . It appears safe to say that the lack of concern and the lack of interest in support enforcement is a political question in Illinois to which the state legislature and governor have never addressed themselves."

KENTUCKY: "There is no enforcement of alimony decrees. Only child support."

KENTUCKY: "It is my impression that Kentucky officials are a few steps behind most other states in support enforcement activities because of the low priority they give to child support matters. The local officers generally view crimes involving force and drugs as much more serious than child support, which is considered a 'domestic law' problem."

NEW MEXICO: "I'm afraid that there is no source in New Mexico which can provide the statistics you require."

NORTH CAROLINA: "Unfortunately, there are no statistics available concerning the extent to which URESA has aided the enforcement of alimony decrees."

OKLAHOMA: "The URESA filled a real social economic need for

the deserted widow and children. We regret that we are unable to give you any percentable figures."

ARIZONA: "Since Arizona had adopted a new no-fault dissolution act which makes maintenance available to either spouse on a basis of need, the courts look more favorably on alimony [maintenance] orders."

MINNESOTA: "It has been the experience of our office that alimony decrees are not enforced through the URESA action in our county or in the majority of counties in the metropolitan area of the Twin Cities."

MARYLAND: "I'm sorry but we are unable to accede to your request to provide information on the enforceability of alimony decrees. The reason being that URESA is used by us only in the context of obtaining support for children. We have no statistical information of any kind that deals with alimony. Our statistics refer only to support orders decreed."

NEBRASKA: "At the present time there is no mechanism in Nebraska for the identification or compilation of data as to increased enforcement of URESA decrees, before or after the amendments of 1959 and 1968."

OREGON: "Oregon courts do not look favorably upon alimony and few are entered of record in Oregon. We have no data on enforcement of such decrees either before or after and I do not know any person or organization who would have information on this matter."

TEXAS: ". . . in Texas there is no alimony collection at all because our statutes specifically prohibit collection of alimony in Uniform Reciprocal Enforcement of Support Actions."

The various states have laws *theoretically* subjecting husbands to various penalties for nonsupport.

MARYLAND: Requires husband who has ability to labor or is laboring and who willfully and without reasonable cause refuses to support his wife or children to be subject to an action for maintenance. Failure to comply with maintenance makes husband subject to civil action and he may be jailed on execution of this default.

ARIZONA: The statute has been amended to read: "A married person having sufficient ability to provide for his or her spouse's support or who is able to earn the means of such spouse's support and unjustifiably refuses to do so is guilty of a felony." (Section 13-803) (Supp. 1973)

NEW YORK (Family Court Act, Section 412): "A husband is chargeable with the support of his wife and if possessed of sufficient means or able to earn such means, may be required to pay for her support a fair and reasonable sum, as they determine, having due regard to the circumstances of the respective parties." The only penal section is Section 260.05: "A person is guilty of nonsupport of a child when, being a parent . . ."

The District Attorney's office in New York County responded to a request for the number of prosecutions under this section by saying, in part, "This office does not record the number of prosecutions under a particular penal law section." However, it is common for the District Attorney's office to release, for example, the number of homicide arrests and prosecutions.

But where penalties exist, they are treated as family situations, not crimes, and prosecutors look the other way, citing extradition problems, which don't seem overwhelming in what they consider "real crimes." The states largely take the position that, despite penal laws, unless both welfare and children are involved, no criminal prosecution can be instigated.

"For every man suffering under the burden of unfair alimony, there are a hundred women whose children are financially abandoned by ex-husbands."[33]

Children

Since most husbands are not faced with having to make alimony payments anyway, in practice the main money problem is child support.[34]

"Unfortunately, too many fathers try to escape the financial responsibility of raising their children once they leave the household.

---
[33] Robert W. Kahn and Lawrence E. Kahn, *The Divorce Lawyer's Casebook* (New York, St. Martin's Press, 1972).
[34] *Ibid.*

Thousands of failure-to-support petitions are filed in our country's family courts each year. They reflect thousands of fathers neglecting financial obligations to their children.
"By some illogic these men feel their children will be mysteriously cared for after divorce."[35]

It is generally felt that men are willing to acknowledge a greater obligation and duty toward supporting their children than their ex-wives. Nevertheless, according to one study[36] based on a 1955 sample of fathers who were ordered in divorce decrees to pay child support in a metropolitan Wisconsin county, after ten years of support, 79 percent of the fathers had not complied at all with the court order; 13 percent had fully complied, and 8 percent partially; *legal action had been taken against* one father.[37]

Feminist Backlash

Where equal rights are for the distinct, direct, obvious, unmistakable advantage of men, states are quick to enact equal rights legislation. Michigan, for example, a state which voted against ratification of the Equal Rights Amendment, succeeded in making alimony "equally" available to men. "There is a clear majority of the 50 states plus the District of Columbia and Puerto Rico, and the Virgin Islands, which theoretically removed sex discrimination from alimony [by providing it for the husband]."[38]

Some Examples:

> ARIZONA: Either spouse may ask for maintenance upon a showing that she/he lacks sufficient property to provide for her/his reasonable means and is unable to support her/himself through appropriate employment or is the custodian of children whose age and condition is such that the custodial parent should not be required to seek employment outside the home.
>
> CALIFORNIA: The court can order either spouse to support the other and for a time and in an amount reasonable with regard to

---

[35] *Ibid.*
[36] Kenneth Eckhardt, *Deviance, Visibility, and Legal Action: The Duty to Support,* 15 Social Problems, 470 (1968); and reprinted, Nagel & Weitzman, *Women as Litigants,* 23 Hastings Law Journal 171 (1971).
[37] URESA Conference Study, 1973.
[38] Henry H. Foster and Doris Jonas Freed, *New York Law Journal* (February 22, 1974).

the ability of the supported spouse to gain employment without interfering with the interests of the children.

FLORIDA: Either party may claim temporary, permanent, or rehabilitative alimony. The court may consider the adultery of the spouse claiming alimony and deny support upon a finding of guilt. And the Supreme Court of the United States has refused to overturn Florida's denial of alimony to an adulterous wife.[39]

HAWAII: Allows alimony to either party. A court order is modifiable upon (1) showing that the supported party, although capable of substantially[40] rehabilitating her/himself financially, has willfully failed to do so, (2) remarriage of the wife. (The statute appears to be silent on the question of the husband's remarriage.)

NORTH CAROLINA: A dependent spouse (whether wife or husband) is entitled to an order for alimony when the supporting spouse has committed adultery or has been imprisoned, or has engaged in an unnatural sex act with a person of the same or opposite sex or a beast, or has abandoned the dependent spouse, or the supporting spouse's conduct of cruel treatment endangers the life of the dependent spouse.

OKLAHOMA: If the divorce is granted to the wife for the husband's fault, wife can get alimony. If the divorce is granted to the husband for the wife's fault, the husband can get alimony.

VIRGINIA: Maintenance allowable to either party. However, court has no authority to grant support or alimony that continues after death of the "father or husband."

And alimony to men is not brand-new. For example, in a 1932 case, Mr. and Mrs. Barnett were married for fifteen years and had two children.

At the time of the marriage, each owned a separate portion of land. Oil was discovered on the wife's land, but not on the husband's, and during the marriage the husband managed the wife's land.

The court, finding Mrs. Barnett guilty of adultery, granted the hus-

---

[39] Pachero v. Pachero 246 So. 2nd 778 (Fla.), 92 S. Ct. 85 (1971) (*Cert. denied*).
[40] The termination of support to the "willfully unrehabilitated" lends itself to grave dangers since it will still be up to courts to decide what is willful refusal to become rehabilitated, and they will not likely consider the lifetime of conditioning and image shattering that has gotten the woman where she is today.

The Myth of Alimony

band a divorce, and child custody; it also awarded him $15,000 a year alimony:

> "If the union has been abandoned by the criminality of the wife without the fault of the husband, it seems just that the innocent husband should not, in addition to the grievous wrong done, by the breach of the marriage vows, be wholly deprived of means to support himself and children; nor viewing the matter of another standpoint, does it seem either just or equitable that funds which were intended at the time of the marriage for the use of both should be borne off by the guilty wife and perhaps transferred to the hands of the adulterer as the dowry of a . . . second marriage."[41]

A myth within a myth is that the disintegration, if not disappearance, of alimony is due to the feminist movement. Or that feminists oppose alimony.

With increasing frequency, male judges—and virtually all judges are male—pontificate that the "official position" of the women's movement is antialimony. They now have a rationalization for their actions. There is a feminist backlash.

Many people contend, "Feminists don't believe in alimony."

Though feminists meet the question of marriage with varying degrees of approval or disapproval, none believe that women are anywhere near a level of economic independence. Judges have not been guided by what the women's movement believes or wants except, apparently, where that posture is useful for the preservation of the status quo. Judges and others often say, "If you want to be 'liberated,' don't ask your husband to support you."

Feminists do not favor the *need* for alimony, but most do not support its abolition while the need exists. Women are coming to view alimony as reparation for the time, years, youth put into the marriage —and the husband's career. In fact, reparations themselves cannot even be adequate because they don't usually contemplate the husband's rising income, his greater pension, Social Security. In light of their inequities, even seemingly fair agreements like a fifty-fifty property division split are not in the wife's interests since it is fifty-fifty of the assets of the past and not the future.

Feminists have made these observations about the complex question of alimony:

[41] Barnett v. Barnett 13 P2d 104 (S. Ct. Okla. 1932).

Jane Galvin Lewis, Director of the National Black Feminist Organization:

"A woman should get paid alimony just for having sat across the breakfast table from him all those years."[42]

Diane Schulder, coauthor of *Abortion Rap*:[43]

"Alimony is a myth perpetuated by the media and the male dominated establishment to becloud the issue of abandoned women and children."

Claudia Dreifus, author of *A Woman's Fate*:[44]

"People think that alimony is one of the great advantages that women have. Well, if it's so great, then why don't we have it? It seems to be inaccessible to most women. I don't think, however, women should give it up until they have equal wages and equal work."

Barbara Seaman, author of *Free and Female*:[45]

"Many feminists are *too* generous. We rush to give up the meager protections we have before we've gained anything approaching the equality that might make such protections unnecessary. A woman who has taken herself off the job market, put her husband through college or graduate school, serviced and served him, raised his children, and failed to develop her own marketable skills, is most certainly entitled to alimony, lots of it—every penny she can get. I am deeply puzzled and alarmed to hear some young feminists denounce alimony. It seems that they have no knowledge or understanding of the plight of many older women, nor do they seem to recognize that even the woman who has good job skills earns about 60 percent as much as a man with the same training, seniority, and competence. A feminist wouldn't even think of giving up alimony until women have truly achieved equal pay for equal work, as well as a genuine codivision of child care and household responsibility in the family."

Robin Morgan, editor, *Sisterhood Is Powerful*:[46]

". . . in the earliest stages of this feminist wave (the antithetical or 'So there!' phase), various feminists publicly deplored alimony 'as prostitution wages.' This is, of course, ridiculous—as well as being a

---

[42] Personal interview, Fire Island, New York.
[43] New York, McGraw-Hill, 1971.
[44] New York, Bantam Books, 1974.
[45] New York, Coward, McCann and Geoghegan, 1972.
[46] New York, Random House, 1970.

The Myth of Alimony

self-destructive attitude born of false pride (and false consciousness). At this time in patriarchal history, alimony is, rather, *'retroactive pay'* for years of free labor. When a woman, untrained and rebuffed by society for any real 'marketplace' job, invests years of work as wife, mother, housekeeper, cook, laundress, chauffeur, secretary, hostess, psychologist, and general 'nurturer'—and then finds herself 'out of work' in, perhaps, her middle age—what means of survival are available for her? Being a file clerk or waitress or other abominably salaried 'unskilled' job?

"As long as decent and *salaried* jobs are not as available to women as to men; as long as marriage remains the major means of economic survival, albeit a dependency means, for women; as long as most men consider "housework" the natural (and free) labor of women; so long must alimony exist—and, in fact, be affirmed by feminists.

"When the above conditions change, then the concept of alimony can alter or disappear, too."

Again, men have seized upon the concept of women's liberation as something that can work to their advantage. Like the so-called sexual revolution.

In an economic, social, and cultural atmosphere in which women are economically independent, there would be no necessity or justification for alimony. However, if women in the United States have achieved a kind of unshackling, perhaps it is sexual, a female "liberation" for the benefit of men. Or at least that is the only struggle for female liberation supported by men. There has been no economic liberation.

Feminists seem in agreement that attacks on alimony, fights for the elimination of alimony are not the place to begin to achieve, for all persons, financial freedom. Before abandoning alimony, there must be a raising of women to a level of economic equality with men, and indeed economic equality of men to other men. This involves a redistribution of the wealth and the control of the wealth, which is now in the hands of the sexual aristocracy.

The idea that women all over America are sitting around collecting alimony is a myth. A convenient myth.

11. Women and Credit: Neither a Borrower Nor a Lender Be

"It is un-American to count a woman's income. . . . The only way a woman's income could be counted would be if she were to have a hysterectomy."[1]

America moves on money. Specifically, on *borrowed* money: credit. The essence of capitalism is making money through the use of money (capital). The keys to our economic system are the ability to make money through nonproductive means, such as lending or investing capital, and through *other* people's labor (which requires having money to invest to open a factory and employ laborers). However, the source of capitalist energy, profit, is in the ability to be a *lender* rather than a *borrower:* That ability is available to only a few, and they are usually men. In fact, even the less desirable status of being a borrower is frequently denied poor white men (unless the interest rate is exorbitant and the amounts of money relatively small),[2] and much more frequently denied women in every economic situation.

"Try the bank—it's good for a laugh. Then go back with a supporter —male—and you'll get your line of credit."[3]

---

[1] Women and Credit Study Group, Oregon Public Group Interest Research Group (February, 1973).
[2] Use of BankAmericard, Master Charge, small personal loans are encouraged; the interest rate is often 18 percent and through such means the banks establish a self-serving web from which the poor person may not escape.
[3] Jane Trahey, founder and President of Jane Trahey Associates, advertising agency.

Economic discrimination against women isn't restricted to wage and employment only; it also consists of closing other avenues of access to money. Women have not been able to borrow capital for purposes of establishing businesses, careers, attending school,[4] purchasing homes, investing or obtaining money for any of the purposes for which men raise funds.[5]

There has long been a pattern of lending practices which discriminate against women. There still is.

Everything used against women to deny credit has to do with the "double bind" situations created by men to deny women access to money; these include low-income jobs, and primary individual responsibility for child care duties.

It is men who have decided to take pregnant women out of the job market and to require them, if possible, to stay out after childbirth, and certainly to deny child care services which would tend to give the mother greater mobility.

> "A woman should not expect to get a credit card . . . if she is too young. But neither should she expect one if she is too old. On the other hand, she should not look forward to improvement in her credit status after marriage. She has gained a husband, but probably lost her credit. Then if she loses her husband by divorce, she is stripped of even his credit rating. And if she loses her husband by death, her credit card may follow him to the grave."[6]

Women as women suffer the penalties of denial of job, loss of job, lowest salaries, denial of benefits, denial of child care, denial of job. Circle.

Women suffer because they are "guilty" of the "social disease" of pregnancy. Despite the large number of households headed by working mothers, and though there is no evidence that women are poor credit risks,[7] banks ponder how a woman could be a good credit risk

---

[4] Margaret J. Gates, *Credit Discrimination Against Women: Causes and Solutions*, 27 Vanderbilt Law Review 432–441 (1974). Women obtain fewer loans for educational purposes. In 53 out of the 54 jurisdictions participating in the Federal Guaranteed Student Loan Program, women have received fewer loans than men. For example, in Alabama, male-female distribution is 63.8-35.6; in Arizona 79.2-20.6; in California 70.4-29.4; in Illinois 77.9-21.8; in New York 63.2-36.7; in Utah 79.1-20.8. Though it is not clear whether women also apply for fewer loans, the result is still the same discrimination once they wake up and do. HEW, "Report of the Guaranteed Student Loan Program, Distribution of Cumulative Loans as of June 30, 1972" (May 14, 1973).
[5] Since the enactment of Title VII of the Civil Rights Act of 1968, mortgage lending discrimination on the basis of *race or ethnic origin* has been unlawful.
[6] Women and Credit Study, p. 6.
[7] A study of risk in installment credit found that both married and single women were better credit risks than men with the same marital status. (Nothing to the contrary exists.) Indeed, a study by the Federal Home Loan Bank Board (March, 1972) could

if she is unable to be a working mother. And they assume she is unable to be a working mother since they, the banks, the employers, are doing nothing to provide child care, educate women, end job discrimination. And women, for the most part, do not have access to such "favorable" credit arrangements as GI Bills and veterans' loans.

A U.S. Civil Rights Commission study of Hartford quotes the *Mortgage Credit Analysis Handbook* as saying, "The mortgagor who is married and has a family generally evidences more stability than a mortgagor who is single because, among other things, he [she][8] has the responsibility holding him [her] to his [her] obligation."

> "What credit would you allow for a working wife's income if she was age 25, had two *school age* children, and worked full-time as a secretary?"

The above question was asked by the Federal Home Loan Bank Board of one hundred savings and loan associations considered "most likely to cooperate."

One-fourth of the seventy-five responding savings and loan institutions said they would count *none* of her income. Twenty-six percent said they would go as high as half of her income. Only 22 percent of those responding would count all of the wife's income![9]

The 1972 study by the Federal Home Loan Bank Board also asked if marital status was a factor in the decision to grant a loan. Sixty-four percent of the savings and loan associations said yes, and 18 percent said that marital status could actually *disqualify* an applicant.[10]

The United States Savings and Loan League asked:

> "Assuming you give weight to a working wife's income, how much will you give?"[11]

---

find no empirical evidence to support the theory that the extension of credit to women would increase risk of default and subsequent foreclosure. Paul F. Smith, "Measuring Risk on Installment Credit," *Management Science,* 1964 (Nov.) II (2), pp. 327–340. Cited by Nancy Felipe Russo, in Report to Assemblyman Lucio F. Russo, Chair, Banking Committee, New York State Legislature, October, 1973.

[8] "Mortgage Money: Who Gets It? A Case Study in Mortgage Lending Discrimination in Hartford, Connecticut," United States Commission on Civil Rights, Clearinghouse Publication No. 48 (June, 1974). Where it is considered desirable to emphasize that a negative factor applies to women, the feminine gender is often used.

[9] *Federal Home Loan Bank Board Survey* (March, 1972).

[10] John P. Farry, President, United States Savings and Loan League, testimony before the National Commission on Consumer Finance, May, 1972, cited by Nancy Russo, *op. cit.*

[11] It is unfortunate that the question was prefaced with "assuming you give weight to the wife's income . . ." for it indeed appears to have been a false assumption. Nancy Russo, *op. cit.*

Seventy-two percent of the respondents reported that they would ignore all or part of the wife's income. The nonresponse rate for this question was 21 percent versus 1 percent for other questions, which implies that there were a considerable number of savings and loan associations that would not have counted any of the wife's income which were not included in the 72 percent figure.

"A spokesman for the Idaho First National Bank testified that thirty-two is considered the 'safe' age for a woman from the lender's point of view. A younger woman is judged to be still likely to marry and have children, thus not a good risk. Much of her income will be discounted. After thirty-two, the prospects of marriage and children are more remote; then, perhaps, she will be deemed reliable, and her total earning capacity will be considered."[12]

"The women with the greatest difficulty in gaining access to mortgage finance are single women—unmarried, widowed, separated or divorced women. It's a complete 'damned-if-you-do-damned-if-you-don't situation' because, as to single women (and, in fact, single men), the LACK OF family is held against them (whereas for the married person the *presence* of family is held against her)."[13]

Notwithstanding that in 1970, 68 percent of all families headed by men nominally owned their own homes (actually, the bank did), only 48 percent of families headed by women did.[14]

In the United States Commission on Civil Rights[15] survey of Hartford, Connecticut, a city which was chosen as a demonstrably typical American city, only 15 percent of families headed by women owned their own homes. Though the Commission found that families headed by women earned substantially less than the median income, still, of those, another 15 percent earned enough money to afford to purchase

[12] Idaho Governor's Commission on Women's Programs, "Hearing on Discrimination in Finance" (May 12, 1972), pp. 22–26, as cited in ACLU Report by Trudy Hayden, "Punishing Pregnancy: Discrimination in Education, Employment and Credit," Women's Rights Project (October, 1973).
[13] If one combines the classifications "widowed," "separated," and "divorced," one finds that in 1970, 5 million men compared with 14.5 million women fit into one of the three categories. (Stephen Rohde, National Center for Policy Review, in testimony before the Joint Economic Committee on Economic Problems of Women, July 12, 1973. Cited by Nancy Russo, *op. cit.*)
[14] Census of Housing: Metropolitan Housing Characteristics, U.S. Dept. of Commerce, 1970.
[15] "Mortgage Money: Who Gets It? A Case Study in Mortgage Lending Discrimination in Hartford, Connecticut," *op. cit.*

housing but were the victims of sex discrimination in credit, which, the study found, was not nearly as subtle as race discrimination.[16]

> "Women of different marital status—married, unmarried, widowed, separated—are all viewed somewhat differently by the mortgage lending committee. No group of women, however, has equal access to mortgage money."[17]

The FHA claims to count all of a wife's income in about 90 percent of the cases. But they also claim to keep records of the mortgages actually granted, and not of those rejected on the basis of wife's income, nonincome, or any other reason.

The Civil Rights Commission study found statements made in justification of more easily extending credit to a male applying for a mortgage than a female, as "A man could make repairs around the house, but a woman couldn't."[18]

Even the Veterans Administration, which denies that it engages in the practice of private lending institutions of requiring a "baby letter" (a statement of contraception), does admit that "if such a medical statement [supporting evidence that a couple is unable to have children] is voluntarily submitted by the veteran to the lender, it cannot very well be refused upon receipt in VA."[19]

The Hartford study concluded:

> "If left to operate in accordance with traditional banking processes and standards, will the system of mortgage finance in the city assure fair treatment for minorities and women? The basic finding of this report is that it will not. For minorities and women, the mortgage finance system is a stacked deck—sometimes inadvertently, often unthinkingly, but stacked nonetheless."

Cases

A New Jersey woman was told by real estate agents that if she expected her income to be counted for a mortgage, she would have to submit written proof from a doctor that she was on birth control pills

---

[16] Information contained in the Hartford Study was gathered prior to June, 1973, when a state law was passed prohibiting discrimination on the basis of sex or marital status in credit transactions, including mortgage lending transactions.
[17] Hartford Study in Mortgage Lending Discrimination.
[18] Ibid.
[19] Allegedly, as of July 18, 1973, all of the Veterans Administration regional offices were instructed no longer to discount the income on account of sex or marital status.

and written proof from her employer that she would be rehired after a pregnancy before they would show her any homes.[20]

Applicants for a mortgage under a federal Veterans Administration loan program were told that the wife's income could be considered if she was sterilized and submitted medical certification of sterilization. (A vasectomy for her husband wouldn't do, they were told, for she could still get pregnant.) Writing of the incident, she noted ruefully that her income "is counted 100 percent by the State of Delaware and the United States Government for the income tax."[21]

A New York woman, after three years at the same job, made $10,000 a year and had a savings account with $5,000. Her husband made $115 a week and had no savings. Chase Manhattan Bank refused to grant her their Uni-Card unless she applied in her husband's name.[22]

A young Virginia couple seeking a mortgage found the bank unwilling to count the wife's income unless (1) she provided a statement from her doctor attesting that she was on birth control pills, (2) she signed a statement promising to have an abortion if she did get pregnant, *and* (3) her husband signed a statement agreeing to an abortion *and* (4) her husband agreed to consider a vasectomy should she become unable to take pills.[23]

A personal credit officer with a Baltimore savings institution explained that if a married couple applies for a loan and the wife is under forty-two, he computes only half of her income. If she is younger than forty-two, he believes, chances are high that she will quit working.[24]

The Federal Housing Administration required a working wife whose income was considered crucial for a loan to submit a letter

---

[20] Hayden, *op. cit.*
[21] *Ibid.*
[22] *Ibid.*
[23] *Ibid.*
[24] Ann F. Hoffman, *Sex in the Money Market*, Maryland Law Forum, Vol. II (1972), p. 136. Cited in Hayden, *op. cit.*

stating that she did not intend to become pregnant and explaining who would care for the child if she did. . . .[25]

A twenty-five-year-old, single New York woman buying her own home applied for an FHA mortgage. The FHA Albany regional office was suspicious of her desire to own a home when she could live inexpensively with her parents. She was asked by FHA to submit a "Letter of Motivation."[26]

The evidence is that discriminatory practices exist, including evaluating credit based on the applicant's sex or marital status and requirements that women produce a "certificate of contraception" (nothing similar is required of men); all women have trouble obtaining credit. Single women have more trouble obtaining credit than single men (especially mortgage credit).[27]

Married women generally lose their own credit standing, are unable to obtain credit in their own names, are excluded from family income in the granting of credit despite their earnings, are considered "dependents" of their husbands for some purposes such as calculating his *eligibility* for credit (though she is not necessarily a dependent when it comes to using his credit). Different standards are applied when the wife rather than the husband is the primary wage earner.[28]

To complete the circle, women who are divorced or separated or widowed have trouble reestablishing credit because accounts are in the husbands' names, because they have not had individual credit before, because they have no job security,[29] and because alimony and child support are often excluded as income to wife for credit purposes, although charged to her for some purposes, such as tax. In fact, alimony is viewed as a liability by the bank credit officers since its existence is uncertain.[30]

And an ex-wife has another problem: credit history. If the husband has a bad credit history, it is used against her.[31] Wives' credit ratings are altered on the basis of the husband's credit performance.

---

[25] *Ibid.* (Hoffman).
[26] Assemblyman Lucio Russo, Report to Assembly, State of New York, Investigation of Sex Discrimination Against Women by Banks in the Extension of Credit (1973).
[27] Women and Credit Study.
[28] Hartford Study in Mortgage Lending Discrimination.
[29] National Commission on Consumer Finance, Consumer Credit in the United States 152–53, reprinted in *CCH Installment Credit Guide,* No. 215 (1973).
[30] See Chapter 10, "The Myth of Alimony."
[31] Women's Equity Action League, WEAL Credit Kit.

"When women marry they become economic nonentities in the eyes of the credit establishment; when they are subsequently divorced or widowed they emerge as unknowns in an increasingly credit-oriented society. This pattern occurs whether or not a wife works outside the home or is, in fact, the principal wage-earner in her family. The current campaign for equal credit opportunity acknowledges that the wife who does not work outside her home is nevertheless an equal partner in the economic unit of her marriage, but it recognizes that unless she has property or income of her own she will not be considered credit-worthy."[32]

However well intended new laws may be, women *do* earn less, *do* have fewer prestige jobs, and certainly have *less* collateral to establish credit worthiness. This subtle, insidious form of discrimination is not legislated away.

"Charge It"

It is commonly thought that a woman who says, "Charge it" can obtain, at her husband's expense, anything she's ever wanted.

Actually, during the marriage, and forever more, it is the husband who determines the family standard of living—more specifically, what money may be spent—and what are necessary expenses. It is those "necessaries" that the husband *may* be liable for.

What constitutes necessaries depends on the couple's standard of living, as established by the husband, and what is viewed as necessary for people in their "station of life," as established by the husband. *Necessaries* are distinguished from objective *necessities*.

Since women have commonly had no credit or money of their own to purchase even necessaries, and since married women were viewed as "incompetent" to enter a contract, and since creditors had to deal with some responsible party—i.e. the man of the house—the theory evolved that a woman could pledge her husband's credit.[33]

However, to the extent that the theory is recognized, the existence and continuation of such credit are largely at the husband's whim. He may inform creditors that his wife has left his "bed and board" and he is no longer responsible for her debts. He may claim that the articles were not necessaries; he may claim that the retailer extended credit to the wife alone.

[32] Gates, *op. cit.*
[33] An unholy alliance of women's groups and creditors was formed to change California's community property laws. Both groups wanted access to all marital property.

What may happen is that merchants will refuse to deal with her. If they do allow her to make purchases, and the husband does not pay for them, she may then be sued.

In community property states the husband is liable for his personal debts and community debts (debts incurred on community credit, community property or on personal security of spouse without assets). However, on the theory that property interests are equally vested in both parties in community property states, the idea that both should be equally able to obtain credit has been pointed out by the Women's Equity Action League and others. However, that is not the case. This would be a departure from the thinking that the only time the community property principle really comes into effect is at the time of marital dissolution.

What a husband can do is borrow on the community property without his wife having a say in the matter. Then if the loan cannot be repaid, creditors can look to the community property (the home), foreclose it, and repay themselves with proceeds from the sale. The result may be a homeless wife with no say in the matter whatsoever.[34]

In a substantial number of states creditors have obtained the enactment of Family Expense Acts, generally making it possible to seek payment from either husband or wife for "family expenses" regardless of which spouse made the purchase and which spouse has income and decision-making powers. The laws do not prevent creditors from collecting from a married woman for debts she has undertaken, as well as family expenses that her husband has charged.[35]

And in Maryland, a husband may petition the court to bar his wife's use of his credit, notwithstanding that she cannot get her own credit on her own money.

> "If the court shall be satisfied that the petitioner is supplying his wife with all necessaries to which she is entitled . . . the said court shall pass an appropriate order . . . sufficient to prevent trades (men) or other person(s) from recovering from the petitioner for any work thereafter done for, or goods, wares or merchandise thereafter furnished to the petitioner's wife or on her order."

[34] Some statutes may protect the homestead from this type of creditor attack, but community property of other kinds is susceptible.
[35] Gates, *op. cit.*

Cases

Hutzler's department store sued[36] a wife for purchases of clothing on a charge account. Mrs. Swanson contended that the credit card was issued on the basis of her husband's credit, not her own.

The court decided that there was a duty of the husband to supply the wife with "necessaries," but that lacking evidence of the husband's failure to support the wife—and since the credit was issued to Mrs. Swanson—she was solely liable.

The Citizens Bank sued[37] a wife for charges on a credit card made during a separation from her husband. The wife claimed reimbursement from her husband on the basis of the "necessaries" doctrine. However, the court found that the card was issued in the wife's name and said that though the wife can still sue her husband for reimbursement for necessaries purchased when the couple was separated, she must show circumstances which still make the husband liable. The decision: *she* must pay the bank.

Sanford Nager notified Sacks and Company that he would not be liable for Jacqueline Nager's debts; Sacks closed the account in the name of "Mrs. Sanford Nager" and sent the wife a new credit application. A new account was opened in the name of "Mrs. Jacqueline Nager" after she filled out the application and presented her own credit references.

Sacks then sued[38] husband and wife for monies due for purchases charged to the new account.

The court decided that the husband was not liable for the purchases, notwithstanding the common-law duty of a husband to provide his wife with "necessaries," and the husband's liability to a third person who supplies his wife with "necessaries." The department store, said the court, looked solely to the wife's personal credit in issuing the card and could not recover from the husband.

---

[36] Swanson v. Hutzler Bros. Co. 135 A2d 151 (DC 1957).
[37] Waxelbaum v. Citizens & Southern National Bank 120 Ga. App. 312, 170 SE2d 333 (1969).
[38] Sacks and Co. v. Jacqueline Nager and Sanford Nager 74 Misc. 2d 855, 34S N.Y.S. 2d 883 (1973).

A Georgia court wrote in another husband-wife credit case:

"In the absence of the husband's signature we think that the legal consequence of the document signed only by the wife is to bind the wife separately and to extend credit solely to her and excludes as a basis of recovery the theory of agency of the wife to purchase necessaries. This agreement does not purport to be a contract by the plaintiff to give credit to the husband for the purchase of necessaries by the wife. The only legal conclusion is that credit was extended solely to the wife, in which case the husband is not liable even for the purchase of necessaries."[39]

And such credit card companies as Carte Blanche, BankAmericard, and American Express have persisted in refusing to issue credit cards in the name of a married woman without the signature of her husband.

New Developments

Varying in degrees of weakness and strength, there are various new state and federal laws "barring" discrimination in the granting of credit. Among the possible penalties are individual lawsuits, class action, litigation, license suspension, fines, actual damages, punitive damages.

Under New York's new law, a woman turned down for credit may request written explanation of why her credit application was rejected. But she may still be badly treated on the "objective criteria" since her earning level is lower, her "prestige," her contacts, her collateral are all less available. This is the circular problem.

New York's legislation[40] bars discrimination in the granting of credit by any creditor because of an applicant's race, creed, color, national origin, sex, marital status, or childbearing potential. The law applies to creditors, including banks and trust companies, private bankers, foreign banking corporations and national banks, savings banks, licensed lenders, savings and loan associations, credit unions, sales finance companies, insurance premium finance agencies,[41] insurers, credit card issuers, mortgage brokers, mortgage companies,

---

[39] Almon v. R. H. Macy and Co. 106 Ga. App. 123, 126 S.E. 2d 641 (1962).
[40] N.Y. Executive Law 296-a (1974).
[41] Not insurance carriers discriminating in the denial or writing or charging of insurance policies.

mortgage insurance corporations, wholesale and retail merchants, and factors.

The New York law makes it an unlawful discriminatory practice for any creditor to make any record or inquiry which

> "expresses, directly or indirectly, any limitation, specification, or discrimination as to race, creed, color, national origin, sex or marital status; *provided, however* [our emphasis] that this section shall not bar creditors from making inquiries and records from which they may compile statistics for the purpose of demonstrating compliance with this section, or for the purpose of establishing and evaluating valid, objective criteria of credit worthiness."

Creditors cannot make any inquiry concerning an applicant's capacity to bear children, or use of birth control.

In addition, the practice of requiring a man to cosign a single woman's application for a loan has been made illegal; it is considered discriminatory if, because of an applicant's sex or marital status, she is "either denied credit in circumstances where other applicants of *like overall credit worthiness* are granted credit OR special requirements or conditions, such as requiring co-obligors or reapplication upon marriage, are imposed upon an applicant in circumstances where similar requirements or conditions are *not* imposed upon other applicants of like overall credit worthiness."

In 1974 Congress passed legislation[42] designed to bar sex discrimination in the granting of consumer credit. The law is effective in part as of October, 1975, and in part during 1976. The federal law comes after similar statutes adopted in many states and is, in fact, much weaker than some state laws.

Under the Federal Equal Credit Opportunity Act, added as an amendment to the Consumer Credit Protection Act,[43] it becomes unlawful to discriminate on the basis of sex or marital status in any credit transaction. However, inquiry regarding marital status is acceptable to ascertain "creditor's rights." For example, it may be permitted to require the signature of both spouses (which could effectively bar credit to the wife of an unwilling spouse).

The law, administered by the Board of Governors of the Federal Reserve System, has limited civil liability, under which actual damage

---

[42] Equal Credit Opportunity Act, 1974. Leonor Sullivan (D.-Mo.) had introduced a bill which would have barred credit discrimination based on race, color, religion, national origin, age, sex, and marital status. A mortgage discrimination law known as Depository Institutions Amendments Act 1974 was signed separately.
[43] Public Law 90-321.

may be awarded, and punitive damages up to $10,000 to an individual; this section does not apply to class actions. The section dealing with class actions limits the total recovery to $100,000 or 1 percent of the net worth of creditor (whichever is less). However, the procedures for using the federal law are so complex and cumbersome as to be considered unavailable, as a practical matter.

Also adopted in 1974 was the Housing and Community Development Act[44] amending the fair housing provision of the Civil Rights Act of 1968 by inserting sex among the previously existing discriminatory categories (race, religion, national origin) in the sale, rental, or financing of housing, and amending the National Housing Act to prohibit discrimination on the basis of sex in connection with a "federally related mortgage loan."

In 1974, the Federal Home Loan Bank Board adopted amendments relating to sex discrimination and consideration of married persons' income within the federal Home Loan Bank System.[45]

These guidelines begin with the position that bank compliance with antisex discrimination regulations is essentially voluntary, but that noncompliance may be unconstitutional. The guidelines simply delete their own statements that sex discrimination is *not* expressly prohibited, and add, "Automatically discounting a wife's income is not favored."

The guidelines also extend to home improvement and maintenance loans, and declare it a discriminatory practice to require a steadily working single woman to have a cosigner on a loan.

As part of their effort to secure a place in the economic mainstream, women have begun to establish their own financial institutions. These include credit unions in New Haven and Detroit, and "women's banks," such as the First Women's Bank and Trust Company in New York.[46]

The purpose of these financial institutions is not to "discriminate" against men, but to make available to women money and credit that they cannot secure from male lenders and to educate women in the ways of money. Women credit officers say, while applying "sound

[44] 88 Stat 633, August 22, 1974.
[45] Federal Home Loan Bank Board, Title 12, Banks and Banking, Chapter V, Subchapter B, Part 528, Part 531.8. 1974.
[46] The First Women's Bank and Trust Company in New York City was unable to raise the requisite $4 million to secure their charter but FDIC approval was forthcoming based on somewhat less capitalization.

banking practices," they are more flexible. "We'd listen to women who *want* to start a tennis school, not throw them out like the other banks did," said one woman banker.

There is considerable ambivalence to such concepts as women's banks and credit unions because of the contradictory views that, on the one hand, women should participate in every possible institution either for the image value or for the power, and, on the other, that women should involve themselves with *women's* issues. But it is difficult to find a corner in midtown Manhattan, for example, that isn't occupied by a bank. Nobody's closing down the banks. And women are in the least powerful position to do so. So there is considerable support for a bank which at least will give women credit, rather than one which will question when she last had her diaphragm fitted or whether she would be willing to have a hysterectomy (since pregnancy might interfere with her suitability as a credit risk).

There is much discussion about the difficulties New York's Women's Bank had in raising capitalization. Some believe the idea of a women's bank was well timed in the sense of "women's role in the seventies," but badly timed in terms of the general economy of 1974. It is academic to discuss what might have been the experience of a new but more traditional-style bank trying to raise capital. It is possible that it would have had even more difficulty than the Women's Bank, since it would not have even had "novelty appeal." *Or,* it is equally possible "the boys" could have gotten up whatever capital was needed (if they wanted to).

But, apart from the 1974 general economy, were the very goals of the bank the real problem? Its near undoing? Was it the fact that they *wanted* to teach women about money, that they *wanted* to help women get into the "economic mainstream"?

Proposal

It shall be unlawful for any creditor to lend money to any business, whether for construction or other purposes, unless and until the applicant shows evidence of an affirmative action plan for the hiring and promotion of women.

Proposal

It shall be unlawful for any creditor to lend money to any business, whether for construction or other purposes, unless and until the applicant shows evidence of inclusion of child care centers in residential housing, factories, offices, schools.

Proposal

In recognition of women's inferior economic status, the United States Government shall establish programs of federally subsidized loans to women.

These loans shall be analogous to student loans, small business loans, etc., and shall have federally guaranteed low-interest funds available to and through banks.

12. The Compassion Urge: The Psychology of Volunteerism

"Money stands for all kinds of things; its purchasing quality isn't limited to diamonds and motor cars."

"Not in the least; you might expiate your enjoyment of them by founding a hospital."

—Edith Wharton, *House of Mirth*

"Volunteer work has helped make this country the greatest country on earth. . . . When the time comes that everything we do in this country has to be paid for, and we've lost our concern for each other, then we're really in sad shape."

—Mrs. Miller, President of the General Federation of Women's Clubs

Women constitute the majority of America's unpaid volunteer workers. Men are rarely expected to work without pay. In 1974, Nelson Rockefeller, one of the world's richest men, did not waive the vice-presidential salary. And despite the occasional "dollar-a-year man"—an industrialist or an industrialist's son who advises a mayor on political or cultural matters—it is mainly women who volunteer to work for no pay.

Within a money culture, people and activities that do not lead to the accumulation of money are not, by definition, valuable. They are treated poorly. For example, when men make financial contributions to charity these donations are treated as tax deductions.[1] When women make human capital contributions to charity—through the donation of their time, skill, and labor—these are not tax deductible. Nor are expenses such as house or child care that women incur in order to free their time to do volunteer work tax deductible.

Given such facts, why would any money-conscious adult in a capitalist culture *not* work for money? Perhaps a revolutionary or a saint might insist on choosing her own work and then refusing to be financially "bought" for performing a necessary labor of love. But most women—and volunteer workers—are not revolutionaries or saints.

Most people do not examine the roots of their behavior, either in relation to money or in relation to whether they are actually doing or accomplishing what they think they are. Of course, this habit is not confined to women. But this chapter—and this book—is concerned with analyzing some of the consequences of leading the unexamined, and powerless, life.

Volunteer work is the great meeting ground for the economically powerless and the economically leisured classes. Volunteers from both classes are seeking spiritual, moral, or social activities that factory work, office work, and manor life do not provide.[2]

How Many Volunteers Are There in America?

From May, 1973, to April, 1974, 37 million adult Americans worked as volunteers. At least 59 percent were women.[3] Economist Harold Wolozin has calculated that volunteer services in America were worth $15.4 billion in 1966 and $26.4 billion in 1974.[4]

---

[1] This means that less tax money is available to pay for services that are essential to the public.
[2] Male factory laborers or white-collar workers probably feel "important" directing male youth in physical or lifesmanship activities, in a way they cannot feel "important" at their salaried positions.
[3] United States Bureau of the Census, quoted in *Action News* and confirmed in a personal interview with Action Director Don Eberly. The figure of 37 million is a projection of a 25,000-person sample. Specifically the 14,750 women sampled were "projected" to 21,830,000; the 10,250 men sampled were projected to 15,170,000. This particular study, like most others, did not survey religious and political volunteerism.
[4] Dr. Harold Wolozin, "The Economic Role and Value of Volunteer Work in the United States; An Exploratory Study," a paper presented at the Annual Meeting of the Association of Voluntary Action Scholars, Denver, Colorado (September, 1974), based on research supported by the National Bureau of Economic Research; personal communication. Dr. Wolozin notes that the government figures on which he based his economic calculations are traditionally low. For example, the government's 1965 figure of 22 million volunteers and its current figure of 37 million do not include many political and

Another study surveyed volunteerism during a one-week period in 1974, from April 7 to April 13. More than 15 million volunteers were counted, 56 percent of whom were women.[5] This study also demonstrates the extent to which sex-role stereotyping—and its economic consequences—is operative even in volunteer work.

For example, women constituted 67 percent of the volunteers in the combined areas of health, education and social welfare—and men 33 percent. Women outnumbered men by more than two to one. However, men constituted 62 percent of the volunteers in the combined areas of justice, recreation and civic/community action—and women 38 percent. Men outnumbered women by nearly two to one.[6]

This study counted more than 400,000 volunteers in the political areas—54 percent of whom were men, 46 percent of whom were women. Although the total of 400,000 is not large—or even representative of the country at large—the figure suggests that men gravitate to appropriately "manly" areas of volunteer work, i.e. areas where their labor gets financially and/or politically rewarded. Working at campaign headquarters—if you are a man—may lead to certain rewards that do not exist within hospital or school settings. Politicians are notorious for rewarding their loyal (male) campaign workers with private business, loans, and paid civil service positions. (Male) political volunteers may eventually be run for public office.

Female volunteers in politics are traditionally expected to remain at their telephone-answering and stamp-licking posts. If they are very lucky, their payment may be husbands for themselves or for their daughters.[7] Traditionally, some female political workers have accumulated great unpaid influence on certain committees—but they were

---

educational volunteer enterprises, nor do they include the less formal or more recent volunteer movements concerned with community, consumer, peace, and environmental issues.

[5] *Action News*, Don Eberly, *op. cit.*; 8,610,000 women were volunteers and 6,845,000 men were volunteers. The figures in this study must be taken as tentative for two reasons: first, because the same person sometimes volunteered for more than one job category—and counted more than once. (Each person was counted only once for the total number of more than 15 million.) Also, the breakdown by job category, although as explicit as any study has been on volunteerism, is still not inclusive enough. Religious and political categories are listed, but a telephone interview confirmed the difficulty of obtaining true figures in these areas.

[6] Nearly 10 million volunteers worked in the above six areas: 53 percent were in the female-dominated areas and 42 percent in the male-dominated areas.

[7] And then they can answer their husbands' telephones at home, in offices, or during their political campaigns.

not supposed to run for public office themselves. When they did, they were not supported.[8]

Why Do Women Do Volunteer Work?

Women usually say they volunteer to "help" others, and because it is needed. Women do not necessarily analyze what doing volunteer work satisfies in *themselves*. Nor do they analyze whether their "helping" actually helps—or not.[9]

The average female volunteer believes that she is not really worth taking seriously. Either her *time* is not valuable, *she* is not valuable— or she is only valuable because her time has already been paid for by her husband. She can be "had" by society for free. More important, the average female volunteer is not, or does not feel she is, a "professional." And she is afraid of being judged too harshly by "professional" standards. As a volunteer she avoids being fired, reprimanded, and competed with. She also avoids the danger of being considered a bad or selfish woman. She is a "good" woman: although she is working outside her home, everyone knows that most female volunteers are *primarily* loyal to their families—and not to their unpaid volunteer work.

Women want to be with other adults in a setting that is socially approved—*for women,* i.e. a setting where their motives are presumably unselfish and asexual; their work unpaid, unskilled, and not too closely criticized; their rewards vicarious, psychological, and nonthreatening to both the male ego and the economic status quo. Volunteer work allows women to leave their homes and children— since they don't really mean it. (It can't lead to anything else.)

Female volunteers cannot translate their volunteer experience into paid employment or great independent wealth for themselves.[10]

---

[8] See Susan and Martin Tolchin, *Clout: Womanpower and Politics* (New York, Coward, McCann, and Geoghegan, Inc., 1974).
[9] Doris B. Gold has cited several examples of the counterproductive nature of female volunteerism: "A New York City family agency sponsors a program of volunteers as one-to-one teachers of English in a ghetto of foreign-born adults, while little or no pressure is exerted on the Board of Education to adapt its sleepy archaism to the needs of thousands of new Americans. A cultural institution uses volunteer assistants for its art exhibitions, while simultaneously, art school graduates trained for similar tasks where state funds might be available go unhired. Six volunteers—four of them women— attempt to raise funds for a community narcotics addiction treatment center, where the placement of one qualified person might make them eligible for foundation funds and/or municipal grants." "Women and Volunteerism," *Woman in Sexist Society,* Vivian Gornick and Barbara K. Moran, eds. (New York, New American Library, 1972).
[10] In the political arena, women who have been active in status-volunteer groups such as the League of Women Voters cannot use their "old girls' club" if and when they wish

"Volunteer work" doesn't often count in the search for paid employment. And it never counts in the search for unemployment benefits. Also, in the female volunteer's capacity as Lady Bountiful, she is not able to really be bountiful, to herself or to others. She usually cannot employ other people for money, nor can she write her own job description. She can do what she is told to do. Her supposed decision-making powers or creativity on the volunteer job are rather limited. It may, however, *feel* creative to be in a place where something "important" is going on and where your work is not too harshly judged.

The volunteer does not and perhaps does not want to force private corporations or politicians into *paying* her for her work. And her unpaid presence in the job market keeps other women who are employed from earning decent wages. If volunteers can work for "free," then money does not have to be allocated to pay workers decent—or even low—wages for performing these tasks. Ultimately, the female willingness and *need* to volunteer make it easy for government and industry to continue assigning a low economic priority to domestic or human welfare areas.

If The Ladies can be counted on to help out, pitch in, clean up, and keep the lid on, there is no need for The Gentlemen in power to alter anything. Daughters of wealth, daughters of poverty: each do volunteer work as mothers and wives; and each volunteer to help the churches, schools, hospitals, medical researchers, politicians, and museums raise money to maintain or expand their empires.

Of course, the daughters of wealth can perform the volunteer labor of maintaining the status quo in more glamorous ways than the daughters of poverty can. But each woman is doing her share of maintaining things as they are. Each is compliant, in some way, in helping men ensure the "triumph of conservatism":[11] the enslavement of class to class, race to race, and sex to sex.

Female volunteers want to be needed—and/or seen as Ladies: women who have been so well bought or "endowed" by men that they can economically afford to dispense the charity of female leisure.

Altruistic compassion—or volunteerism—is considered proof of female "goodness." After the troops move out mothers will always be there to wipe bloodied brows or prepare slaughtered men for burial.

---

to run for elective office. As Susan and Martin Tolchin have noted, "Once these women run for office they must sever their ties with the League [of Women Voters], a handicap not suffered by men, who can benefit from their fraternal ties." Tolchin, *op. cit.*

[11] The phrase is from G. William Domhoff, *The Higher Circles: The Governing Class* (New York, Vintage Books, 1971).

Women as altruistic volunteers are not supposed to wonder too much about why society in general and men in particular are not similarly "altruistic." "Helpers" are not supposed to be concerned with "larger" pictures. Their part, like that of the soldier, is "not to reason why, theirs but to do and die."

Women are geared to an almost other-worldly practicality. Since women are so removed from power networks in this world, they neither understand nor really *believe* that laws, revolutions, and male governments or bureaucracies will ever change anything.[12] Women say, and correctly, that kindness cannot be legislated by governments. Governments are busy men with too many other things on their minds. And people are dying *now*. We can at least comfort them, read to them, visit them.

Psychologically, it is easier for most women to knit socks for soldiers than to believe they have the right either to plan military strategy or to end a war.

Women in America *did* begin to march against the Vietnam War. Women have indeed protested to help or save *men*—when they protested at all. But *most* mothers—and women—didn't demonstrate or protest. And of those who did, only a few, such as Congresswoman Bella Abzug, went into politics on their own, to turn peaceful protest into political power.

Generally, women "minister" to or nurse the wounded, the dying, the outcast—and do not radically question why these people are dying or whether there is any more effective way of helping or saving them. But how can they—if they are emotionally and intellectually bound by the ideology of Love and Maternity—an ideology that religiously upholds the importance of woman's responsibility to or "caring" about only a *few* people in her life. It is easier for women to concern themselves with a few "others" than with themselves; easier to be comforting and "personal" rather than to achieve power to help others in an impersonal, structural, and economic way.

Female identity and the female sense of effectiveness is very fragile and very proscribed. It is psychologically calming to a woman to be able to consider someone else's fate as "worse" or "needier" than her own.

Also, women, as the victims of so many decisions from above, sense the safety of the horizontal spaces, the tiny, private spaces, that

---

[12] In countries outside America various changes have been enormous, but not necessarily to women, and/or not in terms of a *feminist* view of revolution, liberty, or work.

will admit their private acts of mercy—or of tyranny. Women sense the dangerousness involved in attempting structural changes. Psychologically, they would be risking their identities as "givers," as "mothers." Economically, they would be risking survival. Women are therefore more comfortable with the individual approach. It is far less threatening to the status quo.

A Little Help Is a Dangerous Thing

Historically and politically, volunteerism and philanthropy have both had a very specific and obvious function in late nineteenth- and twentieth-century America. Philanthropy initially functioned to keep those upper-class women who wanted more than manors and social life "busy," and out of government, industry and revolution.

G. William Domhoff traces the extent to which upper-class American women, from the 1880's on, dominated settlement-house work and labor reform movements—inspiring the poor to false hope.[13] Domhoff carefully documents the extent to which early American philanthropic and labor reform projects were "entirely financed by the richest men and women of their day." ". . . Jane Addams, for example, was the daughter of one of the richest men in northern Illinois."

> "The situation is similar for Julia Lathrop, Mary McDowell, Alice Hamilton, Lillian Wald, Mary Simkhovitch, and many other of the leading names of the settlement house movement. Mary Kingsbury Simkhovitch . . . was from an "old" family. . . . Her uncle had been with the Pennsylvania Railroad and the Interstate Commerce Commission, and she had a cousin who was the one-time head of Standard Oil of California. . . .
> "In the case of Hull House, the names that would be best-known today are Anita McCormick of the harvester fortune and Julius Rosenwald of Sears, Roebuck. Three of the key angels of the Henry Street Settlement in New York were Mrs. Solomon Loeb, Jacob Schiff (Mrs. Loeb's son-in-law), and John Crosby Brown, a leader of a finance house (now Brown Brothers, Harriman) . . ."[14]

The Women's Trade Union League and other labor reform organizations were also staffed by upper-class women. Their work was not

---
[13] Domhoff, *op. cit.*
[14] Domhoff, *op. cit.*, pp. 48–49.

only invaluable—from a short-range point of view—it was the only such work of its kind. While lower- and middle-class women were active at all levels in these labor reform attempts, upper-class women played the major role.

For example, women of wealth were active in labor reform, often in areas specific to the abuse of women and children: J. P. Morgan's daughters, E. H. Harriman's daughter, Mark Hanna's daughter, Elliot Roosevelt's daughter, Cyrus McCormick's daughter, Jacob Schiff's mother-in-law, Borden Harriman's wife, and O. H. P. Belmont's wife.[15]

So what of it? Simply that the American poor were fooled—and inspired by false hope; and so were the female rich. If their own brothers and fathers allowed, even encouraged them in their "noble" endeavors—well, then they weren't really sharing their beds and homes with murderers or sinners. (Not dear Daddy! *He's* not abusing women, men, and children in order to keep a fine roof over my fine head.)

Volunteers did not—and still do not—realize how much their labor allows private and public wealth to remain out of the hands of those who need it most, the majority of people in the country. Tax dollars and corporate dollars are not used to provide mass quality child, medical, or educational care or to eliminate poverty, famine, war, and planetary pollution. Tax and corporate wealth is used to create more financial profit for the (male) minority, racial and religious conflict, starvation, epidemics, wars—all are either allowed or disallowed as a function of what is good for those who have money and power, and who want more.

It must be noted that there is something *potentially* honorable about the activities of a group that is not owned by either government or business, that is not owned by one political or religious party, and that does not sit in permanent organized session over all matters relating to the body politic.

But the vitality, creativity—and humanity—involved in nonpaid volunteer organizations is rather wasted if such emotions only serve to perpetuate the status quo—and if such organizations are only concerned with perpetuating themselves. The *need* for organized systems

---

[15] I am identifying these women by their fathers' or husbands' names because that is how they chose to or allowed themselves to be identified.

of charity, especially in America, must be questioned and understood. The urge to give "alms" and minister "balms" to the needy should be at least matched by another urge: that of questioning why so many people need so much—and have so little.

13. Sexual Economics: Who Profits?

Prostitution

What about selling sex for money? Can women "lay back," "rake in the money," and retire to a lifetime of leisure in the tropics? Or to a lifetime of corporate enterprise?

Actually—no.

Women, like all mortals, are young for only a short time. Female prostitutes, like models and entertainers, face "aging" as an overwhelming financial liability. Men seem to think that any woman over Lolita's age is old. The greatest percentage of working prostitutes range in age from eighteen to thirty. Recently, in large American cities, prostitutes on the street were found to range in age from fourteen to twenty-one. Those women over twenty-one try to look "younger." They say the men want "younger"-looking girls.

Unlike models, prostitutes are not doing socially approved work. Selling sex for money is illegal in America. Like most illegal activities, it is surrounded with danger, shame, and death. And it is disapproved of even when it is legal.

In the 1974 United States national and state elections, it was not surprising that of three women who ran for state office two—characterized as a "lesbian" and "a nun"—were elected, but the third, a "madam," a woman who legally runs a brothel in Nevada, was not. Women are not *supposed* to be making money from selling sex. And when they *do*, they are not supposed to launder their money in the usual way, by turning to public office.

Sexual Economics: Who Profits?

While the industry of prostitution in America has been estimated as a nine-billion-dollar enterprise,[1] most female prostitutes, like most women, don't understand this kind of money. And they don't get to control or keep it either. As Sheehy has noted, a young, energetic streetwalker can theoretically earn $70,000 a year, but her net income is less than $100 a week.[2]

The low wages for women in all marketplace areas is one way of insuring a steady supply of women for prostitution—and for marriage—in a class and/or patriarchal society. Whatever other deep, "mysterious" or psychological needs are satisfied by these two institutions, one fact is clear: some men are making a cash flow or liquid profit from or because of them—and most women aren't.

Most prostitutes are blue-collar wage slaves and certainly not capitalists. Their ideology or fantasies may be capitalist ones, but their wages and lives are not. The "call girls" who become the mistresses or even wives of wealthy men and who convert their sexual services into liquid assets are very few and very exceptional. Xaviera Hollander does not represent the masses of full-time working prostitutes. She represents their Great Expectations.

There is a very long line of male profiteers who directly and indirectly own, manage, and control both the prostitute and her earnings: her pimp, her hotelkeeper, her landlord, her lawyer, her arresting officer, her judge and the men of organized crime.[3]

Pimps, like other male managers of female money, handle a prostitute's earnings for her. As is known, a prostitute usually receives a small allowance for food, clothes, rent, and drugs—enough money to keep her working, enough money to keep her dependent.

If women who work as prostitutes can spend cash for clothes, vacations, or drugs in a noticeably flashy way, this shows only how little they understand money, and how little money they really have.

Women—or men—may *feel* "rich" when they can do this, but they aren't "rich." Even the (comparatively) economically powerless pimps tend to invest their profits in other legal business and property

---

[1] Gail Sheehy, *Hustling* (New York, Dell, 1974). Sheehy estimated that in 1974 there were 200,000 to 250,000 prostitutes working in America, "committing 10 million different acts of prostitution every week. If 200,000 of these women charged $20 per 'trick' and serviced an average of six men daily, then we are talking about a business gross of 7 to 8 billion dollars annually."

[2] *Ibid*.

[3] There are very few madams: their number, influence, and earnings are nowhere near that of the pimps and the landlords.

ventures. The prostitute only *dreams* of doing so. She rarely does. And she soon stops dreaming.

The question, of course, is why do women work for so little money —*especially* when, as prostitutes, they claim to be primarily interested in making money? The answers are not only psychological. Nor are they simple.

In the spring and summer of 1974, I talked with ten "call girls" in New York and San Francisco. They all found it difficult to stick to the subject of money—not necessarily out of a conditioned sense of secrecy, but because, like most women, they were more interested in talking about boyfriends, emotional and medical troubles, a desire to "run away," a fear of "losing their minds." (Of course, unlike most women, they were able to be more specific about what many different men want—sexually or emotionally—in return for their money.)

Like many women, they seemed to agree that men were "crazy," "sick," or "childlike." But like most women, they also trusted men, needed men, loved men—and could never really "believe" it when male lawyers, politicians, judges, and gynecologists expected sex *plus* high fees for their services.

These women were all between the ages of twenty and thirty-five— but were all reluctant to tell me their exact ages. They did so only after some teasing and some angry and passionate demands for the "truth" from me. Economically speaking, times were not too good, although business was brisk. These women were charging $50 to $100 per man in 1970 and 1971. In 1972, 1973, and 1974, $50 was "good," and $20 or $30 the "going rate." Also, the cost of overhead (rent, furnishings, telephone, medical, legal, and domestic services) was cutting deeply into profits, even before their various male protectors, advisors, and "habits" took their toll of the money.

One woman, who owns her own house, did not think that (young) streetwalkers made less money than she did—"inside." She also "felt sorry" for the aging, pimp-battered streetwalker and the "kids" in the massage parlors who are working for "peanuts."

None of the ten "high-class call girls" I spoke with had either secure or insecure investments. Their savings accounts were rather modest, or nonexistent. Their future business plans were entirely unclear. They were *all* in favor of decriminalizing prostitution and of having unions. They were all against pimps.[4] And they all still ex-

---

[4] This factor may be what makes them "high-class." Their masochistic relationship to men is acted out in the personal rather than in their economic sphere.

pected either to marry for financial security or to be somehow miraculously "set up" in business by a tall dark handsome stranger . . . or they expected to be dead before they were forty.

After I had spent several days in various houses of "ill repute," it was quite obvious that these women, at least, are neither financially wealthy nor secure. They "operate" or "hustle" up only their own financial and emotional insecurity. And they live by crisis-time: one John too many, one girl short; one (suddenly) unpaid bill and no cash; one unexpected legal indictment—and (suddenly!) no trustworthy lawyer.

They are *always* working. They cannot lose a minute or a customer. All clients must be handled or the trade will dwindle. The clock of youth ticks loudly and they have to work—*now*—when they can. They cannot take off and let their money work for them. They *may* travel to the Caribbean in expensive clothes for *business,* and not for *pleasure.* The fact that the *atmosphere* in which they work may sometimes be party-like does not mean that they are partying. Like housewife-mothers, they seem to be "on call" seven days a week and during all their waking hours.

And yet, and yet, the fantasy still persists: don't some women really make a fortune or at least lead "easy" lives by being prostitutes?

Actually—no.

Most prostitutes are streetwalkers, not internationally famous celebrities. And there is nothing easy about walking the streets for ten hours a day, risking, at each step, arrests, fines, imprisonment, and male violence from either customers, pimps, cops, or judges. There is nothing "easy" about being socially and legally condemned and ostracized. There is nothing "easy" about earning too little money for what is often very degrading and dangerous work.

And yet . . . of course: some few women have made "good money"—*for a woman*—in this business. And yes, some women, if they are young, beautiful, and lucky enough, have become rich men's mistresses or wives. And yes, some women who have become madams have run a "good little business"—*for a woman.* But how many prostitutes, any more than women in general, have parlayed their profits into blue-chip stocks or into daring business adventures, or into pleasure palaces in the Caribbean? How many women who sell sex for money have made as much money as men who sell financial wizardry for money? Or men who sell their athletic ability for money? Or men and women who sell their corporate tax skills for money? How many prostitutes have even made as much money as their pimps do? Or as the state governments do in fining them? Or as all their male customers do because they can continue working at whatever financial level, sustained by sexual services?

Sleeping Your Way to the Top

Perhaps some people might concede that the "average" prostitute doesn't get "rich" or doesn't earn "easy" money. But still, people have fantasies about how sex might—or must—be used by women.

People believe that women "sleep" their way into "rich" marriages or into "good" jobs. It is assumed that if a woman is young or beautiful as well as skilled as a physicist or businesswoman, or if she just makes a lot of money "for a woman" or is at all well known, that she has been "sleeping" with powerful men. What other way could she have done it, since (according to unspoken conviction) employers demand this particular pound of female flesh for her right to work—and women don't really *have* anything else to offer.

Recently, a highly successful businesswoman told this anecdote:

> "I said I was attending a feminist meeting and a young woman at the office said, 'Oh, you must be a lesbian!' I replied, 'You know, if it weren't for me, you wouldn't be here at all.' It's funny, in my days of career climbing, I was always accused of sleeping with the men. Now that I've arrived, I'm accused of sleeping with the women. So be it."

A woman does not become the president of a company or an *independent* power-broker because she is beautiful or because she sleeps with her boss. What happens more often is that she loses her job when her boss loses interest in her or when she actually tries to use sexual intimacy with the boss to advance her own position. The point of such "sex" is that it is supposed to be "useful" to him—and not to her. Michael Korda puts it well:

> "In office affairs, as in the politics of the seraglio, women are always in the wrong. When a man makes a fool of himself over a girl twenty years his junior, the odds are that she will be fired in the final reckoning unless the management of the company was looking for an excuse to fire the man anyway. The 'double standard' lives on, indeed flourishes. The aftermath of most office affairs is the departure of the woman—sometimes forced out by a hierarchy of men whose

protective instincts are aroused by the sight of a fellow man in trouble, sometimes, 'cruelest of all blows,' fired by her lover for 'her own good.' "[5]

Unfortunately, whether women want to use sex or not, they have to worry about it. Female students, nurses, employees—and even bosses—must be careful not to offend male vanity; artful in turning down a sexual proposition without losing a job—or an employee; and *equally* artful in "having the sex" without risking their jobs, reputations, and collegial relationships. This artfulness takes time, *extra* time, and doesn't often lead to an increase in either power or pleasure for the woman.

Many men in executive positions expect the physically attractive and/or mentally skilled token woman to "understand" them—as their wives don't—but in "wifely" ways. Unfortunately, "wifeliness" also constitutes a style that is not recognized as financially competent. Women, meeting men as *equal* in professional and business settings, are expected to comply in uniquely "feminine" ways with the male need to be listened to, understood, sympathized with, ego-bolstered, and sexually soothed. If a woman refuses a drink or dinner with a man after a business meeting, she risks offending him or making an enemy of him in a way that another man doesn't. In offending a man by refusing to be a "woman" to him, women risk losing money, job contacts, and their reputations as "good women."

A "good woman" is one who does whatever a man wants. But a "good" woman is also (supposed to be) a virgin, a conservative, and a sexual prude. But this also makes her "uptight" or a "bad" woman. *But,* a woman who sleeps her way "up": is she "good" or "bad"? One can wonder and keep wondering about this, which many women do. It keeps their minds off how little money they are making.

Congreve aside, hell has no fury like a man spurned, especially when *he* thinks his affection is real or selfless. It will cost a woman her job. If the obsessively job-conscious woman notes this and responds by "submitting," the man may wish to *marry* her rather than work *with* her or *for* her.

Most men don't know how to experience "sex" with a powerful or "superior" woman. Despite male masochistic fantasies—or complaints —once a man has "had" a woman sexually, she is, by primitive definition, "less" than him. How can he then work with or for her in the

---

[5] Michael Korda, *Male Chauvinism* (New York, Random House, 1973).

office? He would feel unmanly. (He can work "for" his wife because a wife is, by legal and economic definition, the "inferior" of the two. Also, he doesn't have to take step-by-step public on-the-job orders from his wife.[6] He would from a female colleague or employer whom he has already "had.")

When men adopt fatherly attitudes toward female assistants, the difficulty of being promoted or supported by such a man may even be greater. Father figures need daughter figures to stay "at home," close by, to take care of *their* needs. When office father figures imagine or hear that their office daughter figures are either "fucking around" or want independent power, they react as real fathers do. They commit irrational acts of cruelty: they fire and bad-mouth their office daughters, assistants, or colleagues. They act out of a sense of great betrayal and bitterness. And their acts usually succeed: the office daughter will have a hard time making her way—not only *without* Daddy, but with Daddy's active disapproval. Daddy's friends are often happy to oblige him by not hiring her—or even *believing* her.

There are countless examples within the business, intellectual, academic, and scientific worlds of women who are talented and ambitious in their own right but have not been groomed for "heirdom," whether they withheld or gave sex at the office. Female graduate students at many major American universities all report being punished by male mentors with whom they refused to have sex. One woman told me the following story:

> "I was finishing a degree in sociology. It was 1972 and my [male] advisor, who was just divorced and having a long-time affair with his secretary, began asking me out. I didn't like it and tried to be as nice as I could. I finally had to be very emphatic and he swore he'd be equally emphatic with me. He suddenly began to tell the rest of the faculty that my work was not very good. This—although I'd been his research assistant for two years and had, in effect, been doing his work. . . . He turned down my final dissertation and said, 'How does it feel to be turned down—you bitch?' I had to spend two years waiting, arguing, trying to get other department members to read my work. . . . I'm getting my degree."[7]

Another woman recalled her graduate school experience at a prestigious university in the mid-1960's:

---

[6] What may go on within the home *psychologically* is perhaps another matter.
[7] Personal interview. The discipline has been changed because she has not gotten her Ph.D. yet.

"My dissertation advisor started acting strangely right after I began living openly with Bob [another graduate student]. Before that he'd loved my work—and accepted the fact I'd turned him down [sexually] . . . after all; he saw me as totally devoted to my work. But when he saw I would sleep with *other* men, that was it. He had me out of that program in one year. I lost all my credits and had to start graduate school all over again."

A third woman described a similar situation, but with a male colleague, not a mentor.

"We were good friends—until after he broke up with his wife, his girlfriend, and his analyst. Then he wanted more than friendship. He wanted me to be all three women to him—plus have sex with him. I refused—gently—and with no intention of giving up our friendship. He turned on me—completely. Refused to speak to me at all, bad-mouthed me at administrative levels, lost me one job I know of. . . . When I confronted him he said it was really his problem—but that I'd have to live with it too."

A fourth woman described her long-term love affair with a famous American man of science:

"I worshipped him. He was a genius. His wife couldn't appreciate him and I also understood why he needed her. . . . Yes, I was lonely and sometimes bitter but I was learning so much from working for him. . . . I did whatever research he wanted done—but without him I might never have done any research at all . . . After his wife died I thought we'd marry, but he reprimanded me: there would be too much gossip in the laboratory, it would make certain things difficult for him. . . . It's strange but he would never back any work of mine—he said 'they' would talk. . . . He wouldn't let me travel to certain conventions with him: talk again. He began taking a young man along and eventually gave him more responsibility in the laboratory than me. . . . Maybe I should have pushed him harder."

While powerful men may be hell on other men, eventually there are some or at least one whom they groom or accept as an heir. And that heir is hardly ever a female, hardly ever a beautiful female—and hardly ever a beautiful female who has been their mistress.

The smoky mirrors on the whorehouse ceiling, like the myths and images about sex, attempt to deflect, distort, and soften the facts of sexual economics.

Myth has it that women can sell sex to men—and receive adequate or spectacular financial, emotional, or professional rewards.

Fact has it that most women do not receive adequate or spectacular financial, emotional, or professional rewards—whether they sell sexual or reproductive services, or refuse to.

Women are not the masters of sexual economics: men are.

14. Women and Work: The Crisis of Psychic Survival

If women's economic "payoff" is less than what they need, less than what they deserve, and less than what men receive, how and why have women continued to work for little or no money without demanding—or expecting—more?

Fear keeps women silent: the fear that something "worse" than economic drudgery can happen to them. For example, women fear being forced into whores' lives—or raped—or killed. Women work in order to avoid something "worse," and not to achieve something "better."

Hope also keeps women silent: hope that their husbands or sons will somehow, someday, make up for or take care of things for them.

As women grow older and/or when they realize that they are primarily responsible for their own economic survival, and for that of their children or parents, they do not deny the difficulty of their economic condition. Like poor people everywhere, such women often talk of nothing else but money problems. By this time it is too late. With too little education, time, encouragement, and other resources, women tend to live within the circle of survival rather than on the boundaries of protest or risk.

Denial, Disassociation and Deference

Women at all salary levels usually deny or are unaware that they are being short-changed economically. In 1971, Dr. Teresa Levitin found that a national sample of American women who worked full-time "should have received 71 percent more than [their] current income . . . the average woman received $3,458 a year less than she should have." Ninety-five percent of the women surveyed were underpaid, yet only 8 percent thought they were being "discriminated against" at work.[1]

Most women believe they earn a "pretty good" salary—for a woman. When women notice that a "pretty good" salary is still less than what men receive, they minimize or deny the importance of the difference. How important can such an injustice be, when "even men" suffer economic inequality and tension?

Women say that if they, personally, haven't been aware of or bothered by economic discrimination, ergo, it hasn't affected anyone else. And therefore it doesn't really exist. Women at high salary levels deny or minimize the economic powerlessness of women as a caste as often as women at lower salary levels do.

Mrs. Olive Ann Beech, Chairman of the Board of Beech Aircraft (since the death of her husband, Walter Beech, in 1950), has said:

> "I don't understand this women's lib at all. . . . I think women should be recognized and paid comparable salaries for comparable work, but I don't understand this hurrah about the ways they are discriminated against."[2]

When asked about economic discrimination against women, Madeleine McWhinney, Director and President of the proposed Women's Bank, and a former officer of the Federal Reserve Banking System, neatly sidestepped objectivity for diplomacy. She noted that

> "Well-adjusted, happy people learn how to live through unpleasant things more easily than others do . . . there has been discrimination but it is still possible to ride it out or overcome it, and there are examples of women who have done so . . . women are not facing anything 'special.' If you rise high you'll become more isolated

---

[1] Dr. Teresa Levitin, University of Michigan Survey Research Center. Also reported in *Psychology Today* (December, 1971).
[2] Wyndham Robertson, "The Ten Highest-Ranking Women in Big Business," *Fortune* (April, 1973).

whether you're male or female. . . . I think it is really more a matter of personality" (personal interview).

Muriel Siebert, the first and only woman to buy a seat on the New York Stock Exchange, ruefully admits that "if a woman displays the same aggressiveness as a man, they say: 'Is she an aggressive thing!' . . . and no woman wants to be regarded as a tough person." However, she insists that it is possible for a woman to "make it."

". . . if you just keep on doing what you want to do . . . companies will treat you pretty well—when they see you know what you're talking about and that you've done your homework" (personal interview).

Financially successful women emphasize the importance of optimism, diplomacy, patience, thoughtfulness, ambition, and the ability to make crucial sacrifices. Of course, they happen to be correct—and yet the doctrine of "individualism," or rather the reliance on the "psychological" solution, is a uniquely female mechanism of self-containment. And it is not restricted to a minority of "successful" women.

In interviews with women employed as domestics, secretaries, and factory workers, a similar ideology was apparent. Each of the less financially successful women believed as fervently in the individual's capacity to "overcome"—by herself alone, and by using inch-by-inch strategies of self-improvement.

When women are upset by their low salaries, they tend to first blame themselves (as the victims), and then to seek a purely individual or "psychological" solution to the problem.

"Maybe I haven't been diplomatic or clever enough," a female office worker or professional will think. "Maybe I *have* nagged or cried too much; maybe I am too aggressive . . . *for a woman.*"

Secretaries and waitresses, especially women over forty, reported being afraid to ask for more money. One woman said: "I won't get a raise anyway. And I know ten file clerks in my office who would be happy to take over my job for even less money" (personal interview).

Another woman factory worker pointed out that "women know all about the layoffs they can't stop, all about the low money we're getting. But women are afraid to do anything. Call a strike or union meeting, and the women don't come. The boss, he comes to watch.

The men from the men's union come, to watch. But the women can't stand up to them—and to their husbands too" (personal interview).

Women employed at low salary levels either blame themselves or other women for earning too little money and for not demanding more. They prefer this search "within" to the potentially more dangerous search "without."

One woman, a forty-five-year-old black domestic, was very adamant about "women and blacks not succeeding because they're not trying to." She insisted that "you can do anything you want to if you want to do it badly enough."[3] She also noted that things are worse for women in other countries. "In Bermuda, for example, women doing unskilled labor usually don't make more than thirty dollars a week, while the unskilled male laborers can make from eighty to a hundred fifty dollars weekly" (personal interview).

Another woman, a sixty-two-year-old white widowed secretary who is living quite marginally economically, said that "there's plenty of work for widows if they really want to work—babysitting or otherwise. Babysitting or Grandparents-for-hire would be a way of earning money. . . . perhaps women want things that they're not capable of doing . . . jobs where they'd have to compete and make decisions" (personal interview).

It must be noted that both the domestic and the widowed secretary work as hard and as conscientiously as they can, and for minimum wages. Nothing short of a miracle—or a revolution—will change this fact.[4]

Women who deny economic discrimination, or who rely on personal and "psychological" solutions to deal with it, do so by looking *down*—comparing themselves to other women—rather than by looking *up*—and comparing themselves with men.[5]

Most women, like the wretchedly poor in India or Asia, find it easier to accept their own fate when someone else's is even "worse." It is not so much a matter of secular gloating as it is one of religious fear: as bad as things are, they could be worse . . . and might get worse if the proper thankfulness or perspective is not shown.

Disassociation is also a major way of warding off the specter of misfortune, one's own or another's. Women at all salary levels tend to dis-

---

[3] She is raising three children of her own and her dead sister's four children.
[4] And a divine miracle may rescue them sooner than a political revolution will.
[5] Women don't want to compete with men or be like men, just as men don't want to compete with or be like women. To do so represents a loss of basic ego identity for both sexes, a loss of a familiar way of resting from competition.

associate themselves from other women. If another woman is raped, murdered, or beaten up, that is *her* misfortune and has nothing to do with me. If another woman is fired or not hired or undervalued economically, well, that is her problem. Women sense the trouble in store for them if they start climbing on bandwagons.

Women who have worked hard to make money or achieve status at any economic level sense that they cannot afford to associate with "trouble makers." One woman said:

> "Radicals or bleeding-heart liberals are not interested in working. They don't know anything about the work I do. Which I happen to like. And they're not too good at their own work—economic and social change. I'd rather worry about myself than wait for help."

Female factory workers, business executives, and academics all have tales of (*other*) women's inability to be "trusted," or to really "care." *All* women are more used to going it alone, and surviving, more or less: why risk the unknown, which often turns out to be worse than the known state of things?

Business journals, personnel managers, and industrial psychologists all encourage women to continue in disassociated and "feminine" states. One recent article, for example, told women that:

> "If you personally have done very nicely, then you have no ax to grind. . . . claim only your rightful share of indignation. . . . preoccupations with 'wrongs' can blind you to all 'righting' developments . . . and since the offers to women are proffered gingerly . . ."[6]

Women at work are also advised to "accentuate the positive," and to use their (natural) talent for peacemaking and their knack for small intimate talk.[7]

Disassociating oneself from other women usually extends to disassociating oneself from any sociological or political ideology that might be used to explain one's own relation to economics in America. Such female disassociation from other women is only matched by its

---

[6] Jane F. Templeton and Naomi S. Marrow, "Women as Managers—Still A Long Way to Go," *Personnel* (September, 1972). Similar points are stressed in an article by Lawrence C. Hackamack and Allen B. Solid, "The Woman Executive," *Business Horizons* (April, 1972). Hackamack advises women to pursue their natural ability for tact, diplomacy, detail, perseverance, and the ability to elicit confidential information. This is bound to endear such women to male colleagues and rivals. A more exemplary article has been written by Marshall H. Brenner, *Personnel Journal* (March, 1972). He advises a special educational program for the husbands of management candidates "to provide them with an understanding of the support functions required of them."
[7] Templeton and Marrow, *op. cit.*

paradoxical opposite: the necessity for "deviant" or "different" (money-earning) women, to prove that they are really like other women, i.e. really "feminine."

More Feminine Than Thou

Women are supposed to be at home. If they are not at home, they must act as if they are, or at least as if they regret not being there. Women working at skilled or unskilled labor, *particularly* if they are paid very well—"for women"—must communicate a basic deference to men, a core "femininity" or "maternalism." Deference is supreme female diplomacy. It usually "works," but it never allows a woman to go beyond surviving well economically, "for a woman," to economically succeeding "like a man."[8]

Women in America are nurses; men are doctors. When nurses either know more than or disagree with a doctor they cannot tell him so directly. One nurse put it this way:

> "I have to be careful. I can't let it look like I am trying to tell him what to do. I have to approach him in a manner so it looks like I'm not telling him."[9]

Another nurse said she might "approach" a doctor by asking a question: "I would say that 'I wonder if this drug is helping the patient?' I may think that the drug isn't, but I wouldn't tell him that."

A third nurse said: "A nurse has to be diplomatic. . . . Our observations are important but we can't tell the doctor what to do. We aren't the doctors. They're the ones who are supposed to be right."

Such deference diplomacy is certainly not restricted to nurses and doctors or even to females as subordinates and men as superiors. Female superiors in rank and salary must be even more careful to be deferential. Female physicians, for example, must prove they are as "tough" as men but not too "tough" for a woman. They must also prove to female nurses that they are not bitches or incompetent. (Women expect other women in superior positions to be *more* com-

---

[8] Women defer to the status quo and to what is expected of them; to the financial double standard; to the necessity of not aiming too high, or of having to work harder. Women defer to the necessity of indirect rather than direct action; to false modesty rather than true self-appraisal. Women defer to the necessity of not "screaming rape"; women defer to the necessity of giving up their ambitions, or of having to marry men in order to be allowed the right to work.
[9] She is quoted by William A. Rusing in "Social Influence and the Social Psychological Function of Deference: A Study of Psychiatric Nursing," *Social Forces*, Vol. 41 (1962).

petent than men; men, in general, expect less from women than other women do.) Further, when women occupy superior positions, they are expected to use their power maternally rather than paternally or sadistically. For example, a female physicist said:

> "I supervise five male scientists and ten technicians. They respect me because I've proved myself: I'm knowledgeable and I'm fair. . . . Men are more sensitive to criticism than women are—especially criticism from a woman. So—I use my judgment here. I criticize when I have to, but I say something like: 'Well, boys, I guess *we* made a mistake' rather than '*you* made a mistake'" (personal interview).

Female subordinates, female superiors: both must gently and indirectly "suggest," "question," and "protect" men. Most women do not directly *command* men at work.

Any assumption of control or leadership by a woman, especially over men, is upsetting to both men and other women. Women are expected to support the *man* of ambition or power, not to be him. Women are expected to be "unassertive" and are considered either incompetent or "sneaky" when they get things done.

Women are perceived as "aggressive" when they are seen in places where women are not wanted: in a "male" setting or in a "male" job, receiving "male" financial rewards.

Aggressive women are generally punished. Aggressive women must work harder, for less money. They must wait longer for financial or emotional recognition. Without an information network. Without heroic or surviving role models. Without encouragement.[10]

While waiting, aggressive women are expected to emphasize their femininity. *On the job,* they must communicate deference to men and to the status quo.[11]

Aggressive women must also communicate their deference *off the*

---

[10] There are so many examples of female competence gone unrewarded, or punished, that such tragedies constitute many books. Let me note just a few outstanding American examples: Maria Mayer, Nobel laureate in physics, had a very long wait to become a full professor at the University of Chicago. Ruth Benedict, the brilliant anthropologist, had a long wait for a tenured full professorship at Columbia, where women were not wanted. Lillian Gilbreth, a pioneer in business management, for a long time was not allowed to publish such material under her own—a woman's—name. Mary S. Calderone, physician, and head of the Sex Information and Education Council of the U.S., reports being paid far less for her previous work in medicine than men are. *All* women who were interviewed for this book in the areas of business, politics, art, science, and the service professions report having been totally excluded from male clubs or networks, and not being rewarded for producing superior work on their own.

[11] If they don't, their work lives are made even more unpleasant for them.

job. For example, when women are being interviewed for "male" jobs, they are rated for certain hidden credentials: Is she married? Does she have 2.3 children? Is her husband at least her equal if not her superior?[12] Does *she* extol the virtues of family, husband, and children before her "career"?[13]

Traditionally, most women who earn money are married and/or mothers. Most women with professional training claim never to have questioned the necessity of stopping their careers when their children were young, or having to leave work when their children became ill, or of being primarily responsible for the housework and child care.

Women who work at unskilled labor are equally emphatic about the greater importance to them of home and children: why work hard at two jobs, one unpaid (at home) and the other poorly paid (outside)? However, the ideological tyranny of the Family Romance functions to control female anger and female aspirations at all economic levels.

Women have coped with not being wanted "where they don't belong" by either denying any interest in belonging or by keeping quiet about their achievements.

Women have "hidden" their interests or talents. In the nineteenth century Harriet Martineau, the author, "concealed her writing under her sewing when callers came," because "to sew" was a feminine verb and "to write" a masculine one.[14] Mary Somerville, the English scientific writer, struggled to hide her work from even relatives because mathematics was a "masculine" pursuit.[15] George Eliot and George Sand, as is obvious, published under male names.

Having to hide your talent, your ambition, or your achievement is a particularly perverse and confusing punishment. Today, women must still "hide" their achievements, but somewhat differently.[16] They "hide" them behind a stated preference for their "families" or by attributing their success to "luck" rather than to hard work, or to genius. They hide their competence behind "feminine" and maternal behavior, and by remaining in positions of secondary or indirect power—and by not "complaining" too loudly about it.

[12] Men are judged in similar arbitrary ways. But marriage usually makes a man's "outside" job easier, and a woman's "outside" job harder.
[13] Among top-flight *business* executives the "children" are not supposed to come first, however.
[14] Charlotte Perkins Gilman, *Women and Economics,* Carl N. Degler, ed. (New York, Harper and Row, 1966).
[15] *Ibid*.
[16] I am referring to achievements that are public—not private—achievements that a money culture rewards with money.

The Token Woman

    The token woman gleams like a gold molar in a toothless mouth.

    The token woman arrives like a milkbottle on the stoop
    coming full and departing emptied.

    The token woman carries a bouquet of hothouse celery
    and a stenographer's pad: she will take
    the minutes, perk the coffee, smile
    like a plastic daisy and put out
    the black cat of her sensuous anger
    to howl on the fence all night.

    A fertility god serves a season
    then is ritually dismembered
    yet the name, the function live on:
    so she finds the shopping lists
    of exiled women in her coat pockets.

    The token woman stands in the Square of the Immaculate
    Exception blessing pigeons from a blue pedestal.
    The token woman falls like a melon seed
    on the cement: why has she no star shaped yellow flowers?
    The token woman is placed like a scarecrow
    in the longhaired corn: her muscles are wooden.
    Why does she ride into battle on a clothes horse?
    The token woman is a sandbag plugging
       the levee: shall the river
    call her sister as the flood waters rage?

    The token woman is a black Chicana fluent in Chinese
    who has borne 1.2 babies
    (not on the premises, no childcare provided)
    owns a PhD, will teach freshmen English
    for a decade and bleach your laundry
    with tears, silent as a china egg.
    Your department orders her from a taxidermist's catalog
    and she comes luxuriously stuffed with goosedown
    able to double as sleeping
    or punching bag.

    Another woman can never join her,
    help her, sister her, tickle her
    but only replace her to become her

> unless we make common cause
> unless she grows out, one finger of a hand,
> the entering wedge, the runner
> from the bed of rampant peppermint
> as it invades the next clipped turf
> of the putting green.
>
> —Marge Piercy, *The Token Woman*

"Token women," like Great Ladies, are *used,* with or without their informed permission, to keep other women out of "careers": partly because men won't hire more than one or two women, partly because the price exacted from women for public success frightens and horrifies other women. (Annie has a great job—for a woman—but look how lonely she is. . . . Dr. X does superb work—but isn't it a pity she has no children . . . Judge Y sits in Family Court, while her own husband runs around with other women. . . . President Z is a dedicated leader. She has so much energy; like radiation, I think it killed her husband. . . . and so on.)

Nobody seems to like the "token woman" in an all-male group. Women perceive her as a fire-snorting Dragon Lady whose "success" (for a woman) has limited or ruined other women's chances—or lives. "Token women" are said to be man-haters or woman haters; their style—overly feminine or staunchly mannish. In either case, they are said to steal husbands away from wives—or they steal a husband's money away from his wife. It is felt that "token women," rather than male employers, prevent other women from working at higher economic levels. It is believed that "token women" constitute a militia, an armed guard against female strikers, or female rebels in the act of storming all-male bastions of economic power.

By such descriptions, "token women," like all other women, are first reduced to their sexual parts ("femme" or "butch"), and then reconstituted into a Bad Mother image.

Psychologically, women believe that it is Mommy, not Daddy, who is responsible for their economic and emotional castration. Daddy is too big, too powerful, and too potentially cruel to be blamed directly. Mommy is easier to get at and blame, without endangering one's physical or economic security. It is also easier to *blame* Mommy than to exorcize her in yourself—or to take *her* side against Daddy's.

Both women and men have a difficult time evaluating a woman in terms of her specific work choice, or as just another wretched—or greedy—*human* contender in the inhuman capitalist or nationalist race. Whatever is ruthless or unnatural about competitive economic behavior is rendered a biological crime when women perform it.

Female economic experience (or lack of it) has convinced women that only one woman can "win"—a beauty contest or the richest husband—and that a female "winner" always means a female "loser." Women find it difficult even to visualize joining other women in an attempt to "win" something of value, like better jobs or more money. Women find it difficult to trust any woman with more independent economic power than a woman "should have": If she's got it, then I can't have it; if she's got it, she'll never use it in my interest, but only against me.[17]

Thus, no one is startled to see a room filled with one hundred male judges or priests, business executives or congressmen, military leaders or plumbers. Everyone is startled and defensive when *any* woman is present in this room, or when more than one or two women are there.

"The women are taking over—where will it end? Who'll watch the children? What if they're menstruating? Women are more violent and less competent than men—you'll be sorry."

Or "Well, we've hired two women—what else do you want? Quotas? That's discrimination in reverse, that's illegal."[18]

You can tell who the token women are by how awkward they look without any wives. You can easily spot them as the only two judges flirting or being maternal toward the other judges, and with whom the other women present don't flirt. Or you can spot them as tokens because they are talking only to each other. Mainly, you can tell who is a token by how much more money she earns than other women do.

The important point is that whether the token woman "hates" or "loves" women or men, she does not have enough power to either hurt or help the economic condition of women *in general*. She can—and does—hurt women's feelings and, more than occasionally, individual women's economic lives.

It is true: many "Queen Bees" do not like other women admitted to their all-male group. They refuse to bond with or sponsor other women because of past painful experience or because they are afraid of being replaced rather than joined by a second woman. Only-

---

[17] If women believe that God is a man and not a woman, or that there is no God in heaven, only male heroes and kings on earth, this sort of thinking is understandable.
[18] There are more than two women in this room. There are nearly one hundred female secretaries, one hundred female office workers, one hundred female wives (or wifely nuns), at least twenty cleaning women, ten paid housekeepers, thirty unpaid female volunteer workers . . . perhaps the women *have* taken over.

women also get used to being "preferred" or being treated as exceptional: it has been the only effective survival tactic they could use in the sphere of male success.[19]

It is true: some Queen Bees are genuinely more comfortable working with or for members of the opposite sex, just as some "King Bees" work more closely and "tightly" with women in some areas of their work lives. (Sigmund Freud, for example, preferred intelligent female disciples to intelligent male disciples.) Also, some men have learned how to respect, use, and reward a competent woman in ways that are unavailable, basically frightening, or role-alien to other women.

It is true: most women refuse to sponsor or support other women in the economic sphere, and most women deny each other information or a work-related social life. Such women, who play eunuch to the needs of management—or to the needs of husbands and children—are not behaving in brave or creative or even reasonable ways. They may even be acting against their own self-interest. They are *not* being "good mothers" to the vulnerable daughters of our species (each of whom, like her mother, may prefer Daddy no matter *what* Mommy does).

It is true: the general female preference for a male doctor, lawyer, or Indian chief is, from a feminist point of view, not an honorable preference. But it is not an exercise in power in any way equivalent to the male exercise of power. Women may prefer a male gynecologist, but male-controlled medical schools make sure that very few women are accepted or allowed to graduate as physicians.

Most women are used to serving individual men. A mother serves one infant in his crib; a wife serves one husband in his home; a secretary serves one boss in his office; the token woman, if she has more economic or public visibility, serves the male status quo—as well as individual men. But these four women are performing similar tasks. Any of these women would be quickly replaced and condemned to

---

[19] Arlie Hochschild has described the unwritten job requirements of the highly skilled woman in this way: "If other women are undependable, and unpredictably quit work to have babies, she is different. If other women do not think analytically or can't do math she is different. If other 'different' women are manlike and make poor colleagues, she is different from them. This is close to the 'deblacking' that black professionals undergo: if other blacks are lazy and careless, this one is not. If other blacks are dirty and messy, this one is neat and clean. If other blacks talk too loudly, this one talks softly. If other blacks are incompetent, this one is competent. If other blacks are neat, hardworking, soft-talking and competent, but overly sensitive about their race, this one is different and easy to get along with." *Women and Success*, Ruth B. Kundsin, ed. (New York, William Morrow and Company, Inc., 1974).

some feared "worse" fate if she left the crib or home unattended, the business letters untyped, or the men unsupported at an executive meeting.

Token women do not earn as much money as women at the (female) financial top. Nor do they lead lives that are similar to those of Great Ladies.[20] However, at their economic level, they adopt similar survival tactics: feminine deference; a fetching helplessness, behind which beckons the promise of a protective maternal agent—to a man (against other groups of men, against men in his own group, or against women).

Traditionally, when a *second* Lady enters an all-male group, certain political moves are made.[21] For example, the second woman must communicate to the first that she is even more helpless than she is, and is willing to occupy a position submissive or subordinate to her. Or the second woman can elect to overthrow the first. To do this, she must be more "beautiful" or "sexy" than the first woman or, better yet, the wife or daughter of a powerful man whose support or approval is desired or needed by the all-male group. (Even the "strong" female contender for the only-woman position must communicate that she is at least deferential to *some* man somewhere.) It is this credential—that of having a powerful father or husband—that usually allows her to act as if she is equal to the men in the group.[22] And even then, her pretense to "equality" must be carefully, indirectly, and maternally expressed.

When women employ "feminine" tactics to enter an all-male group —when they sleep with or marry a male boss—they are usually despised and hated by their male counterparts. Men say, and with some justification, that *they* can't sleep with the boss to get ahead. Of course, they *would,* and do, when the boss is homosexual. And homosexual men tend to inherit thrones rather more directly and frequently than heterosexual women do.[23] Men do try to marry the boss's daughter. And male resentment or dissension about this fact quickly dissipates into "bonds" of support for the son-in-law: bonds

---

[20] See Chapter 5, "Wealth: A Tale of Two Sexes."
[21] Trying to analyze the moves when a *third* woman enters an all-male group is somewhat similar to solving the three-body problem in physics. Also, there are fewer data to observe since, traditionally, a third woman has not been present.
[22] Male-male interactions may function analogously, but the point here is that men entering an all-male group do not indicate deference to a powerful *woman* in order to be accepted or feared. Nor is their relation to a powerful male "protector" a romantic or sexual one. It may indeed be a subordinate one, as "male-pecked" son or son-in-law.
[23] See Chapter 13, "Sexual Economics: Who Profits?"

that help both the son-in-law and his newfound "realistic" male allies.

Just as men require "mothers" to protect and clean up after them forever and ever, so women require "fathers" to vicariously "cover" or protect them from the consequences of their own lack of self-worth and confidence. This state of affairs generally exists within the family. And within the capitalist marketplace.

To the extent to which this is not true in either place, there is no *institutional* support for the woman, as either mother or token-only "successful" woman. The more a woman attempts to redefine or control the nature of her unpaid or relatively well-paid work, the more difficult her work life will become. Most mothers who demand wages or more time off are endangering their jobs, or lives, as surely as are women who attempt to organize female-controlled labor unions in factories or offices.

Women in America who give up marriage or other close family ties in order to become economically independent generally cannot count on their parents for financial or emotional support. For every woman who can, there are more whose brother's college education "comes first" or whose parents need to be economically supported.

The family exists to support the rights of men, not of women. An American workingman can count on his mother's, wife's, or girlfriend's unpaid labor: phone calls, typing, cooking, soothing.

A working woman cannot count on her mother's, father's, husband's, or boyfriend's unpaid labor. A mother's husband and sons usually "come first." A boyfriend or a husband needs such services from *her:* and he usually doesn't know how to type or cook anyway.

Outside the family unit, the lack of automatic, familylike support for female economic advancement is just as prevalent. For example, most secretaries are women. They tend not to work overly hard for a woman—who, after all, is not perceived as a "leader" or a potential marriage mate. Secretaries devote nights and weekends to boyfriends and husbands, or children. They are not likely to work overtime, or as volunteers, for female bosses. They might work for a male boss—for "love," especially if the female secretary is single.[24]

Many token women may not fare any better in relation to either male superiors or coequals, or female or male subordinates. One fe-

---

[24] Only women work for (male) "love." Men work only for money. It is perfectly obvious that no man would work "devotedly" for his female boss for low wages for thirty years because she was a "good woman."

male administrator described her working experience in a hospital in this way:

> "My biggest problem was the secretaries. They were able to see right through my attempts at getting power. They didn't like it. They were into protecting the men they worked for, and they reported back on what I was up to. They acted like their bosses, the doctors, were gods. . . . I don't know if it's because they were jealous or if they just weren't used to having a woman like me around. They sure taught me that women have two enemies—men and women. And men really only have one enemy—other men" (personal interview).

The Crime and Punishment of Competent Women

The more ambitious, competent, and skilled a woman becomes at redefining her independent economic status, the more uncomfortable and the more deprived she risks becoming in relation to both men and women. Mothers who abandon their children or who bring their sons up "like daughters" have a difficult time with organized systems of education, religion, and family or neighborhood opinion. Women who achieve "male" skills and who wish to get paid as if they were "men" also offend everyone. Many very competent women—the working token women—in America, have been isolated and denied membership in the "club" of their expertise and have systematically been driven to prolonged bouts of deprivation and self-doubt. Extraordinarily competent women have apparently survived these dry spells with more humor and resilience than ordinary mortals should have. Dr. Margaret Mead, for example, worked hard and became very "successful"—for a woman. However, such "success" often made her personal life harder rather than easier; and like most women, she had too few professional or human escapes or *automatic* systems of support, during difficult personal or professional moments. The job of "wife" often took precedence over Mead's job as anthropologist.[25] For example, after an extended field trip with her

---

[25] However, Mead is a Good Woman: she never "complains" or "blames." In fact, she believes she is different from other professional women in that she is a more "feminine" sort. Perhaps she is correct, and this is one of the many reasons she has been able to survive as well as she has. In her autobiography she notes that she never wished to "compete" with men and so consciously chose an all-female college, and subsequently a comparatively "feminine" career: investigating female adolescence in Samoa is not exactly competing with men—either in anthropology or in banking. Margaret Mead, *Blackberry Winter* (New York, William Morrow and Co., 1972).

anthropologist-husband Reo Fortune, both of them were starved for conversation with another intellectual. Upon meeting their first one, Gregory Bateson (who was later to become her third husband), Mead writes:

> "This time there were three of us and Gregory was, if anything, even more starved for talk than Reo and I were. He had been working alone and was depressed and discouraged at the way his field work was going. He and Reo sat up all night talking, while I kept the conversation going with the young patrol officer who was accompanying us, so that the others could talk without interruption."[26]

Mead notes how careful she had to be when discussing her husband's work with him. She had to tailor her comments to fit her husband's ego, lest his resentment or despair upset the two of them. More important, however, is the kind of resentment felt toward her by *strangers* simply because she is a successful woman. In her autobiography, Mead, who for many years has been associated with the American Museum of Natural History in New York, says:

> ". . . it was a little hard, a few years ago, to find on my desk, accompanied by a rather curt letter of obviously unwilling apology, a skit written by a member of another department. . . . in the skit the writer recorded that although he constantly encountered me in print and on the radio and on television, he had not seen me in a museum for many years. Finally, he penetrated the west tower to find my offices deep in dust. . . . he did find live files. These revealed that I had been dead for years, but that ample funds were still being provided by a series of impersonators, each one of whom was murdered when she asked for a larger share of the take and was replaced by another."[27]

Here, Mead as the "successful" woman is accused of not really existing, of being invisible, of not doing her job, of being an imposter of herself—all thinly veiled wishes for her death. Of course, successful men have their problems too. But they are often better supported and protected by the institution of the family than are women. Also, from a psychological point of view, the envy-hatred fantasies toward successful men are largely a male-male affair. Women do not "hate"

---

[26] *Ibid.*
[27] *Ibid.* Since we have no psychological or pictorial experience of a female Godhead, it is inconceivable to most people that a woman can be fleet-footed, invisible and as omnipresent as a (male) God, doing what she pleases and responsible only to herself and her own powers.

financially or publicly successful men like men—and women—hate publicly successful women.

For example, nearly all of the twelve female scientists who recently participated in a symposium on women in American science told of being systematically discouraged by teachers, excluded by classmates, and shut out of important jobs and inner circles by colleagues and employers.[28]

Women in American politics have generally also been systematically denied (their party's) funding and support and have been excluded from most important meetings, committees, networks, privileges, and patronage because they are women. Congresswomen Martha Griffiths, Sissy Farenthold, Leonor Sullivan, Margaret Heckler, Bella Abzug, Shirley Chisholm, and Pat Schroeder, for example, have all been denied party support at various times—*as a matter of course* and *especially* because they merited it.

Martha Griffiths has noted that the Democratic party did nothing to assist her at various crucial points and really didn't want her to win.

Sissy Farenthold, after establishing the kind of political power and savvy that nearly won her the 1972 gubernatorial primary in Texas, had to wage a bitter struggle for the relatively low-level post of a delegate to the 1972 Democratic Convention.

Margaret Heckler said that

"[my] party did not encourage [me]. In fact, they discouraged me. . . . When I was finally elected they had to accept the fact."[29]

Pat Schroeder was denied both the usual support from the Democratic party and the AFL-CIO funds "normally given a Democratic candidate."[30]

Women's political power has been limited and questioned in very diverse political areas. For example, revolutionary leaders such as Emma Goldman, Alexandra Kollontai, Elizabeth Gurley Flynn, Agnes Smedley, Angela Davis, and numerous women involved in the Russian, Cuban, Chinese, Israeli, and Algerian nationalist-Communist political struggles all report being denied that quality and

---

[28] For example, read Betsy Ancker-Johnson, physicist; Joanne Simpson, meteorologist; Marian Boykan Pour-El, mathematician; Mildred Dresselhaus, engineer, et al., in *Women and Success*, Kundsin, ed.
[29] These particular examples are all noted in Susan and Martin Tolchin, *Clout: Womanpower and Politics* (New York, Coward, McCann and Geoghegan, Inc., 1974).
[30] *Ibid.*

quantity of personal and institutional (party) acceptance or recognition that a male counterpart would have received.[31]

Women who are scientists, artists, congresswomen, and revolutionary leaders are often only-women. They are also token women. They come from all class origins. They have struggled against male bias without female support. They have struggled against female bias without male support. They have struggled against bias, per se, without family support. Their existence demands a careful evaluation or reevaluation of the rather general dislike for the ambitious or aggressive woman who does well—for a woman.

[31] Angela Davis, *An Autobiography;* Elizabeth Gurley Flynn, *The Rebel Girl;* Emma Goldman, *Living My Life* (Dover Press); Alexandra Kollontai, *The Autobiography of a Sexually Emancipated Communist Woman,* trans. by Salvator Attanasio (New York, Herder and Herder, 1971); Agnes Smedley, *Daughter of Earth.*

15. Out of the Supermarket and into the Job Market

"Women's work" is not valued. Our society honors what is paid for, which is not female labor. Women frequently work both in and out of the home, in the "husband's business," at those jobs men are willing to let women occupy, and at the lowest possible pay. When jobs are available at all.

Motherhood is idealized and mothers are idolized—as long as that is what keeps women out of men's jobs. The paradox of the exclusively female characteristics—motherhood, maternity, pregnancy, or the possibility—is that these are idealized in the one sense but become a stigma in the paid work force.

> "The dogma of beneficial motherhood has been handed down by men. If a woman spews out children, she will be sufficiently exhausted by the process never to attempt art, music, literature or politics. If she knows that that is all that is expected of her, if she feels that the fertility, the impregnation, birth cycle validates her credentials as a female human being, she will be driven to this misuse of nature as a standard of her own worth, as a measure of the comparative worthlessness of those who breed less successfully. That will occupy her sufficiently to keep her from competing successfully with male human beings on any other human basis."[1]

The ability to bear children is used as a negative employment factor. Mothers at every level are either kept out of the paid work force

---

[1] Myrna Lamb, *But What Have You Done For Me Lately?* (New York, Pathfinder Press, Inc., 1970).

or kept in low-paying, uninteresting jobs; they are presumed to be uninvolved, unreliable, undependable, uncommitted to anything but their preoccupation with their children. This is presumed true if they are single, married, and formerly married women, women who have children or may have children in the future, women who are "housewives" or "heads of households."[2] In other words, if they are women.

All Pregnant People Are Equal, Regardless of Sex

In June of 1974, the Supreme Court of the United States (on which no woman has ever sat) decided in a now famous decision referred to as the *Aiello* decision that there is no unconstitutional discrimination in a state's refusing to pay insurance benefits for disabilities which may accompany pregnancy and childbirth.[3]

Under challenge was the California disability insurance plan which pays compensation benefits, without regard to cost, voluntariness, uniqueness, or "normalcy" for such disabilities as heart attacks, cosmetic surgery, sterilization, prostatectomies, race-related disabilities such as sickle-cell anemia, preexisting conditions such as degenerative arthritis, cataracts, and "normal" disabilities such as removal of wisdom teeth or orthodontia. But not pregnancy.

In an outstandingly tortured opinion, two-thirds of the Supreme Court justices agreed:

> "There is no evidence . . . that the program worked to discriminate against any definable group or class. There is no risk from which men are protected and women are not.
>
> "The California insurance program does not exclude anyone from benefit eligibility because of gender but merely removes one physical condition—pregnancy—from the list of compensable disabilities. While it is true that only women can become pregnant, it does not follow that every legislative classification concerning pregnancy is a sex-based classification. . . ."

The highest court was not, after all, denying benefits to pregnant women alone, but to "pregnant *people*."

Women do work at "operative" and "service" jobs, but their acknowledged primary function is the reproduction, care, and feeding

---

[2] The government is a coconspirator in the social refusal to unlock sexual roles. As defined by the government, women *cannot* be heads of households or heads of families if they are living with their husbands.
[3] Geduldig v. Aiello 417 U.S. 484, 94 S. Ct. 2485 (1974).

of children. On "masculine," professional, or career levels, women generally can have families only if they are willing to end or diminish their paid work. This conflict causes a familiar refrain: "When I'm at work I feel guilty about not being with my family and when I'm at home I feel guilty about not working."

Though women can and do work in and outside the home, to have rewarding jobs—and America's rewards are cash—usually involves the choice at one time or another between family and career.

Unlike men, who not only *can* but are expected to have career, job, spouse, children, family, and home, women can have these if only they keep the priorities firmly in mind and don't miss coming home for dinner because they have a meeting at the office or must take clients out for dinner or fly to a board meeting. One successful woman who has no husband or children says:

> "I spend a tremendous amount of time on the road. I used to fly to the West Coast, fly right into Los Angeles, then I would go to San Francisco for another day, then I would go to Denver, then I'd go to Kansas City and spend another day there, then I would go to Chicago and spend two days there, and I'd do that for a few times a year. If I had a husband and kids, he'd say you're leaving me with *your* child for two weeks."

Men don't decide to run for Congress by rationalizing: "When-the-legislature-is-not-in-session-I'll-be-able-to-take-care-of-the-kids; politics-is-a-good-career-for-combining-work-and-marriage."

Using politics as an example of the "choice," and looking at New York's elected officials on the state and federal levels, one finds: There are no women in the entire United States Senate. New York has three women representatives in Congress:

Bella Abzug: Married. Children. Did not seek office till her children were grown.
Shirley Chisholm: Married. No children.
Elizabeth Holtzman: Not married. No children.

In the State Executive Branch:

Mary Anne Krupsak: Lieutenant Governor. Married. (Did not marry till after she was a state senator.) No children.

In the Legislature:[4]

Carol Bellamy: Not married. No children.
Karen Burstein: Married. No children.

[4] Prepared with the assistance of Ms. Ross Graham, Manhattan Women's Political Caucus.

Linda Winikow: Married. Young children. (Did not enter elected office until 1975.)
Rosemary Gunning: Married. No children.
Marie Runyon: Divorced. Did not seek office till her children were grown.
Elizabeth Connolly: Married. Four children. (Entered elected office when children ranged between nineteen and nine.)
Estella Diggs: Married. Children. Did not enter office till children grown.
Jean Amatucci: Not married. No children.
Mary Goodhue: Married. One child. Did not enter office until son grown and married.

It is not uncommon to see women in very local elected jobs which do not require travel away from home to constituents or seat of government; in addition, these jobs are often nonpaying. Women are in a damned-if-you-do-damned-if-you-don't situation. Either they cannot even run for office or cannot be elected because of family obligations.[5] Or, if they are not married, or do not have children, they may be regarded as nonwomen or freaks.

Tales of discrimination against mothers or potential mothers, i.e. women, are common. Betsy Ancker-Johnson described what happened to her when she became pregnant while working as an industrial research physicist:

"I wasn't even allowed to enter the laboratory building for three months before the birth or hear or talk or get a book out of my private collection without special permission of the laboratory director. . . . my second baby was born while I was employed [at another, more 'enlightened' laboratory]. My paycheck stopped eight weeks before expected delivery (a company rule) and resumed six weeks after (a state law). . . . however, no one cared that I went right on working. . . . I must say I thought it a bit perverse, though,

---

[5] Susan and Martin Tolchin (*Clout: Womanpower and Politics* [New York, Coward, McCann and Geoghegan, Inc., 1974] wrote:
"Of the women in our book sample—and this included women in a wide range of political roles from the clubhouse to the White House—only 0.8 percent had young children (under ten); 38 percent were unmarried; 29 percent had no children; and 40 percent had older children. Smaller samples selected at random invariably produce similar results. Of the fifteen women administrative assistants in the New York, New Jersey and Connecticut Congressional delegations, the following statistics emerge: Eleven are unmarried; of those who are married, only two have children; and of those who are unmarried, one is a widow, and one is divorced (both have children)."

when the wife of one of my assistants had a baby, and he was given a week's leave *with pay*."[6]

A writer who also happened to be a married woman was told in her interview at Columbia Graduate School of Journalism, "But if you have a baby, we've taken a place away from someone who's serious about his career."

Judge Nanette Dembitz, while seeking to run for a seat on New York's Court of Appeals, was asked by the State Bar Association how she could also manage her family.[7]

A counselor in a drug program was told addicts would be upset at the sight of a pregnant woman.

Two or More Jobs for the Price of One

Equal rights, if meaning "equal pay for equal work," does not change the expectation that women still have double duty. "Working women" are still doing at least two jobs for the price of one; even the woman who fights for equal pay on the job still has the responsibility of coming home to take care of house, children, husband.

What employer questions a male job applicant about taking time from work when the children are ill? His ability to reproduce is not considered relevant to a man's work. As a matter of fact, if anything, fatherhood as proof of virility may be an asset to a man.[8]

And yet, what really is "the bottom line?" After all, on the day the hired housekeeper, nurse, or babysitter can't come to work, who stays home? The mother or the father? And in one-parent families, which parent is usually absent?

Of course, the facts are that women *do* work.[9] Single women work.[10] Married women work.[11] Women with children work.[12] But

---

[6] *Women and Success,* Ruth B. Kundsin, ed. (New York, William Morrow and Company, Inc., 1974).
[7] Although the subject was presumably unrelated to childbearing, Federal Judge Constance Baker Motley was asked in a similar interview what she would *wear* if appointed to the bench.
[8] See, for example, George Gilder, *Naked Nomads* (New York, Quadrangle, The New York Times Book Company, 1974).
[9] 35,320,000. *Marital and Family Characteristics of Workers,* Bureau of Labor Statistics, Special Labor Force Report No. 173 (March, 1974).
[10] 8,230,000. *Ibid.*
[11] 20,367,000 married women workers with husband present; 6,723,000 divorced, widowed, or separated. *Ibid.*
[12] Records are not kept as to how many working mothers are single. But families with children under eighteen with mothers working number 10,907,000. "Children of Working Mothers," Bureau of Labor Statistics, Special Labor Force Report No. 174 (March, 1974).

for women there are variations in the numbers, the job level, and the money, depending on parenthood status.

Adequate child care facilities do not exist. The estimated number of children in licensed day care accommodations is 920,000.[13] Nevertheless, 30 percent of the mothers of preschool children and 50 percent of the mothers of children over six work outside the home as well as inside.[14]

Working against women are attitudes, requirements, practices, and laws which *mandate* certain "protections" and remove from women the option and the right to decide, for example, whether or not to work during and after pregnancy, to have children, whether and when to join the paid labor force.[15]

Interestingly, state courts and lower federal courts do not seem to be adopting the *Aiello* decision. Some judges, on benches less lofty than the Supreme Court, are finding ways to say that discrimination based on maternity status is indeed sex-based.

For example, several months after the Supreme Court opinion, a federal judge in California, the state in which the *Geduldig* v. *Aiello* challenge arose, decided in *Vineyard* v. *Hollister Elementary School District*[16] that loss of wages and sick-leave benefits to pregnant women but not to employees with other disabilities violated Title VII of the Civil Rights Act and Equal Employment Opportunity Commission guidelines. The judge there departed from *Aiello* by saying, in this case, the defendants had not introduced evidence of a rationale for their maternity-leave policy.

> "Here there is no showing of a strong economic justification for singling out pregnant women for exclusion from disability benefits. Moreover . . . this plaintiff has relied on Title 7 . . . [and] may reach more broadly than the Equal Protection Clause itself [relied on in *Aiello*]. In a Title 7 case, the court does not need to go through the balancing process followed by the Supreme Court in *Geduldig* v. *Aiello*. . . . treating pregnancy differently from other temporary disabilities is discriminatory and flatly prohibited."

As many feminists have pointed out, each woman must have not only the option of having or not having children, but also the option

---

[13] *Twenty Facts on Women Workers*, Women's Bureau, U.S. Dept. of Labor (1974).
[14] Howard Hayghe, "Labor Force Activity of Married Women," *Monthly Labor Review*, Bureau of Vital Statistics, U.S. Dept. of Labor (April, 1973).
[15] Immediately prior to the *Aiello* decision it had been widely assumed under Title VII that pregnancy-based discrimination would be illegal.
[16] 64 Federal Rules Decisions 580, 1974.

of arranging her work and child care duties and those of the father to complement each other (until there is universally available child care), as well as the option of taking short or extended maternity leaves. To be sure that there really *is* an "option," the woman who elects to take maternity leave must not be punished economically or otherwise. Protective legislation and other maternity discrimination must not be used to eliminate a woman's choice.[17]

Though the majority of married couples do have two earners, those women who do not work until their children are grown may then be out of the job market for reasons of their own age. By the time women are really available to work outside the home, work is not available to them.

Still, the question of whether women *should* work is beating a dead horse. Women *do* work.

There are more than 35 million women in the United States with jobs outside the home.[18] Sixty percent of them are also wives.[19] More than 73 percent of employed women work full-time. Women constitute 41 percent of the entire work force;[20] they earn 59 percent of what they would earn if they were men.[21] Of nearly 12.7 million working mothers with children in 1972, 35 percent had at least one child under six.

---

[17] In Cleveland Board of Education v. LaFleur 414 U.S. 632, 94 S Ct. 791 (1974), the Court struck down forced leave of absence at six months for pregnant women.

Under the Maternity Law for the Woman Worker in the Republic of Cuba (1974), every pregnant worker shall be obliged to stop working on completion of the thirty-fourth week of pregnancy, and shall have the right to leave from work for a period of eighteen weeks, which will include the six weeks prior to birth and the twelve weeks afterward. This leave will be paid. The worker will be guaranteed a postnatal leave of six weeks necessary for her recuperation, even if, through adverse circumstances of accident or congenital or acquired illness, the child should die at the moment of birth or within the first four weeks of birth. If the worker needs a longer period of rest after the postnatal leave is over, because of complications at partum, she will have the right to collect the illness subsidy established in the prevailing Social Security Law. Complications characteristic of pregnancy or illness coinciding with it that require absolute rest by medical prescription, with or without hospitalization, will give the injured worker the right to the illness subsidy established in the prevailing Social Security Law. The economic compensation that the worker will receive during the period of maternity leave will be equal to the average weekly income in wages and subsidies received in the twelve months immediately prior to the beginning of her leave. During and up to the thirty-fourth week of pregnancy, the worker will have the right to six days' or twelve half days' paid leave for prenatal medical and dental care. In order to guarantee the care and treatment of the child during its first year of life, the working mother shall have the right to one day of paid leave each month to attend a center for pediatric care.

[18] *Twenty Facts on Women Workers, op. cit.*
[19] "Consumer Income," Bureau of the Census, U.S. Dept. of Commerce, Series P-60, No. 90 (1973 based on 1972 data).
[20] *Twenty Facts on Women Workers, op. cit.*
[21] "Consumer Income," *op. cit.*

Nearly two-thirds of all women workers are single, divorced, widowed, or separated, *or* have husbands who earn less than $7,000 a year.[22] They are working for the same reason men work: to make money. But for women, the accepted reasons are boredom, hobby, or "pin money."

Families with more than one worker have increased steadily over the years, and by March, 1972, they accounted for almost 55 percent of all families headed by married men in the labor force (if a male is present, the Census considers him the "head of household"), compared with only 45 percent ten years earlier.[23]

The average woman worker is now forty years old and married;[24] nine out of ten women alive today will be paid members of the work force for twenty-five years or more; at least six out of ten will work full-time for up to thirty years.[25]

But there is a female job ghetto.

When women do enter the paid labor force, they tend to occupy jobs that "can be described as extensions of what women do as homemakers—teach children . . . nurse the sick, prepare food."[26]

It is remarkable that a small number of female physicians constitute nearly 22 percent of the pediatrics field. Of the total number of physicians specializing in child psychiatry, nearly 25 percent are women, and in the field of public health the number of women physicians is nearly 20 percent.[27]

In 1910, over 30 percent of employed women were working as domestics and household workers and nearly 50 percent could be found in three other occupations—farm laborers, dressmakers and seamstresses, and teachers. In 1960, one-third of the women employed in the United States were in just eight occupations—secretaries, saleswomen, retail trade, general household workers, teachers in elementary schools, bookkeepers, waitresses, and nurses. In 1970 more than

---

[22] *Twenty Facts on Women Workers, op. cit.*
[23] Hayghe, *op. cit.*
[24] Nancy Seifer, "Absent from the Majority, Working-Class Women in America," National Project on Ethnic America of the American Jewish Committee (1973).
[25] Betty Howard, Director, Division Women's Affairs, Minnesota Department of Human Rights, in testimony before the National Commission on Consumer Finance, Washington, D.C., May 22, 1972; Report to Assemblyman Lucio F. Russo, "Background Information on Women's Credit," October 9, 1973.
[26] Elizabeth Waldman and Beverly J. McEaddy, "Where Women Work—an Analysis by Industry and Occupation," *Monthly Labor Review,* Bureau of Vital Statistics, U.S. Dept. of Labor (May, 1974).
[27] "Statistics—Women in Medicine, 1973," *Journal of the American Medical Women's Association, Inc.,* Vol. 28, No. 11.

a third of the working women in America were still concentrated in these occupations.[28]

The majority of women workers are employed in traditional "female occupations": clerical, service work, beauticians, nurses' aides, waitresses.[29] This does not include private household workers, almost all of whom are women and where the median income (and no benefits) is $1,800.[30] Of those women in the "professional-technical fields," 40 percent are elementary and secondary school teachers.[31]

Of the women described as being in "white-collar" jobs, 60 percent are doing clerical work, including supermarket cashiering; but 70 percent of men in white-collar jobs are in professional, technical, or managerial positions.[32] Only 5 percent of women in white-collar jobs were managers or administrators.[33]

About 60 percent of all employees in the service industry were women—approximately 75 percent in the medical-health industry and about 75 percent in personal services, including those in hotels and private homes.[34]

The finance, insurance, and real estate industries became predominantly female during the 1960's, and by 1973, 52 percent of the employees were women, *but* about 80 percent were in low-paying clerical jobs. Similarly, nine out of ten bank clerks and tellers are women, but few bank officers are. In the education industry, about 70 percent of the teachers in colleges and universities are men; about 70 percent of the teachers in elementary and high schools are women.[35]

In terms of female job ghettos, there have been no more disadvantaged workers than those doing housework—in other people's homes. According to the National Committee on Household Employment, 97 percent of all such workers are women, "most of whom are partly self-supporting or heads of families. Black women comprise over half of this segment of the labor force."[36]

As a matter of fact, until 1974 this category of workers was not

---

[28] *Women and Poverty*, U.S. Commission on Civil Rights, Staff Report (June, 1974).
[29] *Women and Poverty*, Bureau of the Census, U.S. Dept. of Commerce (1970). Cf. *Women in the Work Force, Underutilization of Women*, Women's Bureau, U.S. Dept. of Labor (1971).
[30] Most recent U.S. Census (1970).
[31] *Women and Poverty*, Bureau of the Census (1970).
[32] *Women in the Work Force*, U.S. Dept. of Labor.
[33] Cf. Carolyn J. Jacobson, "Women Workers: Profile of a Growing Force," AFL-CIO *American Federationist* (July, 1974).
[34] Waldman and McEaddy, *op. cit.*
[35] *Ibid.*
[36] The NCHE Code of Standards for Household Employment, Silver Spring, Maryland.

covered by the Federal Fair Labor Standards Act. Even at that, the established minimum wage was only $1.90 per hour with an escalation to $2.30 in 1977.[87]

Though paid "domestics" may be paid slightly more than nothing, which is what the housewife doing the same job in the "employ" of her family receives, the wage scale has been pitiful and benefits such as insurance, Social Security, vacations, unemployment compensation virtually nonexistent. Domestics, now sometimes known as household technicians, typically black, untrained, needy, have had little contact with one another at the work center itself, and in that sense, if no other, may be worse off than classic slaves, who had some communication and organizational opportunities. There are now attempts both to organize and support, as a feminist issue, the demands of household workers.

On one point *everyone,* men, women, feminists, anti-feminists, agree: women are paid less than men.

No one is poorer than poor women. Not even poor men. Women of all races and ethnicities consistently earn less than white men. And the median wage level of women is pathetically low. Women of all races earn less than men of their own racial-ethnic group, and less than white women. But earnings of women of all races are significantly lower than white men's and that of minority-group men (with the exception of native American and Filipino men).[88]

And the female condition seems to be worsening. In 1955, women's median wage or salary income was 64 percent of men's; by 1970, women's median earnings were 59 percent of men's.[89]

Median Income[40]

White men (over 25)	$ 9,378
Black men (over 25)	5,648
White women (over 25)	3,073
Black women (over 25)	2,730
46.3 million husband-wife families	11,900

[87] *Ibid.*
[88] *Women and Poverty,* U.S. Commission on Civil Rights, Staff Report (June, 1974).
[89] *Fact Sheet on the Earnings Gap,* Employment Standards Administration, Women's Bureau, United States Department of Labor. (Cf. *Women in the Work Force.*)
[40] *Consumer Income,* Bureau of the Census, U.S. Dept. of Commerce. See also Bureau of Census, U.S. Dept. of Commerce, Census Population 1970, Detailed Characteristics PC (1)-D1.

6.6 million women alone with families	5,340[41]
—White	6,815
—Black	4,335
—Spanish surname	4,501
College-educated men	14,350[42]
College-educated women	9,162
Men 5 years after obtaining Ph.D.	18,700[43]
Women 5 years after obtaining Ph.D.	16,400
Men 22 years after obtaining Ph.D.	27,100
Women 22 years after obtaining Ph.D.	21,800

For example, almost half of the women who work full-time, but 14 percent of the men, earned less than $5,000. But this is reversed at the upper end of the scale, where only 7 percent of the women but 40 percent of the men had earnings of $10,000 or more.

Women who work full-time throughout the year earn $3 for every $5 earned by men who are similarly employed.[44]

Seven percent of women earned $10,000 plus, in 1970, compared to 40 percent of men. Only 2 percent of all full-time employed women had incomes over $15,000.[45]

Unequal Pay at All Levels

Unequal pay prevails on the "working class" level as well as in the technical occupations and professions. Women service workers (excluding private household) earn 56.8 percent of what men are paid. And female professional and technical workers earn only 66.7 percent of men's comparable wages or salaries.[46]

And men, in addition to their higher salaries, receive far superior benefits, which are not so fringe, in their freedom from penalty for

[41] Forty-eight percent of the female-headed families which receive wages or salaries had incomes below the poverty level. Bureau of the Census, United States Department of Commerce, *Statistical Abstract of the United States* at 339 (94th ed., 1973).
[42] *On Campus with Women*, Project on the Status and Education of Women, Association of American Colleges, Washington, D.C., No. 9 (June, 1974).
[43] *The New York Times*, January 6, 1975; reporting on "Women, Men, and the Doctorate," published January 5, 1975, by Educational Testing Service, Princeton, New Jersey.
[44] *Fact Sheet on the Earnings Gap*, Employment Standards Administration, Women's Bureau, U.S. Dept. of Labor (December, 1971).
[45] John Kenneth Galbraith, "The Galbraith Plan to Promote the Minorities," *The New York Times* Magazine (August 22, 1971).
[46] Bureau of the Census, U.S. Dept. of Commerce, Current Population Reports, 6–60.

parenthood, in their stock options, profit sharing, telephones, education, expense accounts, including meals (an executive having a martini and full meal for lunch may pay less out of his own pocket than his secretary having a cheeseburger and coffee), cars, vacations (out-of-town conventions), and in the higher strata, clubs, attorneys, accountants, and college scholarships for their children.

In unemployment as well as employment, women fare worse than men. Women generally are the last hired, and, if for no other reason than seniority, the first fired. Traditionally they are among the highest groups of unemployed.

Reported unemployment rates for blacks are about twice as high as for whites. In January, 1975, the rates were 6.4 percent white unemployment and 12.8 percent black. They are considerably higher for black women than they are for white women or black men. The annual unemployment rate for black women in 1973 was 11.1 percent. The comparable rates were 7.9 percent for black males and 5.3 and 4.3 percent for white women and white men, respectively, over twenty.[47] The women hardest hit by unemployment, though, are teenagers and mothers with young children.

Actually, unemployment figures for both sexes are much higher than officially reported. Most women are not included in employment or unemployment figures since "unemployed" means actively seeking employment, as indicated by unemployment insurance figures. Consequently, many wives and welfare recipients not considered as part of the work force are not considered unemployed. Also, domestic workers, for example, who are usually women, when not processed through official channels are not unemployed.

Unemployment insurance, however, is another matter. Women are often considered ineligible when they leave jobs because of pregnancy, responsibilities for their children, or family relocation.

> "In light of the husband's legal right to choose the family domicile, the denial of unemployment insurance payments to workers who leave their jobs to follow their spouses to a new location seems especially unfair."[48]

Women are presumed to be unavailable for job relocations and, as Karen DeCrow, President of the National Organization for Women,

---

[47] *The Social and Economic Status of the Black Population in the United States*, U.S. Dept. of Commerce (1973).
[48] Rep. Martha Griffiths (D.-Mich.), "The Economics of Being Female," *Trial* Magazine (Nov./Dec., 1973).

points out,[49] if one is married and moves, she may be guilty of abandonment.

A recent government-published report showed that industries paying average weekly earnings of less than $100 were female-intensive. Several were paying under $90 a week, while the weekly paycheck for all industries averaged $138.[50] In the service industries, earnings averaged $111 a week. About 1.6 million women worked in hospitals, where weekly earnings averaged $108. Another 600,000 women worked in hotels and laundries-dry cleaners, where average weekly wages were $76 and $87, respectively. Male-intensive industries are on the higher rungs of the wage ladder: Construction—6 percent female, paying $223 average a week; transportation and public utilities (switchboard operators $126, line construction employees $228).[51]

"Not only is the male median income almost twice that of women's," as Caroline Bird wrote in *Born Female*,[52] "the gap widens at upper brackets."

In publishing the names, corporations, and salaries of the fifteen highest paid corporate executives in the United States, *Business Week*[53] "revealed" that none is a woman.[54] In addition, on the magazine's list of the highest paid executives in major corporations within such diverse industries as tobacco, transportation, utilities, retailing, drugs, steel, oil, food, chemicals, banking, agriculture, advertising, aircraft, apparel, and communications among 383 "Chief Executive Officers," the name of only one woman appeared.[55]

And, according to *Fortune* Magazine's study of "The Ten Highest-Ranking Women in Big Business,"[56] eight of the ten were directly

---

[49] *Sexist Justice* (New York, Random House, 1974).
[50] Waldman and McEaddy, *op. cit.*
[51] *Ibid.*
[52] New York, David McKay, 1968.
[53] *Business Week* (May 4, 1974).
[54] Paul B. Hofmann, former Chairman, Johnson and Johnson, $978,000; Richard C. Gerstenberg, Chairman, General Motors, $938,000; Henry Ford II, Chairman, Ford Motor Company, $878,746; Lee A. Iacocca, President, Ford Motor Company, $878,746; Edward N. Cole, President, General Motors, $846,500; Harold S. Geneen, Chairman, ITT, $814,299; Thomas A. Murphy, Vice-Chairman, General Motors, $776,125; Lynn A. Townsend, Chairman, Chrysler, $683,600; Richard B. Sellars, Chairman, Johnson and Johnson, $678,968; John K. Jamieson, Chairman, Exxon, $620,766; John J. Riccardo, President, Chrysler, $590,987; William F. Laporte, Chairman, American Home Products, $540,409; Rawleigh Warner, Jr., Chairman, Mobil Oil, $530,009; Robert W. Sarnoff, Chairman, RCA, $525,000; C. Peter McColough, Chairman, Xerox, $506,461.
[55] Mary Wells Lawrence (Chairman [sic] of the Board and Chief Executive Officer of Wells, Rich, Greene, Inc., advertising agency), who, as the highest paid woman, is paid only approximately half of what male chief executives are paid.
[56] Wyndham Robertson, *Fortune* (April, 1973).

aided by family connection, marriage, or helping to create the organization they now manage.

Male executives—even in such "service" professions as health and hospitals—receive not only enormous salaries but additional "fringe benefits" which, in tax terms, may be preferable to salary. Executives are courted, seduced, bought with executive compensation plans, stock option plans, deferred income, college tuition "scholarships" for their children, limousines, athletic and country club memberships, *full* medical coverage, and financial and tax counseling.

And, according to a "compensation specialist":[57] "Most companies do this secretly because medical insurance is an emotional issue, and if the rank and file found out, they could be upset."

As sociologist Cynthia Epstein has written, "Even women at the top are usually at the bottom of the top."[58]

The Trauma of Exclusion

The "battered woman" may be a victim of more than obvious and literal assault or rape. The experience suffered by girls and then women is ostracism and exclusion from life as it is known to the sexual aristocracy. Its effect on the interests and attainments of women has been profound and explicit. In the case of Myra Bradwell, a woman whose early application for a license to practice law had been denied by the State of Illinois, the Supreme Court of the United States ruled that:

> "God designed the sexes to occupy different spheres of action, and . . . it belonged to men to make, apply, and to execute the laws. . . . In view of these facts we are certainly warranted in saying that when the legislature gave to this court the power of granting licenses to practice law, it was not with the slightest expectation that this privilege would be extended to women.
>
> "It certainly cannot be confirmed as an historical fact, that it is one of the privileges and immunities of women as citizens to engage in any and every profession, occupation, or employment in civil life. . . ."[59]

Courts and government agencies are beginning to recognize the

---

[57] Graef S. Crystal, "Executive Compensation: Getting Richer in '73," *Business Week* (May 4, 1974).
[58] *Women and Success,* Kundsin, ed.
[59] Bradwell v. Illinois 83 U.S. 130 (1873).

"trauma factor" in various forms of discrimination, particularly economic.[60]

Nowhere is the effect, the trauma clearer than when women "go into business."

> "It helps to come from a family where accountants and lawyers are part of the family tree.
>
> ". . . You are involved with leases, lawsuits, credit, statements, income tax, tax payroll, people, etc. There is no mystique to it—but, most women in business let men do it—and there they are right back where they came from. Totally dependent on a male point of view about what they should do or should not do."[61]

In or out of school, women don't get exposure to, or experience in, business or financial matters. Daddy, not Mother, usually takes care of all "those" things. Daughter merely imitates and repeats the pattern with Husband.[62]

Some women are starting businesses as "alternatives" to the establishment; for example, services to fill in gaps and voids, such as the organization of day care centers. Other businesses, including stores, management and consulting firms, light manufacturing, are traditional except that female participation is new.

Most women, even if educated, have not studied subjects having to do with money or economics, the subjects and values most revered in our country.

> "When I was in school I had to carve up a frog for biology and I've never carved one since. But, I was never taught anything about

---

[60] For example, in Humphrey v. Southwestern Portland Cement Company 369 F. Supp. 832 (Texas), U.S. District Court (1973), the court held that in a discrimination case (the facts involved race, not sex) a showing of evidence of and damages from "psychic injuries are proper." (Reversed, but on basis that there was no proof of discrimination, not on psychic injury question.)

[61] Jane Trahey, President of Jane Trahey Associates, an advertising agency.

[62] On-the-job training for women is often the type described in a letter from the State Bank of Long Island, to all female employees:

"I am happy to announce that a team of prominent ladies has been engaged by the bank to give an excellent course in grooming and charm to all of our lady employees. I am quite sure you will find this course exciting, pleasant, and an inspiration for you personally, and ultimately rewarding to our customers as well. . . . All ladies will attend the first class on Tuesday, March 4th, from 5 to 6 P.M.

"It is requested that each lady bring her own: Makeup, eyebrow tweezers, brush and comb, mirror, cuticle scissors. I am pleased to inform you that in addition to coffee and cake, the bank will provide the following: cold cream, eye shadow, eye liner, mascara, cuticle remover, emory boards, cotton, nail polish remover, hazel astringent, nail polish, tissue. Good luck to all of you."

Upon the suggestion of Barbara Shack, Assistant Director of the New York Civil Liberties Union, that such a policy might be discriminatory, the bank made the course an "optional fringe benefit" for all women.

money because I was a girl. Yet, I and every woman have been dealing with money ever since we left school. Now, I ask you, twenty years after college, is it more important to dissect a frog or know how to manage money?"[63]

Very few women are graduated from (or even attend) Harvard Business School, for example, and comparatively few have business or accounting degrees from any graduate school or even college.[64]

Women are not attuned to commercial risk-taking and are ambivalent about being outside the home, about "going into business."

Women have little experience with business structure and financial reality. Many women who would like to go into business have no idea of how to get started. They don't know how much capitalization they need or how they would be able to raise it; they are unfamiliar with contracts, corporations, partnerships, interest, usury, collateral, liability. They are not accustomed to finding, retaining, working with accountants, lawyers, bankers. And what (if anything) does a woman do when she has a good idea? She goes to a man. But how would a woman know? "You don't expect a baby in diapers to go out and play golf or drive an automobile, so why should we expect a woman to know how to run a business?"[65]

At the same time women say they want to make their own decisions, be free of their fathers, husbands, or surrogate dominant figures, they are usually not prepared for and do not necessarily want to make business decisions. But, unlike the businessman who believes in professionalism and specialization and wants the expert to make or guide certain decisions, women, though they have very limited information and experience of their own, may at this point in history be so committed to rejecting control over their lives that they often fail to employ expert resources in meaningful ways. This appears to be especially true when women deal with other women in business or professional relationships; the female expert seems to have many more demands placed upon her by other women than her male colleagues would have.

---

[63] Muriel Siebert, the first and only woman member of the New York Stock Exchange; *Family Circle* (May, 1972).
[64] There were 50 women in the Harvard Master of Business Arts Class of 1974, out of a class of 781, and 32 women in 1973, out of 776. Salaries for the 1974 class showed a median of $17,600; for women, $16,500. Marlene Krauss, of the Women's Action Alliance, was graduated from the Harvard Business School in 1967; there were 11 women out of 700. She reports that women students were always asked to discuss the cases on marketing detergents because "we were supposed to know about stuff like that" (personal interview).
[65] Florynce Kennedy, Attorney at Law. Personal interview, Fire Island, N. Y.

A recent book about the Harvard Business School written by one of its graduates describes various classmates in terms of their skills, talents, backgrounds, ambitions. Here is the author's description of classmate Mary:

> "Mary's short brown hair is parted on the right—a boy's cut, almost—yet with strands of it falling onto a small, frail face. The features are drawn in clear, thin lines as though time, discarding sketches of her youth, had settled too quickly on a definite draft.
>
> "The short line of her mouth, an accountant's double line, balances the sparse but delicate assets of her face with a puzzling finality."[66]

Here is a woman student talking about penetrating the boys' club:

> "The single girls found it very hard to have a normal sort of social life. Either they were treated like one of the guys, which would be fine except that they wanted to be invited out like other girls. Not necessarily that they wanted a boyfriend out of them, but, you know, when the guys went out together on Saturday night, they wanted to be asked along, even if just as one of the group. And that never happened. They found that the guys had trouble dealing with them in that way."[67]

And her experiences looking for a job:

> "What made me particularly angry was the attitude: 'Well, girlie, you have to prove to me that you're serious about this.' Dammit, I've gone through two years of Harvard Business School. I've spent so much money and grief, and you think I'm not serious?"[68]

Ms. Lee Walker holds what is, in some circles, the coin of the realm—a Harvard Master's of Business Administration. She started working at IBM in 1965, while her then-husband was studying for the same degree. According to her, it seemed the value of the currency depended on who was holding it. When the couple moved to New York from Cambridge, Ms. Walker continued to work for IBM and did get an increase. However, her husband's first job at a consulting firm had a starting salary of one-third more than Ms. Walker's. Her employers justified less pay for married women with the popular "You have a husband to support you."

---

[66] Peter Cohen, *The Gospel According to Harvard Business School* (Baltimore, Md., Penguin Books, Inc., 1973).
[67] *Ibid.*
[68] *Ibid.*

In 1970, Ms. Walker was offered a job working for the City of New York, at a salary increase of more than two and a half times what she had been earning; she accepted the job. On the day she reported for work, however, the offer was withdrawn: It troubled the Health and Hospital Corporation that Ms. Walker's spouse had, through his firm, done studies which had resulted in the establishment of the city corporation. And it is not unusual for the husband's possible conflict of interest to be used against a wife who had no role in the "conflict."

At the time she left IBM, after nine years, Ms. Walker's salary had nearly tripled and she was earning "good money for a woman." But her husband's annual income was reaching six figures!

Women in business and in the professions are a minute number. Stories of a 100 percent increase on a corporation's board of directors or a doubling of the number of women judges, for example, usually means an increase from one to two.

But women who have been considered for corporate boards of directors report that they are not appointed if they are really expert in the business of the company or in finance in general.

It is interesting that women are seeking high-paying, though not spectacularly high-paying jobs at a period of recession (if not depression), extraordinary inflation and unemployment. It is a time when factory workers, government civil servants, white-collar workers, stockbrokers, and others with traditionally respected salaries are, in fact, unemployed. This is a surprising time for business neophytes to be entering the job market. On Wall Street, for example, the number of member firms is shrinking. And,

". . . middle management jobs are being 'consolidated,' 'eliminated through attrition.' But while business is cutting down on the Indians, it is bidding UP for the Chiefs. . . . men for senior level positions in the $35,000 category and over are more in demand than they have ever been."[69]

It is obvious that very few top-level positions in the country are available to women. That leaves, at best, middle management, not the place where power resides.

As Stanley Aronowitz has written:

"But most managers, except those involved in the highest councils of the company, make decisions only in their own realm. Even if

[69] New York *Post*, Wednesday, September 11, 1974, Lester Korn, President of Korn Flash Ferry International, an executive research firm.

they are highly paid, and own a small portion of corporate property in the form of stock, they are often unable to comprehend the whole of the corporation's activities, since their own work is confined to a fragment of it. . . . Few ever truly become top managers, that is, those who will coordinate all these functions in conformity with the overall political and economic objectives of the corporation. More often than not, they become victims of shifts in top management or changes in ownership of the corporation."[70]

"Women's" Work, "Men's" Work

Although the number of women employed in professional and technical occupations has almost tripled since 1940, women are a smaller proportion of all professional and technical workers today than they were before World War II. The number of women workers (nonprofessional and nontechnical), however, has increased.[71]

Teaching has always been viewed as a female profession and yet on the level of higher education only 22 percent of faculty and professional staff are women (this is without even exploring the tiny percentage of women who have tenure). Likewise, of course, most women health professionals are nurses, not doctors.

Though on the rise, the number of women lawyers is still only about 3 percent of the profession. Seventy-one percent of women attorneys are practicing; they do not abandon their careers (even though they cannot take their children to court with them). There is a higher percentage of women lawyers working in the government than in other areas,[72] but lawyers, a highly paid professional group, do NOT make their money or achieve positions of "power" by being government lawyers. Of lawyers in private industry, only 1.61 percent of the total are women; private industry is where lawyers make money *and* policy.[73]

In some states[74] court sanction, and in some cases, the husband's consent, has been required for a wife's legal venture into an independent business.[75]

[70] Stanley Aronowitz, *False Promises: The Shaping of American Working Class Consciousness* (New York, McGraw-Hill Book Company, Inc., 1973).
[71] *Underutilization of Women, op. cit.*
[72] American Bar Association Women's Division Report, 1970.
[73] *Ibid.*
[74] Even California did not pass contrary legislation until 1974.
[75] Leo Kanowitz, *Women and the Law* (Albuquerque, University of New Mexico Press, 1969).

"The Florida 'free dealer' law, for example, requires the married woman's petition to set forth her name and age 'and her character, habits, education and mental capacity for business, and briefly set out the reasons why such disabilities [to engage in her own business] should be removed.' She must either procure her husband's consent or serve him with a copy of her petition. Only if the judge is 'satisfied that the removal of the disabilities of such married woman will be for her permanent interest or benefit will he [sic] make a decree removing her disabilities. . . ."[76]

Unfair Choices

But women are still being told how glad they should be that they are not "making it." "The unattached female executive pays heavily for her reward in any case, and at any age. . . . The bright working woman can watch her social invitations decline in direct proportion to the rise in her income tax."[77]

Despite the "complaint" by men that they have no time with their families, men can have families *and* careers. Without even discussing the quality of the time and effort, they can do all things when business takes them away; they know that the wife is home with the children. A woman in the executive suite would have no such assurance. But if she did hire a housekeeper, the "guilt" and the "bottom-line" responsibility would be hers.

It appears that those women who do go into schools and the professions do not "drop out" with any greater frequency than do men. They leave at the same rate and for the same reasons—financial problems, change in career focus, inability to keep up with the work; *not* for marriage or motherhood, as is commonly believed.

For example, of the nearly 30,000 women physicians (7 percent of the total) in this country, 86.7 percent are professionally active, with about the same percentage of men being classified as retired, disabled, or inactive.[78]

After law school graduation, most women practice on a full-time basis. One-half of the full-time women attorneys in James J. White's study of the legal profession in 1965 were married and one-third had very young children.[79]

[76] *Ibid.*
[77] *Harper's Bazaar* (August, 1974).
[78] "Women in Medicine, 1973," American Medical Women's Association, Inc.
[79] B. Dinerman, "Sex Discrimination in the Legal Profession," *American Bar Association Journal* (October, 1969).

But most women, and not men, have at some time chosen between career and family; they have given up or reduced commitments in an effort to balance all their separate lives. Consequently, when women lawyers, for example, have to leave the office to go home and start their home job, their male associates are hustling themselves into partnerships.

Women and the Labor Movement

There is continuous debate as to whether, in the long run, the American trade union movement has helped or harmed workers. There is considerable agreement by all factions, by employers and employees, that unions have frozen the relative positions of the two classes and insured that one would never become the other. There is ongoing debate as to whether, even on a short-term basis and in less abstract terms than the class question, unions have let down the workers, their own membership.

Workers, even men, even union members, are ruled by a class of which they are not a part. It can be said, however, through displays of collective strength, strikes, collective bargaining, men have obtained "benefits" and better working conditions. Women, however, even union members, are, as Charlotte Gilman[80] estimated, thousands of years behind.

Men have long known the power of organizing and collective effort. Women have either not known how to work together, have feared it, have not been exposed to it, or have been kept from doing it.

For a variety of psychological, economic, social, and legal reasons, women workers have not been organized to the extent that men have. It is safe to assume that women have not refrained from unionism on the theory that it strengthens the economic status quo. The most powerful unions are those largely composed of men. Those with considerable—even overwhelming—female membership are led and dominated by men.

> "Some of these explanations are based on the premises that as a young entrant into the labor force, a woman views work as a temporary phase until she marries; married women—who make up close to 60 percent of all women workers—work to supplement the family

---

[80] Charlotte Perkins Gilman, *Women and Economics,* Carl N. Degler, ed. (New York, Harper and Row, 1966).

income or to provide luxuries and savings for the children's education; and the majority of these married women are in the labor force on a less than full-year-round basis. Women have generally been characterized, therefore, as not being interested in the benefits that unionization can bring: representation, job security, pension, and other benefits. Strikes or even the threat of strikes are believed to be a further disincentive."[81]

According to Dorothy Haener of the United Auto Workers' Women's Department,

> "Although it is often implied that women workers are less organized than men because of some unspecified sex-based hostility to unionization, there are in fact more concrete explanations. These relate primarily to the kinds of jobs most women hold and to the legal impediments to organizing that have been set up in the postwar period. . . . sales and domestic workers are especially hard to organize because workers are scattered over small units. But organization is difficult even in industry."[82]

Women workers, laborers, are at the bottom end of the wage scale. And nonwhite women, needless to say, have the lowest incomes, the worst working conditions.

In 1968, less than 20 percent of union members were women, six out of seven were not in unions.[83] At the same time approximately 25 percent of the unions in America had no women members; the all-male unions were in trades in which the work is relatively high paying: construction, mining, firefighting.[84] A few women are beginning to go into these fields, but in such minuscule numbers that it is thus far meaningless. What is clear, however, is that an industry is more likely to be unionized if most of its workers are men.[85]

Moreover, the number of women in unions, while increasing in numbers, has not kept up with the rise in female employment. In fact, the ratio of female union membership to female employment has declined.

---

[81] Lucretia M. Dewey, "Women in Labor Unions," *Monthly Labor Review*, Bureau of Vital Statistics, U.S. Dept. of Labor (February, 1971).
[82] "Women into Unions: Opening Up a Closed Shop," by Dorothy Haener, International Representative, United Auto Workers Women's Department, Detroit, Michigan, *Trial* magazine, November/December, 1973.
[83] Seifer, *op. cit.*
[84] Dewey, *op. cit.*
[85] Edna E. Raphael, "Working Women and Their Membership in Labor Unions," *Monthly Labor Review*, Bureau of Vital Statistics, U.S. Dept. of Labor, Vol. 97, No. 5 (May, 1974).

Many reasons are suggested for the small incidence of female membership in unions, including that women work sporadically, or part-time, and that they are in and out of jobs depending on the needs of their families.[86] Nevertheless, men, 60 percent of the nation's work force, constitute almost 80 percent of union membership.[87]

Again, the problem is circular. Can't work full-time. Don't join union. Don't get power. Don't get money.

Labor unions are often guilty of excluding women from their membership as well as their leadership. In addition, unions may be charged with discrimination in the low priority they give to women's issues as demands in negotiating contracts.

At least as significant as the male/female membership composition of the unions is the *leadership,* which is virtually never female, even where the rank and file are overwhelmingly so. For example, in the Amalgamated Clothing Workers Union, in which women make up 75 percent of the membership, there are only two women on the governing board of twenty-three. "And there are no women on the Executive Council of the AFL-CIO, since the council is made up solely of union presidents, none of whom is a woman."[88] The ILGWU had some 430,000 members in 1973. Roughly 80 percent—344,000—are women. However, Mattie Johnson is the only woman member of the ILGWU General Executive Board. She is a vice-president of the union and heads the San Francisco Joint Board.

According to the 1973 Directory of National Unions and Employee Associations,[89] the number of women officers and officials of all unions for 1972 in the whole United States is thirty-four. If employee associations and AFL-CIO state organizations (including unaffiliated) are added, there are an additional forty-eight.

Interestingly, the unions with the highest percentage of female members have, according to some sources, done the least for their membership. For example, the ILGWU, which, according to Vivian Gornick,[90] is one of the richest unions in the country, "its treasury holding more than a billion dollars, including a sum of $350 million in its retirement fund, has the lowest pension payment of any union

---
[86] *Ibid.*
[87] *Selected Earnings and Demographic Characteristics of Union Members, 1970,* Report 417, Bureau of Labor Statistics, U.S. Dept. of Labor (1972).
[88] Seifer, *op. cit.*
[89] U.S. Dept. of Labor.
[90] Vivian Gornick, "The Failure of the ILGWU," *The Village Voice* (October 17, 1974).

in the country." The $75-a-month pension was raised to $100 in December, 1974.

Ms. Gornick quotes an ILGWU retiree:

> "I will be seventy-four years old in May. I worked approximately fifty-five years as a garment worker. I was always a very good worker but of average speed. Since my piece-work pay was never too high my Social Security therefore is not too much. I get $150.30 a month which includes the new 7 percent increase. Until this month [April, 1974] I was getting only $139.30 Social Security. My union pension [Local 22] is $75 per month. And that . . . is my entire income!"[91]

There is just beginning to be some activity in the area of collective bargaining on demands of particular concern to women, e.g. abortion, child care, maternity benefits, equal pay, equal promotion. But, interestingly, organized labor did not go on record in support of the Equal Rights Amendment until 1973.

Finally, in 1974, over 3,200 trade union women convened in Chicago for the founding conference of the Coalition of Labor Union Women (CLUW) to work within the union structure to better the position of working women in America. The results are as yet unknown.

Pensions

Not only do women suffer in their attempts to join in the paid work force, in their efforts to survive within it, but the suffering lingers long after the last paycheck. Most elderly people in America rely for their income on savings, Social Security, and pensions and government benefits. Pensions, though not as widespread as many believe, are designed to give some security to the working person who has been retired from the job market by age and the economy. Private pensions usually involve (tax deductible) contributions of money by the employer and the employee. The size of a pension is usually arbitrarily related to income, job level, and duration of service, criteria which put women at a great disadvantage. More and more old people are discovering that when they finally reach the "big pension in the sky," they can barely live on it. And poor old women are the poorest of all.

[91] *Ibid.*

Women don't get much in the way of pensions because there are minimal, if any, fringe benefits attached to women's work, whether in the home or outside. Executive pension plans are much more attractive than those of workers, even where hotly negotiated by powerful male unions. And executive pension plans are for men because most executives are men.

While one out of two retiring men gets a pension, only one of five women retiring from jobs in private industry can expect to receive a pension. Women's pensions—for those who do receive them—are a median sum of $970 a year, compared to a median of $2,080 for men. Only 2 percent of all widows over sixty-five are receiving any benefit from their husbands' pension plans.[92]

To the extent that women do have interest or at least funds in pension plans, the money is totally out of the control of their sex. An enormous amount of all invested money is that of pension funds—controlled by men. "Company pension plans are the fastest-growing sector of all fast-growing institutional groups. Already, they account for around 10 percent of total U.S. equities."[93] Pension funds own stocks, bonds, major real estate holdings.[94] Women less frequently get pensions, and certainly are less frequently pension officers, trustees.

In New York City, for example, there are separate pension funds for different categories of employees such as fire personnel, police, teachers. New York's Retirement Fund is the combined pension fund of New York's employees other than teachers, police, and fire personnel. The fund includes, however, the transit workers, uniformed sanitation workers, and District Council 37, which represents the city's clerical workers, the majority of whom are women. The combined Employees' Retirement Fund has a Board of Trustees which is composed of the Mayor, the Comptroller, the President of the City Council, New York's five Borough Presidents, and the Presidents of the participating municipal unions. The actual operation of the funds is managed by middle-level city officials and professional money managers, including major banks. Not one member of the Board of Trustees which decides the investment patterns of the $3.5 billion[95] and

---

[92] Kate Blackwell and Karen Ferguson, "Pensions: Are There Holes in Your Security Blanket?" *Ms.* magazine (October, 1973).
[93] *Business Week* (June 2, 1973).
[94] See Chapter 4, "Who Really Controls the Purse Strings?"
[95] 1974.

selects its own advisors in this, one of New York City's employees' pension funds, is a woman, much less a feminist.

Most of the money is invested in stocks, bonds, mortgages, certificates of deposit, and government bonds. There is no requirement that money be invested only in governments or even private industries that have established affirmative action programs or clear policies of nondiscrimination.

In the pension department, women are losing all around. They receive fewer pensions. The pensions they get are at lesser amounts of money. The money they do have in pension funds is controlled by men and invested by and in other male-controlled institutions.

Social Security

Social Security is an area of legislation which seems like a reasonable, equitable, and creative solution to the problems of the elderly, particularly the elderly poor, the majority of whom are women. Actually, like most other laws, written or not, it is of much greater advantage to the rich than the poor, and it is of the least advantage to women, poor women.

The Social Security pension, which is just deferred income, is calculated on a sliding scale in which higher income means higher benefits. So women, whose wages are lower, arrive at old age with less benefits than the average male. More women than men receive Social Security and government retirement benefits; 56 percent of the total number of recipients of such income are women. However, women receive only 67 percent of the amount of benefits received by men.[96]

"A survey of Social Security beneficiaries who retired in 1969–70 found that 46 percent of the men who had worked in private industry, but only 21 percent of the women, had been covered by a pension plan on their longest job. Women are concentrated in industries and occupations which lack pension coverage.

"Women earners who are lucky enough to receive pensions receive considerably lower benefits than men. Among Social Security recipients who retired in 1969–70 with private pensions, the median annual private pension for men was $2,080, but for women only $970. Since pension amounts are based on length of service, they reflect interruptions in employment due to women's responsibilities

---

[96] *Consumer Income,* U.S. Dept. of Commerce.

in the home. Since pension amounts are also based on earnings, they also reflect the effects of sex discrimination in employment."[97]

Also, since the scheme is progressive but does not escalate after annual income of $12,000,[98] the burden of the contribution falls more heavily on low earners. And there are no lower earners than women.

Low wages lead not only to low pensions but also to low Social Security payments. Among retired workers receiving Social Security payments at the end of 1972, women received a median monthly payment of only $133. (Men received $189.) Forty-two percent of the women, compared to 19 percent of the men, received less than $120 a month.[99]

As former Congresswoman Martha Griffiths wrote,

> "Social Security's method of determining eligibility for disability payments penalizes absences from the paid labor force: In order to be eligible for *disability* benefits, workers not only must be fully insured, but also must have worked five years out of the ten immediately preceding the onset of disability. As a result, only about 40 percent of woman earners, compared to 90 percent of men earners, are insured under Social Security for disability.
>
> ". . . a married woman who pays Social Security taxes all her life will receive retirement benefits no larger than if she had never paid a dime. Even if her earnings do entitle her to a retirement benefit . . ."[100]

The Social Security system has contained a delayed retirement plan under which, for each year one works past the retirement age, the benefit gets larger when retirement does take place. So, if a man works one year after sixty-five, he may get $2 a month more upon retiring at sixty-six. For a woman Social Security spouse benefits may become payable at sixty-two, though 20 percent less.

There are no delayed retirement benefits for women who work past sixty-two and who elect spouse's benefits when they finally do retire. Thus if a man's Primary Insurance Amount (PIA) is $200 and he works to some point beyond sixty-five, he will receive increased benefits. But a wife delaying her retirement gets absolutely no

---
[97] Griffiths, *op. cit.*
[98] 1974.
[99] Griffiths, *op. cit.* From a survey undertaken by the Social Security Administration, analyzed by W. Kolodrubetz, "Private Retirement Benefits and Relationship to Earnings: Survey of New Beneficiaries," *Social Security Bulletin* (May, 1973).
[100] Griffiths, *op. cit.*

increase. If a wife's PIA is $80 and her husband's $200, her own "earned" credits will be subtracted from the sum she would be entitled to from her husband's account. Thus she will have the same sum as if she had not delayed her retirement.

In an effort to "equalize the system" the male-female age distinction is going to be eliminated. This is an example of how "equal treatment" works against women, because, as it is now, women who take their own benefits do get some break in recognition of their lower pay; soon that small advantage will be lost.

Social Security, and court decisions regarding these benefits, keep reinforcing female dependency. Feminists and others who recognize the female condition should, however, be wary about eliminating this type of protective legislation, since, for all the low consciousness it reflects, it is one of the few available defenses.

Illusions

Because of the considerable female-generated activity attacking discrimination against women trying to get into, or already in, a work place other than the home, there is the appearance of success and change.

There is a rumor that women are making great strides in electoral politics. Actually, the number of elected women has not increased significantly. In fact, the number of women in Congress is *less* than the 1962 high point, when the percentage of women in Congress was 5 percent.[101]

One of the major obstacles for women in politics has been lack of access to funds. Women have not had independent wealth, and contributors have not taken women seriously as candidates. Voters still ask: "Why should a woman take up a job that's going to pay $23,000 when a man could use that salary?"

When the New York State Legislature released a list of its non-elected employees earning over $20,000 per year, out of 110, only 10 were women.[102]

> "The lower the salary, the greater the number of women. Only in the state of New Hampshire, where legislators earn $100 a year, have women made a numerical impact: 68 women have been elected to the House, of 400 representatives, the highest number of

[101] Jean Kirkpatrick, *Political Woman* (New York, Basic Books, 1974).
[102] *The New York Times* (January 23, 1975).

any state legislature in the country. . . . Other states with a high percentage of women legislators also conform to the pattern of paying lower salaries: Vermont, a state with 21 women legislators, pays $1.50 a day, plus expenses. . . . Conversely, states whose legislators receive salaries high by the standards of the other states show lower percentages of women, a formula illustrating that as salaries escalate, the jobs become more desirable, and women have a harder time obtaining them."[103]

Much female energy is going into the struggle for job equality; some feminist theorists and activists believe, however, that employment discrimination does not deserve top priority, since it does not really attack the root problems which are so institutionalized.

For example, as Ti-Grace Atkinson puts it:

"As for what the Movement labels 'civil rights' activities, such as fighting job discrimination, it should be evident by now that these are facets of women's oppression, are in that sense secondary and reflect the roles assigned to women within the major sex institutions. Fighting job discrimination, as a primary attack on the oppression of women, is somewhat analogous to the blacks fighting 'job discrimination' as a primary attack on the oppression of blacks in the 1850's."[104]

Nevertheless, there are now city, state, and federal laws dealing with sex discrimination. There is no amendment to the federal Constitution (other than the right to vote) which directly bans discrimination on the basis of sex.[105]

The Laws

Women's groups have shown extraordinary creativity in developing issues and bringing lawsuits. Some of the cases attack very fundamental principles and practices. New ideas are being developed. Looking at other ways to attack roots of inequity (while at the same time "working within the system") may involve using the "enemy's weapons" against them. For example, the very SEC regulations under which publicly traded corporations must list their potential liabilities or sales of their stock may be invoked to bring sex discrimination cases by people other than aggrieved employees or potential em-

[103] Susan and Martin Tolchin, *op. cit.*
[104] *Amazon Odyssey* (Links Books, 1974).
[105] As of January, 1975.

ployees. Carol Murray, Director of Women's Litigation of the San Francisco Neighborhood Legal Assistance Foundation, has suggested derivative shareholder suits for failure to comply with Title VII, thereby indicating bad business judgment and exposure to potential liability, or particularly after a case has been won and damages have been recovered as they have been in numerous sex discrimination cases. Corporations therefore would have to face the potential of attack not only by their mere employees or "disgruntled feminists," but by stockholders.

On the federal level there is Title VII of the Civil Rights Act, administered by the Equal Employment Opportunity Commission; Equal Pay Act; National Labor Relations Act; Executive Orders commonly known as "Affirmative Action." More than one law may be used at a time. Possible remedies include being hired for the job, the promotion, the salary, back pay, damages, affirmative action, injunctions, lawyers' fees, and court costs.

If one seeks help outside the offending employment situation, claims of sex discrimination in employment may be brought before labor unions,[106] administrative bodies and courts. The most celebrated cases are those which are ultimately and finally decided by the Supreme Court. However, litigation is costly in terms of time, money, energy. Those cases that are appealed, and "make" law, take several years; by the time they are over the results may be academic for the individuals or group that initiated the action, though their effects are widespread.

The Civil Rights Act Title VII applies to industries affecting commerce and having fifteen or more employees.[107] Essentially, and theoretically, Title VII bars discrimination on the basis of sex. Period. Except where the individual's sex may be a "bona fide occupational qualification." As attorney Florynce R. Kennedy puts it, "This must mean the job requires a penis or a vagina."

The Equal Pay Act, as its name implies, is concerned with discrimination in the form of unequal pay for equal work. Unequal pay may

---

[106] Which are defendants when being accused of direct or indirect discrimination by union members or would-be members, and plaintiffs when charging management with discrimination against workers.

[107] There are exclusions for religious associates, private clubs, the United States Government. More charges of sex discrimination have been filed against universities than against any other single industry. Kathleen Peratus, "What Have the Courts Done for Us Lately?" *Ms.* magazine (August, 1974). As of November, 1974, 1,600 charges of sex discrimination had been filed with the Equal Employment Opportunity Commission against institutions of higher education. (Project on the Status and Education of Women.)

be the result of such insidious policies as seniority (white men, for example, in a particular employment situation, have seniority and therefore higher pay since no minority-group men, and no women of any race, had previously been hired); such cases come within the law's jurisdiction. The Act, however, excludes many office, retail sales, and service occupations in which women are traditionally employed.

What is known as *"Affirmative Action"* exists on the federal level (local governments may have their own programs) by virtue of Executive Order.[108] The Order requires that contracts entered into with the United States Government contain agreements not to discriminate against certain classes of people, including minority groups and women. Generally, the contractor must agree to and show a commitment to develop programs which affirmatively—through recruitment, for example—eliminate employment imbalances in all job titles.

Affirmative Action to eliminate sex discrimination requires that the employer recruit and advertise for women,[109] make no distinction between the sexes on pay or hours, provide appropriate facilities for both sexes, not discriminate against women for time away for childbearing, make a commitment to including women within management-training programs.

There is perhaps great power in Affirmative Action since, a pledge, at least, is required whenever there is a contract of $10,000 or more, and very rarely would contracts under that amount be entered into by the federal government. That is, the government must not give business to corporations or universities that do not affirmatively display their program for hiring more women and minority-group members. However, barring or voiding contracts on the basis of discrimination is very rare, and the power is no more than potential.

There is considerable controversy about the government's priorities and the effectiveness of Affirmative Action, and about whether loose commitments are used instead of employers' having to pay money damages in settlement of sex discrimination cases. Dr. Cynthia Epstein[110] says, "What Affirmative Action seems to be doing is getting women jobs as Affirmative Action officers."

[108] Executive Order 11246, Revised Order 4.
[109] Though advertising based on sex is prohibited. Pittsburgh Press Co. v. Pittsburgh Comm. on Human Relations 413 U.S. 376 (1973).
[110] Sociologist, professor, author of *Woman's Place* (Berkeley and Los Angeles, U. of California Press, 1970), and member of the President's Advisory Committee on the Economic Role of Women (1972–1974); personal interview, Easthampton, N.Y.

The Equal Rights Amendment, if passed, would, theoretically, eliminate gender-based discrimination. It would also eliminate most female protective legislation, which is usually used against women anyhow. Ideally, in humanist terms, it would *improve* working conditions for all people, but that is unlikely in a corporate state.

Litigated cases have dealt with a variety of sexually discriminatory practices: women receiving less pay than men for substantially the same work, not being hired, not receiving the same fringe benefits, being or not being married, being or not being pregnant, having or not having children. The patterns of discrimination may be subtle or obvious. In either case the employer denies that his acts constitute discrimination.

There is now a race for creativity between seeing the pattern of, and denying, job discrimination. At this point, employers are too sophisticated to say, "We just don't want women." It is more subtle, more insidious: "We would love to hire women in management, only we can't find any who are really tough enough." Or, "If *you* would find us a woman who could stand up to the men we deal with, we'd really like to meet her." Or, "We want more women, but the thing is, we don't really have enough women's restrooms." Or, "We're not discriminating against women, but anybody who has the primary responsibility for taking care of children can't be promoted." Or, "We're not discriminating against women, but we hold all our management meetings at a men's-only club." Or, "We're meeting at the athletic club. No pregnant *people* are allowed."

If a woman's home, husband, marriage, children are keeping her back, does it follow that without them she would now be President of General Motors? And aren't the male corporate, financial, political, and cultural leaders parents?

Some of the Cases

Mary Chamberlain,[111] a cocktail waitress, was fired for being flat-chested and for not wearing her costume in a manner which would accentuate her breasts. But, she argued, men in similar positions had no similar requirements, and she was, therefore, being discriminated against.

---

[111] State Division of Human Rights on the Complaint of Mary Chamberlain v. Indian Valley Realty Corp. State of New York: State Human Rights Appeal Board, Appeal No. 743—Case No. CS-21209-70. Aff'd *per curiam*, 38 A.D. 2d 890 (1970).

The New York State Division of Human Rights found that wearing her costume properly was a requirement of the job which Ms. Chamberlain wrongly refused to comply with. The complaint, decided the hearing officer, was really one of social mores and "sexism" —which is not covered by the Human Rights Law!

In *Sprogis* v. *United Airlines*,[112] the plaintiff, an airline stewardess, was fired when she married, though male stewards were permitted to be married.

United Air Lines argued that this was not sex discrimination, but merely a "distinction" between two classes in a particular position.

The Supreme Court decided that the airline was discriminating, even though its "no-marriage" policy applied only to stewardesses and not to all female job categories.

The Martin Marietta Corporation advertised for factory assembly workers. Mrs. Phillips was rejected because she had preschool-age children. Men with preschool-age children were hired and women *without* were as well.

Not satisfied with this rejection, Mrs. Phillips launched the legal fight that was ultimately decided by the Supreme Court, and known as *Phillips* v. *Martin Marietta*.[113]

The lower, or trial, court had decided that there was no sex discrimination in rejecting mothers of young children. Rather, they said, there was a "sex-plus" requirement. That is, Mrs. Phillips was a woman, *and* had preschool-age children; it was the "sex plus" combination that caused her to be rejected.

The Supreme Court reversed the decision, disallowing different hiring policies: one for women with preschool children and another for men with preschool children.

However, the Supreme Court, the same court that would later decide that not all pregnancy-related discrimination is discrimination,[114] noted that "the existence of such conflicting family obligations, if demonstrably more relevant to job performance for a woman than a man, could arguably be a basis for distinction. . . ."[115]

To be worthy of equal pay, "equal" work need only be substan-

---

[112] Sprogis v. United Air Lines, Inc. 444 F. 2d 1194 (7th Cir. 1971) *Cert. denied* 404 vs. 991.
[113] Phillips v. Martin Marietta 440 U.S. 542 (1971).
[114] Geduldig v. Aiello 417 U.S. 484 94 S.Ct. 2485 (1974).
[115] *Phillips v. Martin Marietta.*

tially the same. Still the Supreme Court did not reverse[116] a lower court decision in which only men were permitted to sell men's clothing, while women worked in other, less lucrative departments of the employer's store. The trial court had found that the higher profitability of the men's department was to be taken into account to justify a pay differential and constituted a legitimate business decision, and there was no denial of equal pay for equal work.

In *Rosenfeld* v. *Southern Pacific*,[117] a federal court in California defeated a weight-lifting requirement for a job as telegrapher. The employer was ordered to consider Ms. Rosenfeld for any future job. However, she was awarded no back pay and no damages.

In *Weeks* v. *Southern Bell Telephone*,[118] a woman was denied a job as a "switchman" ostensibly because of a protective statute saying women couldn't lift over thirty pounds.[119] The federal court held that the employer had the burden of proving that women could not do the work required.

There are also discrimination cases which, though brought on grounds other than sex—for example, racial discrimination—may be applicable in claims of sex discrimination.

Griggs v. *Duke Power Company*[120] was basically a case of discrimination against blacks in which the question was whether it was reasonable to require a high school diploma for a maintenance job. Most of those without diplomas were black janitors. All other job titles were limited to whites.

The Supreme Court said practices, procedures, tests for different classes of people cannot be maintained if they "freeze" the status quo of already existing discriminatory practices that are not reasonably related to the job. Presumably the same theory should apply if all men have high school diplomas, women do not, and only those with diplomas may be promoted.

People in the United States do not have the wide range of life choices popularly attributed to them. Certainly women do not. And

---

[116] Hodgson v. Robert Hall 473 F² 589 (3d Cir. 1973). *Cert. denied.*
[117] Rosenfeld v. Southern Pacific 444 F. 2d 1219 (9th Cir. 1971).
[118] Weeks v. Southern Bell Telephone 408 F. 2d 228 (5th Cir. 1969).
[119] Women have frequently pointed to the ease with which they are expected to carry their babies, and children, and laundry, and groceries.
[120] Griggs v. Duke Power Co. 401 U.S. 424 (1971).

nowhere is the lack of female options clearer than in the area of "use of one's time." Women work. Far too many are working fulltime in and around the home, and outside the home: in post offices, secretarial pools, department stores, hospitals, courts, mines. In fact, in many of the places where men are, but almost always in subservient and poorly paid positions.

Every adult living in a free society should be involved in productive work as his or her means of income. But of course this cannot be "required," demanded, if the economy is such that only a few are being benefited by the work of many. Receipt of welfare in lieu of work should be no less acceptable than "clipping" coupons or living off dividends—equally *unearned* money. But for women, "welfare mothers" and others, whatever the source of their income, it is rarely unearned. While women should not have to do *two* jobs or more, whichever they are doing must be on the same paid basis as other productive and valued work in the society. Moreover, women as the reproducers of the human species should be entitled not only to protective legislation (such as maternity leave), but also to bonuses.

All steps must be taken to make sexism unprofitable. If we truly value human labor, this is as true in terms of discrimination in work as in credit, tax, and the laws of marriage and divorce.

16. Women, Money and Power

"Getting rid of the rich does end up very funnily. It is easy to get rid of the rich, but it is not easy to get rid of the poor. Wherever they have tried it they have got rid of the rich all right and so then everybody is poor. . . . The virgin lands are getting kind of used up, the whole surface of the world is known now and also the air, and everywhere you see organization killing itself by just ending in organization. The more backward countries are still excited about it because they have just heard of it but in their hearts the rest of them know the poor are always there and the very much poorer are always there and what are you going to do about it? . . . One thing is sure. Until there are rich again everybody will be poor and there will be more than ever of everybody who is even poorer.

"That is sure and certain."

—Gertrude Stein, "Money, All About Money, More About Money, and My Last About Money," *Writings and Lectures, 1909–1945,* edited by Patricia Meyerowitz (Baltimore, Penguin, 1971).

Only the powerless live in a money culture and know nothing about money. Ignorance about money and power is not an effective means of acquiring, redefining or redistributing them.[1] A politically "sophisticated" or religious horror of money dangerously avoids the

[1] Ignorance is never freely chosen by the powerless. It is the first of many chains that insure obedience, paralysis, resignation, and self-righteousness. Ignorance or misinformation knows no one class or sex, and is definitely not confined to the formally uneducated. Many educated women have no idea where their self-interest lies, and even less of an idea of the collective good. Many American theoreticians of the collective good have never been able to put anything into practice. Idealism untempered by opportunity—or disaster—is another form of ignorance.

fact that, in a money culture, it is only money that buys the things that all people want—and deserve: life, health, food, land, hope, education, sexual pleasure, and some peace of mind. Money can even buy the sun: or at least an apartment with the space and windows to admit it. In the right hands, money buys freedom from jail, torture, loneliness, wage servitude, and lunatic asylums. (Money, after all, purchases the reputation and appearance that is "above" the law.)

Money buys vacations, leisure time, youth and beauty, desirable company, necessary information, and feelings of well-being. Money pays for abortions, for mortgages, and for child care.

The more money people have, the more important they know it is and they know enough to remain silent about how much money can buy. Shame about not having money keeps poor people silent about it or leads them into denying money's importance. Guilt about having a lot of money silences wealthy people.

Rich people supposedly don't talk about money. It is poor form—"vulgar"—to be preoccupied or anxious about money. It is also dangerous to flaunt wealth. Homes and resorts must be secluded and guarded, membership limited, servants screened. The return to paradise—the longer and safer life that money buys for one man, and his female property—automatically implies a shorter and more dangerous life for another man and his female property. This is murder. And murderers must hide their deed and the very real profits reaped. Some murderers "give away" their "extra" money for this reason; others have wives who lead virtuous private lives and dedicated philanthropic public lives for this reason.[2]

It is a Faustian bargain: all the worldly pleasures money can buy just for the price of a human soul. There is hardly a man who would not strike the bargain and damn the world (for others). Few women leave their Faust when they see how firmly their (female) piety and security are wedded to the misery of others. (There are very few female Fausts.)

Money is not the only power. There are twelve major forms of power. Seven are almost totally controlled by men and are fluid or in-

[2] Such murderousness exists whenever a relationship of the few over the many exists: in capitalist countries, where a small group of individual men own the nation's money and control the state; in Communist countries where the state owns the nation's money—and is composed of a small group of male bureaucrats; in agricultural or "underdeveloped" economies, where a small group of men bound by religion, militarism, or tribalism own most of the land or the natural resources.

terchangeable with each other (Physical, Technological, Scientific, Military, and Consumer power; the power of Organized Religions and Secular Institutions). Two powers may be controlled equally by women and men and are also interchangeable (Social position and Influence). Three forms of power are almost exclusively female and are noninterchangeable or nonfluid spheres of power (Beauty, Sexuality, and Motherhood). Money, the thirteenth power, can buy and control the twelve powers. It is a power sacred to most men—and foreign to most women.

Physical power is the first: this means the physical power to walk, run, run away, hit back, or hit first; hit home runs, make touchdowns, score baskets, and goals; plow the earth; lift cars out of ditches, and children from under heavy logs; it also means the power to intimidate and control other people's actions—and thoughts—through brute physical means. Penniless men with knives, or fists, can rule, rape, and rob entire populations, and individuals. Most men have some form of this power; most women do not.

Technological power is the second: this means knowing how to mechanically survive in the twentieth century: knowing how to fix cars, fuses, guns, computers, and machines. Most women are completely noninformed about—and afraid of—machines, even those in their kitchens. Though many men are increasingly at the mercy of mechanical experts—plumbers or TV repairmen—they are less helpless than women, and in any event the machine experts are almost all men. Most women do not have this form of power. Most men have some degree of it; some men, as experts, have this form of power. Being able to build your own house or fix your car or being able to control an expert who does this for you is a form of power or knowledge that can save time, money, and anguish.

Scientific power is the third: this means the ability to define, understand, and solve problems in a scientific way. It has led to the invention of gunpowder, armaments, and nuclear bombs and to the invention of "miracle" drugs, "miracle" surgery, and a "miraculous" (male) control over crop failure, drought, famine, plague, hurricanes, etc. Scientific knowledge is both intrinsically and socially valuable. It commands some money, some prestige, and some influence, all of which are other forms of power. Very few women have this form of highly exchangeable power.

Military power is the fourth: this means the control of all modern armies of the world, including guerrilla and terrorist groups. Military power contains the first three powers. Foot soldiers employ brute force and some technical proficiency in the use of guns and machines. Officers have access to a scientific approach to killing, winning—or saving lives. They are usually somewhat proficient at brute force and technical know-how. Military power is almost exclusively male. Men pay for armies, men have political power over armies, men compose armies. Women may function in token numbers or in traditionally "feminine" capacities within the army setting. In countries such as China, North Vietnam, Cuba, and Israel, individual "exceptional" women may, in times of great danger, occupy structural positions that are coequal with men's. Military, like scientific, power is exchangeable. Armies can, up to a point, command food, clothing, shelter, sexual pleasure, art treasures, homes, etc. without any exchange of money. Militarists born in material and spiritual poverty can rule people and countries by reason of military force. Military juntas or terrorist bands can take over, kidnap, imprison, and kill politicians, scientists, pacifists, and the majority of people within a nation-state. They need some economic backing to do this.

Religious power is the fifth: this means the control of the world's organized religions. Institutions of religion have very little to do with intrinsic or spontaneous saintliness or spirituality, honor, ethics, or morality. (Although such institutions, on rare occasions, may include, encourage, or refuse to torment or destroy such traits.) Religion dominates legal codes and political and educational behavior. Large religious institutions are economically wealthy and can offer a life of comfort, security, and pleasure to their officials. The control of organized religion in the modern world is almost exclusively male. Many women may be "religious," but no woman is the Pope, or the spiritual leader of Islam, Judaism, Protestantism, or Hinduism. Religion has great social and political power. It is a highly exchangeable power: it buys respect, trust, favors, money, tax-free land, the minds of women and children, the praise of artists. Next to money, institutionalized religion is probably the greatest international "conspiracy" in the world.

Secular organized institutions compose the sixth: this means the power of existing structures to rather mindlessly continue with "business as usual." Political, legal, economic and educational institutions, together with military and religious institutions, compose what is known as civilization. Each of these forms of power can be bought with money; each of them is highly interchangeable (or exchangeable) with each other. Judges, lawyers, businessmen, and educational administrators are bought by political power, which in turn is purchased by economic and religio-economic power. The control of civilization's major public institutions is almost exclusively male, although many women are used to carry out its dictates.

The power of consumption is seventh. Buying things is presumably a woman's province. Women *do* buy the daily domestic necessities and luxuries, but they are "small" items in terms of price, importance, the value of decision-making and its effect on the economy in general. Most men control or at least share in the buying of "large" domestic items at home and even "larger" items for industry and government. Consumer power is real—when the consumer is organized, knowledgeable, and powerful enough to require "large" items such as nuclear warheads. Consumer power is only a myth when consumers, like housewives and mothers, are unorganized, uninformed, and only require "small" items.[3]

Social position is the eighth power. It is usually inherited by men and women, or acquired through marriage, more often by women than by men, except among royal and ruling class aristocracies, where family dynastic power is doubled by marriage. Social position for men is almost synonymous with money and political power. A woman of "social position" uses it in ways that are different from—and unequal to—her father's or husband's use of it.[4]

Influence, ideology, or charisma is the ninth power. Artists, intellectuals, politicians, priests, rabbis, atheists—public "personalities"—each may have something of this mercurial, mysterious transforming power. Influence is almost always purchased and controlled by money power, or silenced and killed by brute force, by technical and military force, or by political and religious opponents. People with money can often purchase talent and use it for their own entertainment or as propaganda for the status quo. More men than women have public influence, but many women *do* have this power. Therefore, it is a form of power that is more tightly controlled by money power than any of those previously listed.

Physical beauty is the tenth power. It is often synonymous with youth and is almost an all-female province. Women who are considered "beautiful" can presumably get jobs as secretaries—or wives—more easily than "ugly" women and more easily than "beautiful"

---

[3] See Chapters 7 and 3.
[4] See Chapters 4, 5, and 15.

men, who don't want such jobs anyway. A woman, however, is not voted into the Vatican's College of Cardinals because she is "beautiful"; no man is kept out because he is "ugly." Beauty is short-lived and noninterchangeable or nonfluid. It is hard to convert into some other form of power.[5]

The use of sex is the eleventh power. Like beauty, this is considered a female province. It is a relatively non-exchangeable and short-lived power.[6] Sexual power also means the power of sexual enjoyment. Very few women have this power. Those that seem to, or actually do, are usually scorned, punished, and feared. Women are not supposed to make the magic of money from sex—and are also not supposed to initiate or enjoy sex. As of 1975, only a handful of women in the world have real sexual power.

Motherhood is the twelfth power. It is an exclusively female province. It is noninterchangeable, nonfluid, and nonvalued in a money culture.[7] Jessie Bernard has summarized the situation correctly:

"Actually the hand that rocks the cradle has not ruled the world. In fact, rocking the cradle has been precisely what has prevented the hand from ruling the world. However much truth there might have been in the old saying, such private, fragmented, interpersonal power did not add up to genuine, public—political—power.... Almost by definition, the role of mother has been incompatible with the exercise of political power, although not incompatible with interpersonal domination and control.... But the power of a million such mothers with great power at home does not amount to much if they are not organized.... Unorganized, they cannot sway policy. They cannot have an input in public decisions. They cannot exert pressure. They cannot protest the outside environment of children. That calls for genuine political power, and the will to use it humanely."[8]

Motherhood is the quintessential female experience—and it stands completely outside the money culture, which, after all, is world culture.

Money is the thirteenth power. Money is human energy trapped and counted in measures of gold, silver, and paper. Money is love. Money is sex. Money is life—or time. Money is human and animal blood. Money is bloody. For all its magical powers, money has not

---

[5] See Chapter 3, "I'd Rather Be Dead Than Ugly: The Psychoeconomics of Beauty."
[6] See Chapter 13, "Sexual Economics: Who Profits?"
[7] See Chapter 8, "Marriage and Motherhood: The Psychology of Total Commitment," and Chapter 9, "Survival Tactics: Marriage and Divorce."
[8] Jessie Bernard, *The Future of Marriage* (New York, World Publishing, 1972).

been able to legislate violence out of human existence. Human energy protests its imprisonment into coins: it engages in bloody riots, it creates chaos, it deflates the value of currency and of its own energy. Money is highly sacred to men. It represents the male's ability to reproduce himself through the accumulation of coins, bills, financial empires, women, and heirs. It represents the male's ability to perform alchemical magic. Men can turn land—or ideas—into gold. Men make money by making a phone call, or by shaking hands. Money can triumph over the forces of nature and of (other) men. Money keeps men awake. Money turns men "on." Making a financial "killing" is what men believe will solve the problem of alienation—and mortality.

It is no accident that stock exchange floors—in addition to bedroom floors—bring out the noisy blood, the flushed cheek, and the passionate cries of men. Most men are making love when they make "magical" amounts of money. To the money priest, money is more sexual and sacred than is earthly sex with women. It is no accident that bank boardrooms are "hushed": the lovemaking is over, conception and delivery have taken place, now there is well-earned rest, and growth ahead.

Although money is the most powerful of forces, it is less so in the hands of a socially "inferior" race or sex. For example, the same amount of money purchases *less* and *different* value for a Black man or woman in America—as it did for a Jew in Nazi Germany, or does now for a woman anywhere in the world. Individual wealthy Jews in Nazi Germany could sometimes purchase their own lives—and a limited number of other Jewish lives—provided they fled the country, leaving their property behind. All the Jewish money in the world could not buy a respected or safe place, in the Nazi—or world—scheme of things, for individual Jews or for Jews as a group.[9] All the Black money in the world cannot buy a respected or safe place within white racist countries for individual Blacks, or for Blacks as a group. All the female money in the world cannot buy a respected or safe place for individual women—or for women as a group—in misogynist countries. As of this writing, there is no feminist embassy or mission that can grant women—or men—political asylum. Understanding this concept, or putting it to any use, is a measure of how well women understand the use of money and power on earth.

[9] This is both an example of the power of (Nazi) ideology and world anti-Semitism or influence, plus the power of brute force and military strength overthrowing "money," as well as an example of *more* money overthrowing *less* money.

Epilogue

In every existing society in the West and, in fact, most of the world, female destiny has been subjugated by male power, and therefore male desire. And throughout history, male use of power has been disastrous for much of humanity, especially for women.

There is a sexual aristocracy,[1] a male aristocracy, a boys' club which has compromised and controlled women without ever yielding power or permitting females to reach its lofty ranks.

Although there may exist the *appearance* of revolution, little has changed in the balance of power. Women have not yet acquired the means of change, much less the ends.

Where major decision making is involved (decisions that will affect many) men are at the top. When, for example, the Council of Economic Advisors meets, it is men deciding how money will move.[2] If it is decided that what the economy needs is a war, men make war. And then a mother who has no voice in "to war or not to war" has no power even to keep her son out of the military.

What may be said is that a closed caste system has opened into an aristocracy with *some* possibility of entry from outside. The potential for female penetration into male bastions of power has been recognized. However, power in the abstract does not really exist.[3]

Where women have what *looks* like power, it is usually derivative.

---

[1] Aristocracy: ". . . a community . . . whose members are born to positions of high prestige and assured dignity because their ancestors have been leaders [elite members]." E. Digby Baltzell, *The Protestant Establishment: Aristocracy and Caste in America* (New York, Random House, 1964).
[2] Hortense Calisher, *The New York Times*, Book Review, September 22, 1974.
[3] A. A. Berle, *Power* (New York, Harcourt, Brace and World, 1969).

They may get close to power; but as Gilman wrote,[4] "the female obtains her share in the social advance only through [the male]."

It appears that women have great power as consumers; wives may make certain decisions on the spending of money, but usually in domestic areas: home decoration, clothing, food. It is personal expenditure and personal consumption.

While it is true that women are needed to keep money in circulation, women are not the people who decide, for example, what products they will be able to choose from. There is very little difference in being able to choose between one male-developed, male-marketed, male-profiting soap and another. Women are not the people who plan the financing of products, the sales, the campaigns which will dictate what desires and needs the public will then have to spend money on, much less general economic policy. So they are an important conduit for money, but their consumerism as such is not a power. And even though women are in factories and at typewriters, the place where they get their real encouragement is at the point of purchase. "Potentially," there is enormous consumer power, but it has been barely utilized, barely successful thus far.

"There's No Advantage to Having a Sow Instead of a Pig"

"If you can't destroy the positions of power you certainly can't participate in them."[5]

"Having a woman President of General Motors earning $50,000 a year wouldn't be doing much for the woman making $100 a week cleaning General Motors' offices after midnight."[6]

"Even one is a very important number if it means that children and adults see that a woman *CAN* be governor OR can be a plumber."

"*Some*body's going to be the President of General Motors, so why not a woman?"

The need for change is clear, but among feminists and other women, there are varying priorities. There are no "party line" answers to the question, "What is it that women want?" Some women

---

[4] Charlotte Gilman, *Women and Economics,* Carl N. Degler, ed. (New York, Harper and Row, 1966).
[5] Ti-Grace Atkinson, *Amazon Odyssey* (New York, Links Books, 1974).
[6] Charlotte Bunch, *Quest,* Vol. I, No. 2 (Diana Press, Summer, 1974).

are seeking personal, immediate, temporary "first aid" for female suffering: their own, and sometimes that of others. Sometimes the search is for "equality," within which there are short-range and long-range varieties. To some, "equality" within the existing system is a long-range goal. Others say the system would not allow equality, to which some answer, "But for women to be truly equal *means* a different system"; in other words, as long as our major institutions exist, by definition equality does not. Still others support equality, provided it is recognized as first aid. Some feminists say "equality" is not the issue and that, in fact, its pursuit can only be used *against* women.[7]

Others, who give priority to an economic political revolution and the destruction of capitalism, hold that *all* of our existing patriarchal, capitalist, and sexist institutions must be eliminated. Some find that for women, the distinction in the various economic political systems are irrelevant, especially in light of the widespread recognition that no economic political system has given priority to the elimination of sexism.

The controversy continues with the argument that women should be making gains in whatever ways and places they can, including "within the system," since that is how power is gained. That is, some say that since America's major powers are corporate, women need to assume power within corporations; others hold that corporate entities demand oppression of other people, especially women.

A woman President of General Motors, even though possibly a more "human" corporate President than her male predecessors, would still be committed to the success of General Motors. She might be able to make a few changes (for example, having day care centers in the plants) but it would be against her self-interests, at least her corporate self-interests, to take any steps to, let us say, reduce profits.

Gaining access to or control of resources and institutions of power, in other words, gaining power, is only a means to an end, and it is an uncertain means because power, once achieved, is not voluntarily relinquished; rather, it is dedicated to its own preservation.

Women rising to relative or absolute power within the existing

---

[7] Ti-Grace Atkinson puts the equality question into perspective with, "Could you maintain slavery if you equalized the roles of master-slave to master-master?" Atkinson, *op. cit.*

I had argued the slavery question from a feminist perspective in 1969 in "the women's abortion case," in taking the position that compulsory motherhood constituted involuntary servitude and therefore violated the 13th (antislavery) Amendment. E.J.G.

structure might just imitate men, and in the process become the oppressors of other people, including other women. As an example, Margaret Thatcher, now leader of England's Conservative party, made the budgetary decision to terminate the distribution of free milk to schoolchildren.[8]

Or, is there some possibility that once in power, women would overcome the established economic and social system and would be more humanist? As Melina Mercouri said, "The Greek *junta* were not women."[9] Do women lust for power? Do they really resist the pressure of ambition? Do they not care about working for themselves, for society? Do women possess greater moral, more substantial values than men, or are they just so conditioned to relate to short-range personal goals, or do they just lack information?

Do women not want the control, in some way, of human beings by other human beings? Do women resist job promotions *because* of their understanding of the moral compromises? Do women question the moral justification, if any, for such control—power? Cinda Firestone, whose family founded the Firestone Tire and Rubber Company, but who has chosen to use her access to wealth to make films about the Attica massacre and the poor of Appalachia, says: "Gaining power is okay if you can still be the same person when you reach the top. I think women are less success-programmed and that there are certain things that may make me a bad director but make me more of a person, like inability to fire people, concern for other people."[10]

Cecily Selby, Executive Director of the Girl Scouts of America, and also *the woman* on two corporate boards of directors, says that "men who have played the power game develop a tunnel vision."[11]

> "Because women come into the pyramid at different levels, we can bring into that, a different kind of vision. By bringing people like us into the decision making, we bring our different backgrounds. These new women bring in the human side and don't concentrate completely on profits."

It may, in fact, be that female needs *are* different and that women do not become the kind of people *men* are en route to, or in the face of, power and success. But there can be a different standard of moral

---
[8] *The New York Times,* February 5, 1975.
[9] *The New York Times,* November 13, 1974.
[10] A personal interview.
[11] Statement at Women's Forum (November 19, 1974, New York City).

expectations from women—should we really *expect* women to be less selfish, indulgent than men?

> "It's no trick to make a lot of money, if all you want is to make a lot of money."[12]

Making money has not been a female pursuit. Few women have thought, much less dared to say, "Men are making money, why can't I? I'm so much better, so much smarter than they are. I love power. I can't tell you what it's like when someone calls and says we got that job contract! Money and power—that's what the country is about. Why should it be any different for women?"[13]

Women's values, or the values attributed to women, are different from those which run America. This may be out of politics, ignorance, fear, or conditioning. Whatever the values women have pursued—have been allowed to pursue—they are not the same as men's.

There are double standards all along the line. Success in this country relates to money, but a woman making money is suspect. If power in men is an aphrodisiac, the opposite seems true of power in women.

When women are in positions traditionally occupied by men, more is expected of them. They are expected to be smarter, less corruptible. *And* "feminine."

Women don't control any of the institutions of society—religious, political, economic, educational, media, health, legal, cultural, military, corporate—and cannot expect to achieve any significant change in their lives without radical change, if not the *destruction* of the existing forms of social and economic power and nonpower (i.e. female) institutions (marriage, motherhood). In fact, if these institutions survive, as we know them, women will be lucky to do the same.

Capitalism, however offending, is not the only guilty system. In varying degrees, anticapitalist movements—socialism, communism—have also been oppressive to women. The lack of women in power is not limited to the United States. Women have not been particularly visible in decision-making levels in the Soviet Union, Cuba, Algeria or China (except very occasionally through husbands). Women in socialist countries not only are given "equal opportunity" but are expected to do several jobs for the "price" of one; they are institu-

---

[12] From the shooting script for the motion picture *Citizen Kane*, Herman J. Mankiewicz and Orson Welles, quoted in Pauline Kael, *The Citizen Kane Book* (Boston, Little, Brown and Co., 1971).
[13] Rochelle Rosenberg, Film Directors' Representative, Easthampton, New York (personal interview).

tionally given the "chance" to work at many jobs, as long as one is the housework. "Women's work" can keep a woman from being on an equal basis with men. Whether in the form of merit promotions or special revolutionary recognition for volunteer work, a Socialist or Communist wife is still the one with the fundamental responsibility for the home.[14]

Women in our country receive the least of capitalism's benefits, but can hardly be said to abstain from capitalism. Getting *less* from an economic system does not separate one from it. Even without being involved in speculation, trading, and other financial manipulation, women are not divorced from capitalism. But the system gets more from women than it gives. Women are indeed participants in all of our system's *worse* aspects as victims of poverty and discrimination. Women free men to work in the marketplace by managing the home, tending the children; women are America's favorite robot consumers, carrying money to market when it is "made available" to them. They are the country's best source of cheap labor on demand.

But whether through guerrilla struggles or "sophisticated warfare," whether through electoral politics or dictatorship, corporate economic or military process, whether through organizing unions or consumer boycotts, every forceful redistribution of power involves access to resources which women are far from controlling.

The Circle

For women to gain control over their own lives and have some noticeable effect on the decisions of the country requires achieving certain positions of power in both personal and political arenas. If women don't get into positions of power, how can they ever do anything? And would women in existing positions of power choose or not choose to, or be able to, turn the economic institutions into tools of justice and equity? And on and on the circle goes.

The dilemma is how women can "make it in a man's world" but reject, as a condition for that success, becoming part of the machinery that keeps this a man's world. In other words, making a woman president of an association or corporation, the American Medical Association, does not mean that entities which have decreed that some people shall not have decent food, clothing, shelter—not to mention

---

[14] However, see Cuban Family Code, 1975.

Ph.D.'s, stocks and bonds, real estate—will no longer be *insensitive* to women.

One of the dangers in disbanding too early certain elements of existing institutions such as alimony, protective labor laws, even certain etiquette is that it could be a kind of rape, a little like "liberating" the women of Algeria by the stripping of their veils. Women may be left defenseless without alternatives.

If wealth is redistributed, will it still be among men? And if there is a redistribution of some wealth to women, will there still be monopoly by the upper classes, even if it becomes domination by the men *and* women of that class? Likewise, a displacement of men by women within the corporate hierarchy would still leave a *class* pyramid with women at the top, or men *and* women at the top.

People of different classes have very different interests. But the women of any class are in an inferior position to the men of that same class. Even if women have "equal rights with men," that would still mean equal with the men of their own class, and disparity with men and women of other classes. Equal rights within each class would still result in a societal pyramid.

Power, if defined as the ability to influence or control other people, may not be a desirable goal of the women's, or any other movement. However, in the case of women, even if we speak about power only as meaning power to control one's *own* life, that would be a radical departure from what now exists.

Women, of whatever class, are in trouble if they are dependent on the income which they have through a man, for the love of a man, or the pleasure of a man; they must now approach the psychosexual economics of our political structure in their interests as women.

Women's lives have been and are manipulated by male greed, profits, power, war, and madness. Without an understanding of money and power and institutions, women can never be prepared for capitalism *or* its successor.

A NOTE ABOUT THE AUTHORS

DR. PHYLLIS CHESLER is a noted author and lecturer. Her most recent book was *Women and Madness*. She has just completed a book about men, which will be published later this year.

EMILY JANE GOODMAN is a New York lawyer who specializes in representing women in divorces and other legal matters. She is also the author of *The Tenant Survival Book*. Ms. Goodman frequently writes and gives lectures on women's rights. "The basic dilemma," she says, "is how women can gain enough money and power to literally change the world, without being corrupted, co-opted and incorporated, on the way, by the very value systems we must change."